PR4487.R
Co

3 9367 03293040 4

S0-BKB-420

COLERIDGE AND CHRISTIAN DOCTRINE

COLERIDGE AND

CHRISTIAN DOCTRINE

J. Robert Barth, S.J.

HARVARD UNIVERSITY PRESS

CAMBRIDGE, MASSACHUSETTS

1969

LIBRARY — COLLEGE OF SAN MATEO

© Copyright 1969 by the President and Fellows of Harvard College

All rights reserved

Distributed in Great Britain by Oxford University Press, London

Publication of this book has been aided by a grant
from the Hyder Edward Rollins Fund

Library of Congress Catalog Card Number 75–75426

SBN 674–13961–8

Printed in the United States of America

78192

To My Father and Mother

❀ PREFACE

This study is an attempt to present in an organized way, as Coleridge himself did not, his matured views on Christian doctrine. They are found in a wide variety of places: in published works like the *Aids to Reflection*; in his numerous unpublished notebooks, now in process of publication; in marginal notes on works of theology and doctrine; in the still unpublished manuscript of his so-called "Opus Maximum"; in letters; and even in the random conversation recorded by his nephew in *Table Talk*. At times these passages take the form of a fairly lengthy discussion of one or another doctrine; at other times they are only hints and guesses, suggestions or promises of a treatise to come. Generally speaking, Coleridge's views on Christian doctrine are not organized, but they have within themselves the principles of organization. The present work, therefore, is one primarily of synthesis.

The only other recent work to treat extensively of Coleridge's religious ideas, James Boulger's *Coleridge as Religious Thinker,* had quite a different purpose. It was concerned with Coleridge's "religious philosophy" or even his "philosophy of religion." It was a work of analysis rather than of synthesis. Although my aim is different, Boulger's study has been helpful to me at several points, and I am happy to acknowledge my indebtedness.

Something should be said about the scope and method of the present work. With a writer like Coleridge, whose ideas were constantly developing, one is hesitant to draw chronological lines; they are no sooner drawn than they must be crossed. Some chronological focus is necessary, however, if one is to talk with any clarity, and the procedure is safe enough as long as one remembers that the lines drawn are only guidelines, not fences. With this in mind, it seems reasonable to refer to the period until 1802, the period of great poetic achievement, as the "early Coleridge" and the period 1802–1815, culminating in the composition of the *Biographia Literaria,* as the "middle Coleridge." The primary chronological focus of this study is the "later Coleridge," during the period 1815–1834.

The time around 1815 is a convenient line of demarcation for several reasons. First of all, the *Biographia Literaria* (not published until 1817, but almost completely written by September of 1815) was the high point of his criticism and literary theorizing. Coleridge continued through the next several years to speak and write occasionally about literary subjects (witness the Shakespeare lectures of 1818–1819), but there was a noticeable change of emphasis in his work, until by 1819 we find that he had turned his attention rather completely to other things. Secondly, this change in the bent of his work after 1815 was strongly in the direction of religious preoccupations. Even in the *Biographia Literaria* itself, in chapters V–X, Coleridge retraced the development of his own thought and closed chapter XXIV with an affirmation of his faith in redemptive Christianity. In 1816 appeared *The Statesman's Manual* (the first "Lay Sermon") and in 1817 the second Lay Sermon, Coleridge's attempts to apply, as he had done on Unitarian principles almost twenty years before in the Bristol Lectures of 1795, the principles of the Bible to the needs of modern society. Finally, as I shall suggest during the course of this study, there is evidence in Coleridge's letters of a deep religious experience which took place during the closing weeks of 1813, when he lay desperately ill at Bath, when "a new world opened to me, in the infinity of my own Spirit." After this time, his reflections on religious belief, especially on sin and redemption, seem to become even more frequent, more personal, and more deeply concerned. I trust it will become apparent, then, as the work progresses, that it is more or less during this twenty-year period, 1815–1834, that Coleridge's matured views on Christianity are to be found.

This is not to exclude Coleridge's earlier theologizing, however, especially during the period 1805–1815. The year 1805 is, in fact, another useful point of reference: in this year, during his stay in Malta, Coleridge wrote for the first time in one of his notebooks that he had definitely abandoned Unitarianism for Trinitarianism. If our primary focus is the period 1815–1834, the period 1805–1815 remains very much in the "periphery of advertence." In all, then, the body of this study covers the years from 1805 to 1834.

The method of this study has been to some extent, necessarily it seems to me, a shifting one. In some cases, the development of Coleridge's thought about a doctrine has had to be traced; in other cases, this has not been necessary. On the question of faith, for example, it is quite clear that there was a profound evolution in Coleridge's thinking, and this development has had to be taken very much into account. In treating the Trinity, on the other hand, Coleridge made little or no basic change in his position or insight from 1805 to the end of his life, but his understanding of it deepened; in this case it has been necessary, therefore, to keep all the aspects of his Trinitarian thought in balance, but there was little need to trace chronological development.

The main body of this study, then, will be the presentation of the views on Christian doctrine of the later Coleridge, with continual reference to the middle years. Chapter I will present the main lines of his earlier religious development as background and context for the formulation of his matured views. A brief epilogue will suggest some of the points of tangency of Coleridge's ideas on Christian doctrine with modern Christian theology.

Several points of mechanical procedure should be noted. I have generally followed Coleridge's punctuation, but occasionally, especially in quotations from manuscript sources, I have normalized the punctuation for the sake of clarity. Very occasionally, the spelling has also been silently normalized where I felt that Coleridge's spelling would be merely a distraction for the reader. Italics which appear in quotations belong to the original unless otherwise noted. Finally, quotations from Scripture (except, of course, those included in quotations from Coleridge) will be from the Revised Standard Version; quotations from the Thirty-Nine Articles are from the text given by E. C. S. Gibson in his commentary, *The Thirty-Nine Articles of the Church of England*.

I am happy to be able to express my gratitude for the kind assistance of the staffs of a number of libraries: the Andover-Harvard Theological Library of the Harvard Divinity School; the Beinecke Library of Yale University; the Berg Collection of the New York Public Library; the Boston Public Library; the British Museum; the Huntington Library of San Marino, California; the Victoria College Library of the University of Toronto; the Widener Library of Harvard University; and the theological library of Woodstock College. I am indebted to Mr. John Peter Mann of Leeds University, co-editor of the forthcoming critical edition of Coleridge's *Lectures on Politics and Religion,* for calling my attention to the manuscript prospectus of Coleridge's Bristol Lectures, which is now in the Beinecke Library of Yale University. I am particularly grateful to Professor Kathleen Coburn, of Victoria College in the University of Toronto, for having made available the manuscript and photostat materials of the Coleridge Room in the Victoria College Library. I am happy to acknowledge a special debt of gratitude, too, to Mr. A. H. B. Coleridge of Whitford, Axminster, Devonshire, great-great-grandson of the poet, for having graciously granted permission to quote from the unpublished notebooks and from the "Opus Maximum" manuscript. For permission to quote from Coleridge's *Collected Letters,* edited by E. L. Griggs, I am indebted to the Clarendon Press, Oxford.

I was greatly assisted at many junctures by the encouragement and incisive criticism of my friend and colleague Philip C. Rule, S.J., now Assistant Professor of English at the University of Detroit, and by the generous counsel of Thomas E. Clarke, S.J., Professor of Theology at Woodstock College. For advice on specific points I am indebted to Walter J. Burghardt, S.J., Avery Dulles, S.J., and John W. Healey, S.J., all of whom are members of the theological faculty of Woodstock College. I am particularly grateful to one of my students, Donna M. Smith, for her exceptionally capable assistance in the work of proofreading and indexing. Kristin M. Brady, John A. Driscoll, S.J., and Dr. Richard J. Thompson also gave welcome help with mechanical details. And I was fortunate to have the services of a very able typist, Mrs. Martha Robinson.

Finally, it is a very special pleasure to acknowledge my large indebtedness to two Professors of English at Harvard University whose substantial work with Coleridge has so much influenced my own: David Perkins, in whose exciting Coleridge seminar the seed of this work was planted, and whose advice and encouragement at many stages has meant much to me; and Walter Jackson Bate, whose own recent book on Coleridge is by far the best general critical study of Coleridge yet to appear, the work of a true Coleridgean writing in the spirit of Coleridge. My debts to these two men, both personal and scholarly, are past counting.

J. R. B.

Canisius College
January 1969

❋ CONTENTS

COLERIDGE AND CHRISTIAN DOCTRINE

ABBREVIATIONS USED IN NOTES

Aids   *Aids to Reflection*, ed. Shedd, I

BL   *Biographia Literaria*, ed. Shawcross

CCS   *On the Constitution of the Church and State*, ed. Shedd, VI

CL   *Collected Letters*, ed. Griggs

Confessions   *Confessions of an Inquiring Spirit*, ed. Shedd, V

FR   *The Friend*, ed. Shedd, II

LR   *Literary Remains*, ed. Shedd, V

LS   [Second] *Lay Sermon*, ed. Shedd, VI

LSTC   *Letters*, ed. E. H. Coleridge

NED   *Notes on English Divines*, ed. D. Coleridge

NTPM   *Notes, Theological, Political, and Miscellaneous*, ed. D. Coleridge

PL   *Philosophical Lectures*, ed. Coburn

SM   *The Statesman's Manual* [First Lay Sermon], ed. Shedd, I

TT   *Table Talk*, ed. Shedd, VI

UL   *Unpublished Letters*, ed. Griggs

Full citations for these works will be found at the end of the book.

❃ I. THE PATTERN OF DEVELOPMENT

It has often been assumed that there is something anomalous about Coleridge's religious development: early education in the orthodoxy of the Church of England; adherence to liberal Unitarianism; return to Trinitarian Christianity; and finally, what Hazlitt contemptuously referred to as a "decline into orthodoxy." At first glance, the Unitarian period seems strangely out of place, and one may be tempted to dismiss it, as some have done, as an undergraduate's flirtation with liberalism. In fact, however, there is more pattern in this development than may at first be apparent. And this pattern is, even when the Unitarian period is included, all of a piece. Although this early religious thought—of Coleridge's Unitarian period—is not part of the main burden of the present study (see the Preface), a brief sketch of his early development is necessary as a background against which to view his matured beliefs and the nature of his later theologizing.

The fact that Coleridge was born the son of a sound if unimaginative Church of England clergyman assured his early and thorough exposure to orthodoxy. There was little to lead him away from it in his early schooling at home in Ottery St. Mary and after 1782 at Christ's Hospital in London. He did taste briefly the forbidden fruits of Voltaire and shortly after declared himself an infidel. The Reverend James Boyer's "wise and sound" response, as Coleridge recalled almost a half century later, was to administer a sound flogging, which ended once and for all any temptations in that direction.[1]

When Coleridge came up to Cambridge in 1791, he was destined, as he had always been, for the ministry in the Church of England.[2] He brought with him his orthodoxy, still intact. But when one looks more closely at the nature of the orthodoxy he brought, it seems like

[1] S. T. Coleridge, *Table Talk,* in *The Complete Works of Samuel Taylor Coleridge,* ed. W. G. T. Shedd, 7 vols. (New York, 1856), VI, 321 (May 27, 1830). This work will hereafter be cited as *TT.* For the sake of simplicity, in the notes the abbreviations p. and pp. will be omitted in all references to works of Coleridge.

[2] E. K. Chambers, *Samuel Taylor Coleridge: A Biographical Study* (Oxford, 1938), p. 17.

light baggage indeed. Under the tutelage of his father (until his death in 1781), Coleridge's early upbringing in the Established Church had been devout and deeply personal, involving a profound sense of individual moral responsibility. This upbringing combined with Coleridge's temperament, which was composed of two seemingly contradictory characteristics: a strong sense of the transcendent, that is, an intuitive sense of the mysteries of nature, of folklore, of human beings; and at the same time, increasing as he grew to young manhood, a skeptical and rationalistic bent. One healthy result of this combination was that Coleridge never accepted religious belief uncritically. However, even including his brief boyish encounter with Voltaire, with its briefly painful aftermath, it can hardly be said that Coleridge was ever an unbeliever. Once, in 1796, he intimated as much in a letter to John Thelwall, but he seems to have been too concerned about proving a point to his atheist friend for the inference to be taken seriously.[3]

All in all, the religious baggage Coleridge carried on his journey to Cambridge was, as J. A. Appleyard suggests, "a matter of assent to a reasonable natural theology, with enough home truths thrown in to warm a heart of rather limited capacity." [4] At that time Coleridge held, together with these beliefs, a vague adherence to the Gospels, especially their moral precepts, and an equally vague allegiance to the Established Church for whose ministry he was destined. Taken all in all, it might be called an untheological, mildly Trinitarian brand of deism in the line of Archdeacon Paley. As Coleridge wrote in a moment of retrospection to his brother George during his Cambridge years (at the end of his ill-fated escapade with the Dragoons), his early faith had been "made up of the Evangelists and the Deistic Philosophy—a kind of *religious Twilight*." [5]

At Cambridge Coleridge underwent much the same experience students have had in every age: the testing of his religious beliefs. Beginning for the first time the adventure of deep exploration into

[3] *Collected Letters of Samuel Taylor Coleridge,* ed. Earl Leslie Griggs, 4 vols. (Oxford, 1956–1959), I, 205 (Late April 1796). This collection is hereafter cited as *CL.*

[4] *Coleridge's Philosophy of Literature: The Development of a Concept of Poetry, 1791–1819* (Cambridge, Mass., 1965), pp. 17–18. In the following pages, I am particularly indebted to Fr. Appleyard, whose long first chapter, "Coleridge as Democrat and Physico-Theologian" (pp. 1–42), is the best available study of the development of Coleridge's thought during the period from 1791 to 1800.

[5] *CL,* I, 78 (March 30, 1794).

human knowledge, into realms he may have only glimpsed before, the student starts to feel the exciting power of his own mind. In this context of new knowledge, he will soon look in a new and different way at his religious beliefs and the commitment they imply, and realize that his intellectual grasp of them has not kept pace with his new knowledge. They must be questioned, tested, deepened. Finally, they will either be deepened and integrated intellectually with his new knowledge in other areas, or they will be discarded. The second alternative can be accomplished in an instant. The first is a long and difficult but ultimately rewarding process, and this was the path into which Coleridge instinctively moved.

It was not only Coleridge's religion which came into question but his politics as well. Because religion and politics were very much bound up together for Coleridge, they should not be unduly separated in discussion. Coleridge's instincts were democratic and his sympathies were with the poor and suffering, and so his early espousal of the cause of the French Revolution was inevitable. This cause was not with him merely a matter of politics and diplomacy but of basic human rights and therefore of profoundly religious import. Coleridge's religion and his political thought were then, as later in his life, closely intertwined. As his religious conviction deepened, so did his concern with individual responsibility in the conduct of society.

The most profound personal influence on Coleridge's deepening of his religious faith, and with it his political faith, was probably that of William Frend. Frend was a Fellow of Jesus College at the time of Coleridge's arrival there, and Coleridge was soon under his spell. Frend was a Unitarian in religion, a radical democrat in politics, and it was not long before Coleridge too was, as Thomas Poole wrote of him in 1794, "in religion . . . a Unitarian, if not a Deist; in Politicks a Democrat, to the utmost extent of the word." [6] Unitarianism, with its belief in the merely adoptive sonship of Christ, was in Coleridge's day a fairly acceptable form of dissent from the Established Church. The simplicity of its creed relieved one of the burden of a systematic theology and accorded well with the rationalistic kind of natural theology that was still in its heyday. In addition, Unitarianism's social

[6] Quoted by Mrs. Henry Sandford, *Thomas Poole and His Friends*, 2 vols. (London, 1888), I, 95.

concern made it a useful form of dissent from the evident injustices of England's political and economic structure. Frend, with both his Unitarianism and his politics, became a cause célèbre at Cambridge in 1793, and Coleridge was ready to go to the wall with him.[7] Ultimately Frend was expelled, but he had left his mark on Coleridge. By insisting on the principles of social justice, especially in support of the French Revolution, Frend had evoked a deep response in Coleridge's already profound sense of moral responsibility. It was no doubt during these years at Cambridge that the principle of individual responsibility came to be a focal point for much of his thinking in politics, economics, philosophy, and religion. Already the role of the individual will had come to the fore.

Even more deeply influential on Coleridge during his three years at Cambridge and during the several years following was one of the patron saints of English Unitarianism, David Hartley. The influence of Hartley is clear enough from Coleridge's lengthy discussion of him in the *Biographia Literaria.* Although Coleridge refutes Hartley's associationist psychology at some length in the *Biographia,* during the 1790's he still accepted Hartley's mechanistic explanation of the origin of ideas. There was no contradiction in Coleridge's mind between acceptance of the necessitarian philosophy dictated by Hartley's associationism and acceptance of Christian revelation in the Unitarian understanding of it. Coleridge calls Hartley, in fact, the "great master of *Christian* Philosophy." [8] For even though Hartley denies man's free will in the theoretical order, he can admit it in the practical sense of the power to do what one desires to do, since one's very desires have been formed by the mechanical association of ideas. As a Christian philosopher, Hartley can point to several admirable results of this mechanism: solution of the seeming contradiction between God's foreknowledge and man's free will; confirmation of belief in universal redemption; and the added motive of being able to strive earnestly toward a goal that is already assured.[9]

Appleyard's summary of the ultimate Hartleyan influence on Coleridge's religious thought is admirable. Appleyard finds the source of this influence particularly in "the moral and religious principles

[7] Chambers, *Coleridge,* pp. 20–21.

[8] *CL,* I, 236 (September 24, 1796).

[9] On all this, as well as on the possible influences on Coleridge of Hartley's follower, Joseph Priestley, see Appleyard, pp. 20–29.

4

which are implicitly assumed in Hartley's work." These principles are summarized as: "the theistic conception that underlies the work, the idea of the perfectibility of man, the mechanism of necessity by which this process toward happiness is accomplished, and the confidence in rational analysis which pervades the study. These are the themes of Coleridge's theology and his politics in the early 1790's. They define what was the precise attraction and the most enduring, though sometimes negative, influence of Hartley's 'Christian Philosophy.' " [10] Man is necessitated, but he is necessitated ultimately by a benevolent God who will bring him to happiness. For that rationalistic age, Coleridge's combination of philosophical necessity with religious optimism during these years seemed an eminently reasonable one. As Coleridge wrote to Southey in 1794 about Charles Lamb's acceptance of his sister's illness: "He bore it with an apparent equanimity, as beseemed him who like me is a Unitarian Christian and an Advocate for the Automatism of Man." Coleridge wishes the same for Southey himself: "I would ardently, that you were a Necessitarian—and (believing in an all-loving Omnipotence) an Optimist." [11]

Coleridge left Cambridge at the end of 1794 a convinced and professed Unitarian. His mind was filled with the celebrated scheme for a Pantisocracy in America, the impractical communist society he and Southey had begun discussing a year or so previously. It was Coleridge's certain cure for the social evils he saw around him. How much the scheme was bound up with his current Unitarian beliefs becomes clear in the six Bristol Lectures of 1795, part of several series of lectures given in Bristol by Coleridge and Southey as a means of defraying the expenses of their venture in America.

The six theological lectures delivered by Coleridge at Bristol are, in effect, a presentation of Unitarian apologetics on behalf of revealed religion.[12] The sources he draws on, though not all Unitarian, are generally of the rationalistic tradition: Joseph Butler's *Analogy of Religion* (1736); Archdeacon Paley's treatise on the *Evidences of*

[10] Appleyard, *Coleridge's Philosophy of Literature*, pp. 28–29.

[11] *CL*, I, 147, 145 (December 29, 1794); see also p. 205.

[12] The manuscript (in Coleridge's own hand) of the theological lectures given at Bristol in 1795 is in the Coleridge Room of the Victoria College Library in the University of Toronto, and it is to this manuscript that references are given. In discussing the Bristol Lectures, I am much indebted to the unpublished doctoral dissertation of Paul A. Lacey, "Samuel Taylor Coleridge's Political and Religious Development: 1795–1810" (Harvard, 1966).

Christianity (1794); Hartley's *Observations on Man* (1749); Joseph Priestley's interpretation of Hartley. Quite intentionally, Coleridge's lectures constitute an example of the same type of "evidence-writing" which he was to attack so strenuously in later years.

Coleridge's thought in the Bristol Lectures was still predicated on the basis of a profound interrelationship of religion and political thought. The announced topic of the sixth lecture says so expressly: "The grand political Views of Christianity—that far beyond all other Religions, and even sects of Philosophy, it is the Friend of Civil Freedom—The probable state of Society & Government if all men were Christians." [13] Coleridge begins the lectures with the rational evidences in proof of God's revelation and ends with the application of Christian revelation to political and social problems. The approach is typically Unitarian.

Coleridge's evidences for revealed religion include: arguments for the existence of God, particularly the standard teleological arguments used by Paley; arguments for the necessary benevolence of the Deity, from the very nature of the idea of God; the problem of evil, insoluble except in the context of revealed religion; miracles, in which he follows Paley's and Priestley's arguments against Hume, arguing in such a way that he can at the same time give a natural explanation of miracles and admit their logical possibility even as exceptions to the natural order; and the historicity of Scripture, using the internal and external criteria employed by Warburton, Paley, Hartley, and Priestley.[14]

Not surprisingly, it is the problem of evil which affords Coleridge his entrée into the political and social ramifications of revealed religion. First of all, he prefers not to speak of anything as evil, since in the long view everything has its place in God's plan. He would rather speak in terms of pain, arguing that the function of pain in the divine plan is to chasten man for his moral evil and return him to the path of virtue. Even vice and its pains are means for man to learn virtue. By association, involving trial and error, man slowly learns the relationship between virtue and happiness, that is, that his own ultimate happiness is associated with his virtuous actions. Thus man's fall was

---

[13] The manuscript prospectus for the lectures from which this is quoted is now in the Tinker Collection (#656) of the Beinecke Library of Yale University.

[14] These "evidences" are found in the MS. of the Bristol Lectures, ff. 12-91.

actually a gift of God's kindness, a part of the divine plan for man. This view of evil "allows Coleridge to argue, first, that God is entirely benevolent, second, that man, though compelled by necessity, is still responsible for his actions and will suffer punishment or enjoy rewards for them in the next life, and finally, that man is in such a state of depravity that he cannot be recalled from it by natural religion or natural wisdom alone." [15] Natural religion must be supplanted by revealed religion, accompanied by miracles as confirmatory signs.

In terms of his belief in the evolutionary character of history, Coleridge can go on to point out that natural religion and the "Mosaic dispensation" are both propaedeutics for the New Testament revelation. The revelation of the New Testament moves beyond that of the Old Testament, because it makes a more direct appeal to man's feelings and because it holds out to man the motive force he needs, the certain hope of a future life. The strong belief in a life to come is obviously of crucial importance if virtue is intimately bound up with man's feeling for his own self-interest.

It is clear, then, what Coleridge finds at this time to be the essence of the Christian gospel: it is an appeal to man's feelings, motivated by the hope of future life as the reward for virtuous actions. This is borne out in a letter to John Thelwall in the year following the Bristol Lectures. "Now the Religion, which Christ taught, is simply ı that there is an Omnipresent Father of infinite power, wisdom, & Goodness, in whom we all of us move, & have our being & 2. That when we appear to men to die, we do not utterly perish; but after this Life shall continue to enjoy or suffer the consequences & natural effects of the Habits, we have formed here, whether good or evil.— This is the Christian *Religion* & all of the Christian *Religion*." [16] Clearly, as Paul Lacey points out, "these two principles, the cornerstone of Unitarian theology and the starting place for all its arguments for the necessity of the Christian revelation, substantiate Coleridge's faith in the gradual melioration of society." Coleridge is still following the Hartleyan associationist psychology. Both the fatherhood of God and the motivation of future reward or punishment

---

[15] Lacey, "Coleridge's Political and Religious Development," p. 135.

[16] *CL*, I, 280 (December 17, 1796).

are addressed to man's affections, and for Coleridge "feelings have more influence on human motivation than the reason has, especially those feelings which lead to active benevolence or philanthropy." [17] What Coleridge hopes for, then, is the moral re-education of the feelings and affections of society, according to the teaching and example of Jesus. This was ultimately his hope for Pantisocracy: the creation of a situation in which man's moral feelings could be regenerated.

Within this context of thought, as Coleridge presented it in the Bristol Lectures, there was obviously no place for an orthodox idea of the Redemption. Coleridge believed that, like much of what was called orthodox Christianity, the doctrine of the Atonement was an aberration of early Gnosticism in its attempts to accommodate to Platonic philosophers. He felt that sacrifice in the Old Testament was not conceived in terms of any propitiatory effect it might have on God but as a means for man to change his own attitudes and feelings. Analogously, Jesus may be spoken of as this kind of sacrifice, "as a necessary means relative to man, not a motive influencing the Almighty . . . Christ offered himself—i.e. he evidenced his sincerity by voluntarily submitting to a cruel Death, in order that he might confirm the Faith or awaken the Gratitude of Men. Such is the moral sense of Atonement in Scriptures." [18]

From the same period as the Bristol Lectures, Coleridge's long poem "Religious Musings," begun in late 1794 and revised several times between then and March 1796, is a kind of epitome of his religious and social thinking during the Unitarian years. It all seems to be there: the deep sympathy with the French Revolution; the hopes for man's future, especially as a result of the Revolution; optimism for the victory of social justice; ultimate beatitude for all men; and trust in the loving example of Jesus. As always, Coleridge's religion necessarily involved political and social consequences.

It is perhaps this same link between religious and political commitment which became instrumental in moving Coleridge slowly away from Unitarianism. By 1798 another poem, "France: An Ode," announced his disillusionment with the French Revolution and its ex-

[17] Lacey, "Coleridge's Political and Religious Development," pp. 27–28.
[18] MS. of Coleridge's Bristol Lectures, ff. 122–123.

cesses. It may have been this disillusionment which drew him away from direct confrontation with political and social issues to a search for general principles and religious truths on which to build his life. Disillusionment was probably a factor, too, in the growing sense of guilt, his own and mankind's, which led him away from necessitarianism to a fuller acceptance of the principle of human responsibility. To this were added a number of other factors: growing evidence of the failure of his marriage with Sarah Fricker; the beginnings of his problem of drug addiction; and before long, the at least seeming decline of his poetic power, lamented in the "Dejection" ode of 1802. In 1802 his topical writing for the *Morning Post* also ended, and in effect, his political activity was over.

The effect of all of these events may have been to turn him in upon himself; surely, it involved a growing realization of his own weakness, a sense of guilt, and a need for inner regeneration which he could not himself achieve. His religious needs began to be focused more clearly than ever on man's diseased and guilty will. If this was a time of deepening theological understanding, it could not come but by anguished prayer. He wrote in his notebook in February 1805: "O me miserum!—Assuredly the doctrine of Grace, atonement, and the Spirit of God interceding by groans to the Spirit of God (Rom. VIII.26) is founded on a constant experience . . . Deeply do I both know and feel my Weakness—God in his wisdom grant, that my Day of Visitation may not have been past!" [19]

In the *Biographia Literaria,* writing of his Unitarian years, Coleridge said that he was "at that time and long after, though a Trinitarian (i.e. ad normam Platonis) in philosophy, yet a zealous Unitarian in Religion." He explained: "These principles I held, *philosophically,* while in respect of revealed religion I remained a zealous Unitarian. I considered the *idea* of the Trinity a fair scholastic inference from the being of God, as a creative intelligence; and that it was therefore entitled to the rank of an *esoteric* doctrine of natural religion. But seeing in the same no practical or moral bearing, I confined it to the schools of philosophy. The admission of the Logos, as *hypostatized* (i.e. neither a mere attribute, or a personification) in no respect re-

---

[19] *The Notebooks of Samuel Taylor Coleridge,* ed. Kathleen Coburn, 2 vols., Bollingen Series L (New York, 1957–1961), II, 2437.

moved my doubts concerning the incarnation and the redemption by the cross." [20] It would seem that during these troubled years—especially those following 1802, culminating in his unhappy escape to Malta in 1804–1806—Coleridge discovered the "practical and moral bearing" of the Trinity, bound up as it always was in his mind with the doctrine of the Redemption. In February 1805, during his sojourn in Malta, he recorded in one of his notebooks what Kathleen Coburn says "appears to be his first recorded explicit statement of Trinitarianism as having supplanted his earlier Unitarianism." There he spoke of "the adorable Tri-unity of Being, Intellect, and Spiritual Action, as the Father, Son, and co-eternal Procedent, that these are God (i.e. not mere general Terms, or abstract ideas) and that they are one God (i.e. a real, eternal, and necessary Distinction in the divine nature, distinguishable Triplicity in the indivisible Unity)." [21] Here, and in the following long notebook entry, Coleridge uses basically the same "intellectual analogy"—God, the Reason or Word of God, and the Spiritual Action—which he will build upon in later years, especially in the Trinitarian speculations of the "Opus Maximum." And yet, although Professor Coburn very rightly points out here that "Coleridge's return to orthodox Christianity is through the Logos, not the Gospels, a metaphysical rather than a historical approach," [22] surely he was led to the Logos partly by his own personal realization of man's need for redemption. Then, as always, Coleridge's was a "practical Christianity," and the role of man's moral being was paramount.

A letter of Coleridge to George Fricker on October 4, 1806, retraces the path that led him from Unitarianism to Trinitarianism. It is worth quoting at length by way of summary:

I was for many years a Socinian; and at times almost a Naturalist, but sorrow, and ill health, and disappointment in the only deep wish I had ever cherished, forced me to look into myself; I read the New Testament again, and I became fully convinced, that Socinianism was not only not the doctrine of the New Testament, but that it scarcely deserved the name of a religion in any sense. An extract from a letter which I wrote a few months ago to a sceptical friend, who had been a Socinian, and of

---

[20] S. T. Coleridge, *Biographia Literaria*, ed. J. Shawcross, 2 vols. (Oxford, 1907), I, 114, 136–137. This work will hereafter be cited as *BL*.

[21] *Notebooks*, ed. Coburn, II, 2444; and see Professor Coburn's note on this entry.

[22] *Notebooks*, ed. Coburn, II, 2445 n.

course rested all the evidences of Christianity on miracles, to the exclusion of grace and inward faith, will perhaps, surprise you, as showing you how much nearer our opinions are than what you must have supposed. "I fear that the mode of defending Christianity, adopted by Grotius first; and latterly, among many others, by Dr. Paley, has increased the number of infidels;—never could it have been so great, if thinking men had been habitually led to look into their own souls, instead of always looking out, both of themselves, and of their nature . . . Still must thou repent and be regenerated, and be crucified to the flesh; and this not by thy own mere power; but by a mysterious action of the moral Governor on thee; of the Ordo-ordinians, [sic] the Logos, or Word. Still will the eternal filiation, or Sonship of the Word from the Father; still will the Trinity of the Deity, the redemption, and the thereto necessary assumption of humanity by the Word, 'Who is with God, and is God,' remain truths . . . Believe all these, and with the grace of the spirit consult your own heart, in quietness and humility, they will furnish you with proofs, that surpass all understanding, because they are felt and known; believe all these I say, so as that thy faith shall be not merely real in the acquiescence of the intellect; but actual, in the thereto assimilated affections; then shalt thou KNOW from God, whether or not Christ be of God." [23]

For more than a decade Coleridge had been a Unitarian. It is clear that he left his former beliefs with a sense of relief or, rather, that he embraced Trinitarianism with a profound sense of fulfilment. He had, after all, found his way to it by a dark and difficult road. It must not be thought, however, that he brought nothing of his former belief along with him. It is all too commonly implied that there is a radical discontinuity between these two phases of Coleridge's life. I should think rather, as I suggested at the outset, that there is a distinct pattern in Coleridge's growth from Unitarianism to Trinitarian Christianity, that the former was a stage through which, for his spiritual growth, he had to pass. It was his experience with Unitarianism, after all, which helped to arouse his sense of social responsibility, and which brought home to him the relevance of religious belief to political action. It was this experience that deepened his realization of the importance of the affections in the context of religious faith, perhaps paving the way for his later emphasis on the priority of will

[23] CL, II, 1189–1190. See also the letter written to Fricker several days later on the same subject; CL, II, 1192–1193 (October 9, 1806).

over reason. With a growing realization of evil and guilt and his own inadequacy in the face of them, he moved beyond Unitarianism to the redemptive strength of a more orthodox Christianity, but he carried with him much of the richness of his earlier experience. It was not lost; it was transfigured.

As I do not accept the idea of a dichotomy between the Unitarian and the Trinitarian Coleridge, neither do I accept the dichotomy of two Coleridges proposed by J. B. Beer in his otherwise splendid book on Coleridge: one Coleridge who embraces the glorious idea of man made in the image of his Creator; the other weighed down by a sense of spiritual guilt. "So wide is the gulf between the two views," Beer says, "that it is no exaggeration to say that their respective protagonists speak different languages. Those who put their faith in the divinity of mankind talk of building the new Jerusalem, of striving towards the ideal, of choosing right courses of action, of responsibility; while those who hold the other speak of sin and redemption, of man's insufficiency and God's mercy, of necessary evils and the protection of innocence." [24] Beer feels that many people are afflicted with a dichotomy between the two points of view and that Coleridge is one of these. "Yet it is clear that in terms of pure logic at least, each attitude is ultimately exclusive of the other, and admits of no compromise. Coleridge was one of those who find themselves torn between an awareness of this and an unwillingness to choose." [25] To begin a study of Coleridge, or of any Christian thinker for that matter, with such a conception, almost vitiates from the start the possibility of getting at his essential thought. These two "points of view" are precisely the point at issue. They are not to be resolved in terms of "pure logic." The inevitable and perpetual balance, or rather tension, between them is the central mystery of Christianity. To say that Coleridge was caught up in this tension is only to say that he was a Christian. Indeed, this is man himself: "In doubt to deem himself a God, or Beast."

Like most Christians, Coleridge sometimes felt the joy of being a Christian, perhaps more often the guilt or the pain. But he accepted it all, reflected on it, and tried to see more deeply into the meaning of the mystery. In a sense, that is the story that follows.

[24] *Coleridge the Visionary* (New York, 1962), pp. 32–33.
[25] *Coleridge the Visionary*, p. 33.

There is another tension, too, that will be seen to run like a kind of leitmotiv through much of Coleridge's religious writing. It is the conflict between his "dynamic philosophy" and his Christian faith. On the one hand there is his conception of reality as organic process, prompted by his reading of Spinoza and deepened by his reading of Kant and later of Schelling. It is the spirit of, for example, the "conversation poems" with their sense of "the one life within us and abroad." For all its lurking possibilities of pantheism (which he shunned all his life), this philosophy attracted him strongly both emotionally and intellectually. On the other hand there is, very simply, his commitment to the Christian faith.

In a sense, much of Coleridge's religious thought is an attempt to reconcile the dynamic philosophy and the Christian faith. His speculations about the Trinity, for example, are to some extent a function of this struggle: for Coleridge, the Trinity offered the only viable alternative to pantheism; in this way alone can God be conceived of as at once "the same and other," and in this way alone can dynamic process be compatible with the Immutable. His conception of the Logos, too, is part of this tension: the Logos is the eternal pattern of Creation, but this pattern is still to be worked out toward its perfection in the "divine humanity." Coleridge's notion of symbol, too, and of "consubstantiality," as an attempt to confront the dynamic problem of the One and the Many, will be seen to be of crucial importance for his idea of faith, Redemption, and the Sacraments.

In these instances—as in so many others—we will find that, although the problem is not resolved and a final synthesis constructed, usually a balance is achieved. And this is probably how it should be, after all, when one is dealing with what he admits to be, as Coleridge does, ultimately mystery. This is why Coleridge's religious writings must be seen as—to use Walter Jackson Bate's words—"brilliant, searching, conservative, boldly speculative, and (increasingly) humble—humble before the mystery of the unknown, and the mystery, in particular, of Christianity." [26] But all this, too, is part of the story that follows.

[26] *Coleridge,* Masters of World Literature (New York, 1968), p. 213.

❈ II. THE NATURE OF FAITH

In beginning an analysis of Coleridge's views on the nature of faith, there are two pitfalls around which one must walk warily. The first is the matter of Coleridge's relationship to the German Idealists, especially to Kant. Just as there have been critics who have virtually ignored Coleridge's unquestionable debts to Kant and the Germans, so there are those who have enormously overemphasized this debt.

The danger of ignoring the debt is evident: incompleteness, and consequent misunderstanding of what Coleridge actually meant. Overemphasizing the debt can also lead to misunderstanding, however, because it can cause the critic to lose sight of the particular bent of Coleridge's mind. Coleridge absorbed ideas like blotting paper: the ideas were absorbed, but they were somehow never quite the same afterwards. He may have kept the same terms, but he made of them, quite deliberately, what he would. Consideration of Coleridge's sources is important, of course, and often crucial in understanding his own use of a word or an idea. But the important element, for the critic of Coleridge, is ultimately what Coleridge himself meant, whatever his source and whatever his departure from his source.

The second pitfall is to approach Coleridge with rationalistic presuppositions, an approach which has prevented some of his critics from meeting Coleridge on Coleridge's own terms.

Even such an outstanding critic as René Wellek, to whom every critic of Coleridge is in debt for his remarkable studies of Coleridge's German sources, has not kept wholly free of these pitfalls. In his approach to the problem of the assent to religious truth, Coleridge was influenced, and profoundly so, by Kant's *Critique of Practical Reason*. Ultimately, however, his commitment to Christianity makes him move beyond the postulates of Kant's Practical Reason, to faith. Wellek's response is not to bring into focus the further problem thus raised by Coleridge, the nature of faith and its possible relationship to rational knowledge, but simply to deny the possibility of knowledge beyond the merely rational. Coleridge was driven, Wellek tells us, "into a fatal dualism of a philosophy of faith, which amounted to an intellectual justification of this bankruptcy of thought." [1] Wellek insists that Coleridge " desires the breakdown of human Intelligence in order to substitute pure Faith" (p. 91), and that in going beyond Kant's Practical Reason in his pursuit of religious knowledge, Coleridge "seduced the struggling spirit to acquiesce in immediate knowledge and faith, he lured it to enjoy a mere feeling of mystery and to give up the labor of thinking penetration into problems" (p. 134). If the student of Coleridge allows rationalistic presuppositions to color his approach to Coleridge, he has cut himself off from the possibility of understanding and attempting to evaluate what was really the heart of Coleridge's religious thought: the problem of faith. One cannot have Coleridge either on Kant's terms or on one's own terms; Coleridge can only be apprehended on his own terms.

What I have referred to as the problem of faith in Coleridge is, properly speaking, two problems. The first is the problem of the nature of assent to religious truth; it is the question of the nature of faith, and in Coleridge it must be formulated in terms of his concept of the faculty of reason. The other is the matter of the relationship of religious faith to natural reason; it is the traditional problem of "faith and reason." The two problems are obviously closely linked, but they are not the same problem, and they must be kept clearly distinct from the outset. The first must be considered separately, precisely so that it can then be used to shed light on the second. In this analysis, we shall find the element of will to be of crucial importance, and it is ultimately this element which can help to explain why it is, in Coleridge's mind, that faith is allowed to complement, to go beyond, reason.

The development of Coleridge's notion of reason was a complex one and will be discussed at length in the course of this chapter, but for the moment its main lines can be briefly indicated. After early accepting the classic distinction between reason and understanding, Coleridge came to see the need for a distinction within reason itself between the speculative reason and the practical reason. The latter, which he occasionally referred to as the "higher reason," came to

---

[1] *Immanuel Kant in England:1793–1838* (Princeton, 1931), p. 69. J. H. Muirhead criticizes Wellek's reading of Coleridge in this context in his essay "Metaphysician or Mystic?" in *Coleridge: Studies by Several Hands,* ed. E. Blunden and E. L. Griggs (London, 1934), pp. 177–197.

include more and more of the higher human faculties, notably conscience and will. Thus practical reason came ultimately, in Coleridge's thinking, to be identified with faith.

Coleridge's formulation of the distinction between reason and understanding clearly owes much to Kant. By the time of Coleridge's first extant reference to the distinction (in a letter to Thomas Clarkson on October 13, 1806),[2] he had already known Kant's writings for several years.[3] Coleridge knew well the *Verstand* and *Vernunft* of Kant, and he explained the terms in a way that sounds very much like Kant: the understanding is the faculty which organizes sense impressions into manageable coherence, which "apprehends and retains the mere notices of Experience . . . all the mere φαινόμενα of our nature"; the reason is the faculty which reaches beyond mere sense impressions to apprehend the necessary and the universal, "which are evidently not the effect of any Experience, but the condition of all Experience, & that indeed without which Experience itself would be inconceivable."[4] One might place side by side with this earliest expression of the distinction, its formulation almost twenty years later in the *Aids to Reflection*. There understanding is called (following Archbishop Leighton) "the faculty judging according to sense," and reason is "the power of universal and necessary convictions, the source and substance of truths above sense, and having their evidence in themselves."[5] Taken *tout court*, these formulations sound much

---

[2] *CL*, II, 1198.

[3] Wellek, *Kant in England*, pp. 71–74.

[4] *CL*, II, 1198.

[5] S. T. Coleridge, *Aids to Reflection*, in *The Collected Works of Samuel Taylor Coleridge*, ed. W. G. T. Shedd, 7 vols. (New York, 1856), I, 241. Hereafter this is cited as *Aids*.

Another excellent explanation of the distinction is found in *The Friend*, ed. Henry Nelson Coleridge, in *The Complete Works*, ed. Shedd, II (hereafter cited as *FR*): "Whatever is conscious self-knowledge is reason: and in this sense it may be safely defined the organ of the supersensuous; even as the understanding wherever it does not possess or use the reason, as its inward eye, may be defined the conception of the sensuous, or the faculty by which we generalize and arrange the *phenomena* of perception; that faculty, the functions of which contain the rules and constitute the possibility of outward experience. In short, the understanding supposes something that is understood. This may be merely its own acts or forms, that is, formal logic; but real objects, the materials of substantial knowledge, must be furnished, I might safely say revealed, to it by organs of sense. The understanding of the higher brutes has only organs of outward sense, and consequently material objects only; but man's understanding has likewise an organ of inward sense, and therefore the power of acquainting itself with invisible realities or spiritual objects. This organ is his reason" (145).

For other discussions of the reason/understanding distinction see: *FR*, 143–150, 164, 184; *The Statesman's Manual* (1816), ed. Henry Nelson Coleridge, in *The Complete Works*, ed. Shedd, I, Appendix B, 456–461 (hereafter cited as *SM*); *BL*, I, 109–110; *Aids*, 115 (Preface), 241–243, 246–253, 259–265, 367 (Appendix A), 368–372 (Appendix B); *On the Constitu-*

like Kant transported, and the temptation, too often succumbed to in the past, is to let the matter rest there.

The fact, however, seems to be otherwise. As J. A. Appleyard says of Coleridge's use of the reason/understanding distinction: "He employs it not in its Kantian sense but rather more according to the traditional significance it has had since Plato's time. Coleridge was never prepared to admit that the deliverances of the reason had subjective value alone, nor that the reason was bereft of all contact with an external reality." [6] The distinction is indeed as old as the western philosophical tradition. Plato distinguished between νοῦς and διάνοια; Thomas Aquinas, and the Schoolmen after him, distinguished *intellectus* from *ratio*; [7] Bacon, the Cambridge Platonists and a stream of other English writers distinguished the discursive function of reason (Hamlet's "discourse of reason") from its intuitive exercise. [8] In each case the faculties are distinguished, but both are faculties of real knowledge.

It seems equally true that Coleridge was never satisfied to use reason in the Kantian sense to the extent that reason achieved knowledge only of phenomenal reality. As early as 1809, he writes to Humphry Davy of "the moral connection between the finite and the infinite Reason, and the awful majesty of the former as both the Revelation and the exponent Voice of the Latter" [9]—surely a more

tion of the Church and State According to the Idea of Each (1830), ed. Henry Nelson Coleridge in *The Complete Works*, ed. Shedd, VI, 61–62, 132–134 (hereafter cited as *CCS*); *TT*, 336, 371–372, 453–454, and passim; *Literary Remains of Samuel Taylor Coleridge*, ed. Henry Nelson Coleridge in *The Complete Works*, ed. Shedd, V, 81–82, 90, 163, 181, 206–207, 208, 272, 286, 364, 365–367, 375–376, 412–413, 484, 514–515, 545–547, 561–562 (hereafter cited as *LR*); *CL*, IV, 688–690.

[6] Appleyard, *Coleridge's Philosophy of Literature*, p. 121.

[7] It should be noted that the Schoolmen used *intellectus*, the faculty of intellectual insight, as the higher faculty, in distinction from the discursive *ratio*.

[8] John H. Muirhead, *Coleridge as Philosopher* (London, 1930), p. 65. One must agree with Shawcross, however, when he points out that "this distinction, as a distinction of terms, is not clearly made by the seventeenth century divines, nor indeed before Kant; but they recognize the distinction of things to which it corresponds." *BL*, I, 249, notes on chap. x. Coleridge suggests this himself when he says: "In Hooker, and the great divines of his age, it was merely an occasional carelessness in the use of the terms that reason is ever put where they meant the understanding; for, from other parts of their writings, it is evident that they knew and asserted the distinction, nay, the diversity of the things themselves . . ." *Notes on English Divines*, ed. Derwent Coleridge, 2 vols. (London, 1853), I, 18; this work will hereafter be cited as *NED*. See also *NED*, I, 60, where Coleridge finds the distinction in Richard Field, and *Aids*, 240–241, where he discusses it in Bacon. He faults Jeremy Taylor and Archbishop Leighton (two of his favorite seventeenth-century divines) for not having sufficiently clarified the distinction; see, respectively, *NED*, I, 263 and II, 139.

[9] *CL*, III, 172 (January 30, 1809).

"noumenal" sort of knowledge than Kant would have cared to admit for reason. A decade later, in discussing Scotus, Coleridge speaks strongly of the objectivity of ideas, which are for him the formal object of reason: "Now whether the objectivity given to the Idea belongs to it in its own right as an Idea, or is superinduced by Moral Faith, is really little more than a dispute in terms, depending on the Definition of Idea. It is enough for Scotus's purpose that the Objectivity is and must be admitted, and what more cogent proof can we have, than that a man must contradict his whole human Being in order to deny it. What should we think of a Physiologist who should deny the objective truth of the Circulation of the Blood, because it could not be shewn by the arteries alone without the veins? And yet the Kanteans argue not much unlike this, when in the Idea they separate the Reason from the Reason in the Will, or the theoric from the practical Man." [10] In 1825, in the *Aids to Reflection,* reason and understanding are still, each in its own kind, faculties of confident assertion about reality: "Understanding in its highest form of experience remains commensurate with the experimental notices of the senses from which it is generalized. Reason . . . affirms truths which no sense could perceive, nor experiment verify, nor experience confirm." [11] Reason and understanding never have a merely subjective validity for Coleridge. Within their proper limitations, they afford knowledge of the external world both of sense and of spirit.

A word should perhaps be added at this point about the interrelationship of reason and understanding. While it is true that Coleridge insisted on the necessity of the distinction, the two faculties do not act, nor can they, independently of one another. Whatever his exaltation of the role of reason, Coleridge never minimized the role of understanding; it is indeed a part (although a distinct and inferior part) of reason. Following Kant, Coleridge saw that the understanding affords categories which make it possible for the mind to grasp sensible objects conceptually and to conceive relationships between them. Without the understanding, there would be no coherent

10 Note on Tennemann's *History of Philosophy,* VIII, 765; quoted by Kathleen Coburn, ed., *The Philosophical Lectures of Samuel Taylor Coleridge* (New York, 1949), p. 438 n. 38; this collection will hereafter be referred to as *PL.* This note was probably written in 1818, since Coleridge used Wilhelm Tennemann's *Geschichte der Philosophie* (12 vols., 1798–1817) in preparation for his philosophical lecture series of 1818–1819. See also Coburn, *PL,* Intro., p. 18.

11 *Aids,* 252 n.

knowledge of the sensible world. As D. G. James expresses it, understanding is "the intelligence in its knowledge of the physical world, whether in common sense or in science." [12] And this is precisely its limitation, as well as its utility: "It organizes the world for us, but is helpless to explain it." [13]

Understanding is implied in different degrees in animal instinct, common sense, and scientific knowledge.[14] Beyond all of these, and of a different kind, is reason. Only such a faculty can explain the supersensuous knowledge involved in art, in religion, and in any morality that is beyond the merely prudential. The higher knowledge, the ideas derived by reason, must be expressed in terms of the sensible knowledge given by the understanding, but their substance goes beyond it. Man's knowledge is limited by the fact that his insight into suprasensible ideas must be expressed in terms of analogy with what he knows on the merely sense level, but he knows at the same time that the sense level is not the whole of his knowledge. In other words, when man speaks in such a way he is aware, at least ideally, that he is speaking by analogy.

The nature of reason and understanding and their mutual relationship is, indeed, deeply bound up with Coleridge's conception of the "consubstantiality" of all being, which is much akin to what has traditionally been referred to as "the analogy of being" and, since the sixteenth century, as "the great chain of being." [15] Coleridge was familiar with the philosophical concept of analogy, of course, since it had been a stock-in-trade of the *philosophia perennis* from Aristotle to Hegel. It is present in his work, however, not as a formal philosophical tool but rather as an accepted premise underlying his thought. It is rarely discussed by Coleridge but is everywhere present by implication or indirection. Nor is this surprising. When one considers that the notion of the analogy of being was formulated by the Schoolmen to counter the problems of pantheism on the one hand

---

[12] *The Romantic Comedy: An Essay on English Romanticism* (London, 1963), p. 174.

[13] *Ibid.*

[14] *Aids*, 242–243.

[15] A classic work on the analogy of being is T. L. Penido, O.P., *Le Role de l'analogie en théologie dogmatique* (Paris, 1931); for a shorter treatment, see E. L. Mascall, "The Doctrine of Analogy," *Cross Currents*, I (1951), 38–57. See also Battista Mondin, *The Principle of Analogy in Protestant and Catholic Theology* (The Hague, 1963). For the Renaissance ideas that grew out of the doctrines of analogy and participation, see Arthur O. Lovejoy's *The Great Chain of Being* (Cambridge, Mass., 1936).

and scepticism on the other, it is only reasonable to expect that Coleridge would have come to a similar position, since these were two of his favorite bugbears as well. The problem is posed primarily in terms of man's knowledge of God. Like the Schoolmen, Coleridge would not admit that there was no difference between created being and the Being of God; this would be pantheism, against which he inveighed all his life. Nor would he admit that there was nothing in common between created being and Uncreated Being; this would be to abdicate the possibility of any knowledge of God. The answer had to be that created being and Uncreated Being are somehow the same yet somehow different. Both have properly the attribute of being, but each in its own degree. An attribute found in a created being (beauty, strength, brightness, or love) can be predicated of God, and properly not merely metaphorically, but predicated in an eminently greater degree without the imperfections and limitations of created being. One does not see the face of God, but one does know something real and proper about His perfections.

It should be remembered that this whole notion of the consubstantiality of all being, both for the Schoolmen and for Coleridge, has its roots deeply in the Platonic tradition.[16] It developed directly out of the philosophical doctrine of Participation, the Platonic conception (followed and developed by Plotinus and the Neo-Platonists) by which the Many derive their being from the One. Because created beings "emanated" by degrees from the One, it is possible for them later to retrace the path, in knowledge and in action, back through the hierarchical degrees of emanated, created being, to reunion with the One. Meanwhile, though distinct from the One, they "participate" in the being of the One, each in its own degree. Thus, in knowing the various degrees and attributes of the Many, one knows in some measure something of the attributes of the One.

Coleridge's idea of the consubstantiality of all being may perhaps best be seen in his attitude toward symbols. In discussing a passage of Archbishop Leighton, Coleridge insists on the importance of distinguishing symbolic and metaphorical. Leighton had written: "The

16 Coleridge's relationship to Platonism and Neo-Platonism is discussed by Muirhead, *Coleridge as Philosopher*, pp. 110–117. As for the Schoolmen, it is curious that it is only in recent years that the strongly Platonic elements of Aquinas and other medieval philosophers have been discovered; see, for example, W. Norris Clarke, S.J., "The Platonic Heritage of Thomism," *Review of Metaphysics*, VIII (1954), 105–124.

Platonists divide the world into two, the sensible and intellectual world . . . According to this hypothesis, those parables and metaphors, which are often taken from natural things to illustrate such as are divine, will not be similitudes taken entirely at pleasure; but are often, in a great measure, founded in nature, and the things themselves." On this, Coleridge comments: "I have asserted the same thing, and more fully shown wherein the difference consists of symbolic and metaphorical, in my first Lay Sermon; and the substantial correspondence of the genuine Platonic doctrine and logic with those of Lord Bacon, in my Essays on Method, in the Friend." [17]

The reference to the first Lay Sermon (the *Stateman's Manual*) falls beautifully to the point. We shall find the year of its publication, 1816, marks a distinct new advance in Coleridge's thinking about the faculty of reason. For the moment, suffice it to say that the *Stateman's Manual* has as one of its leading ideas the intimate relationship between symbol and imagination and by extension (in the beautiful and brilliant Appendix B) the relationship between symbol and reason.

A symbol is for Coleridge an idea, which is by nature supersensuous, incarnated in images of sense. A symbol is the result of the joint functioning of reason and understanding (the faculty of the supersensuous and the faculty of sensible knowledge), both working under the aegis of the imagination. As Coleridge wrote in the *Biographia Literaria,* written the year before the *Stateman's Manual,* "an IDEA, in the *highest* sense of that word, cannot be conveyed but by a *symbol*." [18] Some of this interrelationship of the faculties emerges

---

[17] *LR*, 380. The passages Coleridge refers to are in *SM*, 465, and *FR*, 442–448.

[18] *BL*, I, 100. The several emphases are, of course—and typically so—Coleridge's. There is another interesting discussion of the nature of symbols in Notebook 29, ff. 57–62.

There will be reference throughout this work to the Notebooks which Coleridge kept through much of his adult life, and even more faithfully and assiduously during his last decade. The Notebooks are being edited by Professor Kathleen Coburn of the University of Toronto and published by the Bollingen Foundation. We have already referred to Volumes I and II, which cover the period up to 1808. Using both the collection of photographic reproductions of the Notebooks in Victoria College Library in the University of Toronto and the original manuscripts of them there and in the British Museum, I have examined carefully all the as yet unpublished Notebooks, with special attention to Notebooks 20–55, most of which were written between 1818 and 1834.

The main sequence of Notebooks is numbered 1–55; the originals of these, with the exception of Notebook 29, are in the British Museum. There are also a few other Notebooks, generally smaller and less important, which are not part of this sequence; the original manuscripts of most of these are in the Victoria College Library. Some of these have been assigned additional numbers up to 65; others have been lettered F, L, M, N, P—of which the most

from the classic definition of the imagination in the *Stateman's Manual*. Speaking of the human elements of Scripture, history, political economy, and the like, Coleridge says they are "the living educts of the imagination; of that reconciling and mediatory power, which incorporating the reason in images of the sense, and organizing (as it were) the flux of the senses by the permanence and self-circling energies of the reason, gives birth to a system of symbols, harmonious in themselves, and consubstantial with the truths of which they are the conductors . . . its contents present to us the stream of time continuous as life and a symbol of eternity." [19] The suprasensible truths that are the objects of reason can be "incorporated" (that is, "bodied") in "images of the sense" precisely because there is a community of being between them. This is why it is true to say that "true natural philosophy is comprised in the study of the science and language of symbols. The power delegated to nature is all in every part: and by a symbol I mean, not a metaphor or allegory or any other figure of speech or form of fancy, but an actual and essential part of that, the whole of which it represents." [20] Both the temporal, the world of the senses, and the eternal, the suprasensible world of the ideas, partake of the same reality; both can thus be apprehended, through symbol, in the same act of knowing, for a symbol is "characterized by a translucence of the special in the individual, or of the general in the special, or of the universal in the general; above all by the translucence of the eternal through and in the temporal. It always partakes of the reality which it renders intelligible; and while it enunciates the whole, abides itself as a living part in that unity of which it is the representative." [21]

---

important by far is Notebook F. In addition, there are several Notebooks in the Berg Collection of the New York Public Library. Notable among these are a "clasped vellum" Notebook of 1814–1825, which is actually Notebook 29 of the above-mentioned sequence, and which somehow became separated from the rest (it will be referred to as Notebook 29); and a Notebook of 1833–1834, which is called Notebook Q. In all references to the Notebooks I have used the customary folio references. Where dates are known and are thought to be of interest in the immediate context, they have been included with references to the Notebooks.

The Notebooks are as varied in content as Coleridge's own interests: literary criticism, philosophy, scriptural commentary, theological speculation, prayers, recent scientific discoveries, notes on the state of his health. But by far the greatest part of the later Notebooks, especially Notebooks 30–55, is focused on religion, and more often than not takes the form of extended commentary on the Old and New Testaments.

[19] *SM*, 436–437.
[20] *SM*, Appendix B, 465.
[21] *SM*, 437–438.

In terms, then, of the consubstantiality of all being, the faculties of reason and understanding are seen to be deeply interdependent. The reason's idea cannot be expressed except by symbol, the suprasensible in terms of the sensible. At the same time the reason, by 1816, is very much the dominant faculty. Even the imagination, which as the symbol-making faculty might seem to supersede it, is really at the service of reason: "This reason without being either the sense, the understanding, or the imagination, contains all three within itself, even as the mind contains its thoughts, and is present in and through them all; or as the expression pervades the different features of an intelligent countenance." [22]

We have already remarked that the period around 1816 marked a deepening of Coleridge's concept of reason. Before the publication of the *Stateman's Manual* in 1816, references to the distinction between reason and understanding had been sporadic, and it had been used in a relatively limited way, simply as a means of explaining man's knowledge of both sensible objects and immaterial realities. Coleridge had been occupied in no small measure with literature and literary criticism—among other things, a series of lectures on Shakespeare (1811–1812), his successful play *Remorse* (1813), his unsuccessful play *Zapolya* (1815–1816), the preparation of his volume of poems, *Sibylline Leaves* (published in 1817)—and hence his chief epistemological concern had been with the faculty of imagination.[23] Now religious problems began to come more than ever into the forefront of his attention: in the *Stateman's Manual* Coleridge focused on the Bible; in the *Biographia Literaria* he was as much concerned with his own religious development as he was with his "literary life"; and his extensive *rifacimento* in 1818 of *The Friend,* originally subtitled simply "A Series of Essays," now became "A Series of Essays, In Three Volumes, To aid in the formation of Fixed Principles in Politics, Morals, and Religion, with Literary Amusements inter-

---

[22] *SM*, Appendix B, 461.

[23] It has often been assumed that the distinction between imagination and fancy grew out of Coleridge's reason/understanding distinction. This seems hardly likely, since the imagination/fancy distinction is enunciated as early as 1802, long before Coleridge's formulation of the reason/understanding distinction. The first clear enunciation of the imagination/fancy distinction is in a letter of September 10, 1802 (*CL*, II, 865–866). See Appleyard, *Coleridge's Philosophy of Literature*, p. 65. Of course, it remains possible that Coleridge's reading of Kant, which dates at least from 1801, may have suggested a distinction which is at least analogous to that between *Verstand* and *Vernunft*.

spersed." [24] With the exception of the last great series of Shakespeare lectures in the winter of 1818–1819, this is the way it would be from now on: politics, morals, and religion, with "literary amusements" interspersed.

With his deepened religious concern in mind, particularly a growing sense of the need for personal religious involvement,[25] Coleridge began to see the need for a further distinction beyond the reason/understanding distinction, within reason itself. Personal commitment to spiritual realities demanded not only knowledge but also will. There was reason beyond the merely speculative; there was a practical reason.

The touch of Kant is unmistakable here. Kant had already shown the need for a Practical Reason which, with the aid of will and its "categorical imperative," could go beyond the merely theoretical dic-

[24] *The Friend* of 1809–1810 was a one-man periodical published, more or less weekly, during Coleridge's Grasmere days. It almost died a-borning, then came briefly to a fitful life, only to die quietly after the twenty-eighth issue. In 1812, the issues were bound together and published as a single volume. It was greatly expanded in 1818 and published in three volumes. The most notable addition was the "Treatise on Method," originally written in 1817 for the ill-fated *Encyclopaedia Metropolitana*.

[25] Witness, for example, the deeply personal tone of chap. x of the *Biographia Literaria* and the beautiful peroration of chap. xxiv, or the *Stateman's Manual*, especially Appendix B. I think it may not be fanciful to link this renewed sense of personal involvement with a religious experience, a kind of conversion, which Coleridge seems to have undergone at the end of 1813. He was seriously ill—near death, it seems, at one point—for a period of two weeks (December 5–19) during a stay in Bath. The experience is recounted in three moving letters (*CL*, III, 462–464), one of which says: "The Terrors of the Almighty have been around & against me—and tho' driven up and down for seven dreadful Days by restless Pain, like a Leopard in a Den, yet the anguish & remorse of Mind was worse than the pain of the whole Body.—O I have had a new world opened to me, in the infinity of my own Spirit!—Woe be to me, if this last Warning be not taken." *CL*, III, 463–464 (December 19, 1813, to Mrs. J. J. Morgan). The *Biographia Literaria* (written in 1815, though not published until 1817) and the *Stateman's Manual* are the first works written after this experience.

The experience was more than a passing one. Four months later (April 26, 1814) Coleridge wrote to Joseph Cottle: "You have no conception of the dreadful Hell of my mind & conscience & body. You bid me, pray. O I do pray inwardly to be able to *pray;* but indeed to pray, to pray with the faith to which Blessing is promised, this is the reward of Faith, this is the Gift of God to the Elect. O if to feel how infinitely worthless I am, how poor a wretch, with just free will enough to be deserving of wrath, & of my own contempt, & of none to merit a moment's peace, can make a part of a Christian's creed; so far I am a Christian—" *CL*, III, 478. Another month later he wrote to J. J. Morgan: "My main Comfort therefore consists in what the Divines call, *the Faith of Adherence*—and no spiritual Effort appears to benefit me so much, as the one, earnest, importunate, & often for hours momently [repeated], Prayer: 'I believe! Lord, help my Unbelief! Give me Faith but as a mustard Seed: & I shall remove this mountain! Faith! Faith! Faith! I believe—O give me Faith! O for my Redeemer's sake give me Faith in my Redeemer.' " *CL*, III, 499 (May 27, 1814).

tates of Pure Reason to be the foundation of a legitimate morality.[26] Once again, however, one should not overestimate Kant's importance in Coleridge's thinking. Kant was ready at hand in the baggage room of Coleridge's mind when the need arose, but Coleridge was content to adopt Kant's terminology, without at the same time becoming a Kantian in morality. In the first place, the dictates of Coleridge's practical reason are much more than postulates; however legitimate Kant insisted they were, they remained postulates for him. Secondly, Coleridge was interested in much more than morality alone in his use of the practical reason. Kant's Practical Reason yielded the three postulates—God, freedom, immortality—which he felt were necessary as conditions for true moral action. These postulates gave no increase in speculative knowledge even of themselves. They were principles of action alone, not of knowledge; to this extent at least, there was an effective dichotomy between Kant's Pure Reason and his Pure Practical Reason.[27] Coleridge on the other hand was interested not only in principles of morality but also in religious knowledge, and he was now, profoundly unlike Kant, to conceive of reason as at once cognitive and volitional. Further, speculative reason and practical reason

26 "The theoretical use of reason is concerned with objects of the merely cognitive faculty . . . It is quite different with the practical use of reason. In the latter, reason deals with the grounds determining the will . . ." *Critique of Practical Reason*, transl. Lewis White Beck (New York, 1956), p. 15.

27 ". . . a thorough analysis of the practical use of reason makes it clear that the reality thought of here implies no theoretical determination of the categories and no extension of our knowledge to the supersensible." *Critique of Practical Reason*, p. 5. In reading Coleridge's 1819 lecture on German philosophy, one has the feeling that there is an element of wishful thinking in his treatment of Kant. See also *PL*, 388–391. Coleridge speaks there of Kant as having "determined the nature of religious truth" (p. 390). Surely "religious truth" is too broad an expression for the limited aim Kant set himself, that is, to validate a workable morality on the basis of the three postulates of God, freedom, and immortality. To push his notion of "religious truth" beyond these postulates would be to run counter to such attitudes as this: "Everything which, apart from a moral way of life, man believes himself capable of doing to please God is mere religious delusion and spurious worship of God." *Religion within the Limits of Reason Alone*, transl. T. M. Greene and H. H. Hudson (Glasgow, 1934), p. 158. Elements of Christianity are accepted, not as "religious truth," but only as morality—and that only insofar as they can be made to fit within the categories of Kant's rational morality. Thus Frederick Copleston speaks of Kant's "strong tendency to strip away, as it were, the historical associations of certain dogmas and to find a meaning which fits in with his own philosophy," and "to retain Christian dogmas while giving a rationalistic account of their content." *A History of Philosophy*, 7 vols. (New York, 1962–65), VI, part II, 136–137. Coleridge's concept of what could be known as "religious truth," on the other hand, included not only a broad spectrum of religious truths derived by man apart from revelation —far more than the three moral postulates of Kant—but also the whole of Christian revelation.

would be distinguishable in function, but they would work in harmony one with the other.[28]

The first treatment of this broadened concept of reason (and it remains a brief one) is in the *Stateman's Manual*.[29] First, the role of the will in reason comes into play: "Neither can reason or religion exist or co-exist as reason and religion, except as far as they are actuated by the will . . . which is the sustaining, coercive and ministerial power." [30] Then, reason is seen as the integrating faculty of man, drawing together in itself all man's higher faculties. It is "reason (not the abstract reason, not the reason as the mere organ of science, or as the faculty of scientific principles and schemes *à priori;* but reason), as the integral spirit of the regenerated man, reason substantiated and vital, *one only,* yet *manifold, overseeing all, and going through all* understanding" (p. 461). Finally, the terms of the distinction are used (once only, and that by indirection) in a reference to "that undivided reason, neither merely speculative or merely practical, but both in one" (p. 462). Clearly the distinction is to be one of function, and the emphasis is to be on their conjoint action.

By 1825, Coleridge's conception of reason seems to have come close to full flower. The role of the will had continued to be stressed more and more, as in the 1819 lecture on German philosophy in which Kant is praised for having "made it felt to the full that the reason itself, considered as merely intellectual, was but a subordinate part of our nature; that there was a higher part, the will and the conscience." [31] But it is in the *Aids to Reflection* (1825) that Cole-

[28] D. G. James has discussed very tellingly the similarity between this distinction and Newman's distinction between "notional assent" and "real assent." The comparison is an enlightening one, for their focus on the problem is very much the same. See *The Romantic Comedy*, pp. 188–191. For the distinction in John Henry Newman, see *An Essay in Aid of a Grammar of Assent* (Garden City, N. Y., 1955), chap. iv.

[29] There is a brief glimpse of the speculative/practical reason distinction in one of the notes by Coleridge published in Southey's *Omniana* in 1812. Coleridge there distinguishes "the speculative reason, *vis theoretica et scientifica,* or the power, by which we produce, or aim to produce, unity, necessity, and universality in all our knowledge by means of principles" and "the will or practical reason." *Notes, Theological, Political, and Miscellaneous,* ed. Derwent Coleridge (London, 1853), 331; this collection will hereafter be referred to as *NTPM.* The distinction seems, however, to have been undeveloped at this time.

[30] *SM*, Appendix B, 458. Perhaps even more insistent is the following passage: "There exists in the human being, at least in man fully developed, no mean symbol of tri-unity in reason, religion, and the will. For each of the three, though a distinct agency, implies and demands the other two, and loses its own nature at the moment that from distinction it passes into division or separation." *Ibid.,* 457.

[31] *PL*, 390. In the *BL*, I, 135, Coleridge insists—again in a rather general way, without linking it with the faculty of reason—on the importance of the will, particularly in religious

ridge seems to have fully accepted the distinction between speculative and practical reason, and the role of the will in practical reason has become paramount:

Hence arises a distinction in reason itself, derived from the different mode of applying it, and from the objects to which it is directed: accordingly as we consider one and the same gift, now as the ground of formal principles, and now as the origin of ideas. Contemplated distinctively in reference to formal (or abstract) truth, it is the Speculative Reason; but in reference to actual (or moral) truth, as the fountain of ideas and the light of the conscience, we name it the Practical Reason. Whenever by self-subjection to this universal light, the will of the individual, the particular will, has become a will of reason, the man is regenerate: and reason is then the spirit of the regenerated man, whereby the person is capable of a quickening intercommunion with the Divine Spirit. And herein consists the mystery of Redemption, that this has been rendered possible for us.[32]

Among other things, this remarkable passage brings conscience to the fore; Coleridge had written of it before, and he would write of it often again.[33] Its intimate link with will connects it inevitably, and closely, with practical reason. Conscience is neither will nor the practical reason but is bound up with both. "The conscience is neither reason, religion, or will, but an experience *sui generis* of the coincidence of the human will with reason and religion." [34] It is "a spiritual sense or testifying state of the coincidence or discordance of the free will with the reason." [35] But Coleridge's analysis is faithful to the general Christian theological tradition in seeing conscience both as a faculty of judgment of the rightness of one's actions and as a motive faculty. Once again, we come back to Coleridge's insistence that volition and cognition function together, or, putting it in Kan-

---

experience. "I become convinced, that religion, as both the corner-stone and the key-stone of morality, must have a *moral* origin; so far at least, that the evidence of its doctrines could not, like the truths of abstract science, be wholly independent of the will." An interesting corollary to this is the notion (which Coleridge includes among the "great Religious truths") that "Religion has no *speculative* dogmas—but all practical—all appealing to the will." In harmony with this, Christ "is not described primarily & characteristically as a Teacher, but as a *Doer*." Notebook L (1809–1818), f. 40.

[32] *Aids*, 241–242.

[33] See, for example, NTPM, 315–316; FR, 106–107, 148, 530; *Aids*, 185–187; TT, 370; LR, 312, 486, 551–552, 557–561.

[34] SM, Appendix B, 459.

[35] FR, 148.

tian terms (and for conscience reading "categorical imperative"), conscience is not regulative alone (as Kant would have it) but constitutive as well. Conscience may not be formally a cognitive faculty, but, by acting upon the will and the reason, it is instrumental in yielding true knowledge:

> The Christian . . . grounds his philosophy on assertions; but with the best of all reasons for making them—namely, that he ought so to do. He asserts what he can neither prove, nor account for, nor himself comprehend; but with the strongest inducements, that of understanding thereby whatever else it most concerns him to understand aright. And yet his assertions have nothing in them of theory or hypothesis; but are in immediate reference to three ultimate facts; namely, the reality of the law of CONSCIENCE; the existence of a responsible WILL, as the subject of that law; and lastly, the existence of EVIL . . . The first is a fact of consciousness; the second a fact of reason necessarily concluded from the first; and the third a fact of history interpreted by both.[36]

Conscience is for Coleridge, then, a distinct but not separate faculty from reason and will. It is the faculty which provides the element of "ought" in the acceptance of truth; it is then (to put it chronologically) joined by the action of the will, which chooses to respond to the imperative of conscience by accepting the ideas presented to it by the reason. Actually, Coleridge sees these faculties as working in harmony in a kind of mutual causality. They are distinguished from one another by their special functions, and it is important to conceive them in this way for the sake of philosophical clarity. In fact, however, they work as one, under the aegis of the practical reason, which we have seen is "the fountain of ideas and the light of the conscience," through which the will becomes "a will of reason," and which is ultimately "the spirit of the regenerated man." [37]

Here at last the lines of thought begin to come together; with "the spirit of the regenerated man," we are in the realm of grace. As always in Coleridge, there remain areas of ambiguity and confusion, but the conclusion can be drawn (though it will require further exploration) that practical reason has become one with faith.

---

[36] *Aids*, 195.
[37] *Aids*, 241–242. See above, p. 27.

Coleridge's only extended discussion of faith as such is the "Essay on Faith," first published in the *Literary Remains* (1836–1839), but probably written during the 1820's.[38] Faith is defined first of all as "fidelity to our own being" and by implication "to being generally, as far as the same is not the object of the senses." [39] This fidelity in turn is seen as a manifestation of conscience, which is referred to as a "categorical imperative." Indeed the very act of becoming conscious of a conscience is called "an act, in and by which we take upon ourselves an allegiance, and consequently the obligation of fealty; and this fealty or fidelity implying the power of being unfaithful, it is the first and fundamental sense of Faith" (p. 559). The second sense of faith is "the preservation of our loyalty and fealty" in the face of objects that are contrary to conscience (p. 560). In this sense "faith is fidelity, fealty, allegiance of the moral nature to God, in opposition to all usurpation, and in resistance to all temptation to the placing any other claim above or equal with our fidelity to God" (p. 564).

Conscience is, of course, inextricably linked with will, and it is through conscience that God's Will (and hence his Intelligence) become present to man's will. And this conscience may (coming full circle) "legitimately be construed with the term reason":

The will of God is the last ground and final aim of all our duties, and to that the whole man is to be harmonized by subordination, subjugation,

---

[38] The date of the "Essay on Faith" is uncertain, but from its contents it may fairly safely be assigned to the last decade of Coleridge's life. A note of Shawcross (*BL*, I, 236) refers to the essay as "supplementary to *Aids to Reflection*, pub. 1825," but he offers no source for this comment.

Most of the material which came to rest in the "Essay on Faith" appears in a three-volume manuscript which is sometimes referred to as the "Opus Maximum," since it contains the major part of what remains of that long projected but never completed work. This manuscript, probably in the handwriting of Dr. Joseph Henry Green, was dictated by Coleridge during the Highgate years. It is now part of the splendid Coleridge collection in Victoria College of the University of Toronto. The manuscript consists of three clasped vellum-bound volumes, together with a smaller unbound "supplement" and some loose papers. The volumes were misnumbered by C. A. Ward, who interchanged volumes II and III. I shall follow throughout the corrected numeration used by Alice D. Snyder in *Coleridge on Logic and Learning* (New Haven, 1929), p. xii: B₁, B₂ (marked Vol. III), B₃ (marked Vol. II), and B Supplementary. The material of the "Essay on Faith" appears in B₂, ff. 106–152 and B₈, ff. 1–25. Actually, the essay seems to be nothing but a rewritten version, somewhat amplified, of this material.

Other passages which treat briefly of faith as such include *BL*, I, 135–136, II, 215–217; *PL*, 280, 365–366, 389–390; *LR*, 91, 317–318, 527–528, 530–531, 552–554; *NTPM*, 138; Notebook 18, f. 43.

[39] *LR*, 557.

or suppression alike in commission and omission. But the will of God, which is one with the supreme intelligence, is revealed to man through the conscience. But the conscience, which consists in an inappellable bearing-witness to the truth and reality of our reason, may legitimately be construed with the term reason, so far as the conscience is prescriptive; while as approving or condemning, it is the consciousness of the subordination or insubordination, the harmony or discord, of the personal will of man to and with the representative of the will of God. (p. 564)

After his definition of "the last and fullest sense of Faith" as "the obedience of the individual will to the reason," Coleridge summarizes in a passage which shows him at his luminous best, and which makes it abundantly clear that for "faith" one can read "practical reason":

Thus then to conclude. Faith subsists in the *synthesis* of the reason and the individual will. By virtue of the latter therefore it must be an energy, and inasmuch as it relates to the whole moral man, it must be exerted in each and all of his constituents or incidents, faculties and tendencies;—it must be a total, not a partial; a continuous, not a desultory or occasional energy. And by virtue of the former, that is, reason, faith must be a light, a form of knowing, a beholding of truth. In the incomparable words of the Evangelist, therefore—*faith must be a light originating in the Logos, or the substantial reason, which is co-eternal and one with the Holy Will, and which light is at the same time the life of men.* Now as life is here the sum or collective of all moral and spiritual acts, in suffering, doing, and being, so is faith the source and the sum, the energy and the principle of the fidelity of man to God, by the subordination of his human will, in all provinces of his nature to his reason, as the sum of spiritual truth, representing and manifesting the will Divine.[40]

[40] LR, 565. There is a similar, perhaps even clearer, passage on the same matter in the "Opus Maximum," immediately preceding and continuous with a passage which became the major part of the "Essay on Faith." "We have seen that the reason in man, as far as it is reason, i.e. on the supposition that the word [?correctly] is the same with the divine reason considered objectively, and subjectively it is no other than the knowledge of the divine reason quoad hoc vel illud: further that the divine reason is one with the absolute will, consequently A being = B & B = C, A is = C, i.e. that the reason in man is the representative of the will of God. It follows therefore that the conscience is the specific witnessing respecting the unity or harmony of the will with the reason, effected by the self subordination of the individual will, as representing the self, to the reason, as representing of the will of God." Victoria College MS. B₃, ff. 6–7. I have modified the punctuation slightly for the sake of clarity; the absence of Coleridge's characteristic capital letters is explained by the fact that the manuscript is in the hand of Dr. Green, to whom Coleridge dictated it. The passage is followed in the manuscript by what is substantially the last half of the "Essay on Faith," LR, 561–565.

In summary, then, let it be said that the ideas in which we know immaterial realities, whether they be arrived at by man's unaided intellect or given by special revelation of God, are known by an act of faith, which is to say by an act of man's practical reason. In addition to the speculative reason, this act involves will and conscience as well, because it is an act of imperative commitment and fidelity posited by the whole man.

It would be difficult, to be sure, to locate Coleridge's conception of faith with any exactitude within the tradition of Christian theology. In a sense, he has managed to bring together something of the best of several traditions.

The problem of the conception of faith is, of course, as old as Christianity itself.[41] Serious theological reflection on the idea of faith, too, began early, as early as the Apologists of the second and third centuries. Almost from the start, two traditions, or rather two emphases, were present. Clement of Alexandria (c. 150–215), for example, insisted on the freedom of the commitment of the will in faith: free commitment of oneself to revelation precedes the knowledge that faith can give. It is the Christian's commitment to revelation which is of first importance. Side by side with this tradition (and, of course, not contradictory to it) was the description of faith as an enlightenment of the mind by God. By this enlightenment—as it is described, for example, by Justin Martyr (d. 165) and Cyril of Jerusalem (c. 315–386)—God illumines the mind of the Christian and gives him new knowledge. The emphasis here is not so much on man's act of will as on the enlightenment of his intellect. In Augustine the two aspects are brought together into synthesis. For Augustine faith is a matter of both intellect and will. Through man's free act of commitment and the illumination given by God, the Christian grows in

[41] The word faith, as a religious term, seems to belong to the Judaeo-Christian tradition alone. In the Old Testament, the notion is generally expressed by the words *aman* and *batah,* both of which connote security and confidence in man's response to God's revelation; the note of trust in God is clearly predominant. In the New Testament, the essential note of man's response to God remains, but in this response the notion of intellectual acceptance becomes equally as important as trust, the commitment of the will. Christ demands acceptance of the Word of God as much as of the action of God, or perhaps more accurately, the action of God *is* His Word, the Logos. The notions are often expressed in the New Testament, in fact, by two distinct Greek words: ἔλπις, hope or trust, and πίστις, faith. The words are often not adequately distinct, πίστις especially carrying connotations of both intellect and will, but the desire to emphasize both elements is clear. See *Vocabulaire de Théologie Biblique,* ed. X. Léon-Dufour (Paris, 1962), cols. 389–399; and P. Antoine, "Foi (dans l'Ecriture)," *Supplément au Dictionnaire de la Bible,* t. II (Paris, 1938), cols. 276–310.

knowledge of the truth. The medieval theologians (notably Thomas Aquinas), although they realized the complexity and richness of the scriptural meanings of faith, were generally influenced—by the Aristotelian psychology within which they worked—to stress the intellectual aspect of faith as an assent. At that same time, they did admit a voluntary element in the formation of an act of faith. In the late Middle Ages, however, the voluntarism of the Nominalists stressed more strongly the role of the will and thus remotely paved the way for Luther's analysis of faith. Especially in his reading of the Epistle to the Romans, Luther felt that the Pauline conception of faith was, as Gustave Weigel has summarized it, "an act of trust in a good God Who wrought our salvation in spite of our sinfulness . . . It was no longer an act of the intellect but an act of the will, wherein man grasped a loving God and in this grasp found his peace." [42]

From the time Luther's conception of faith became more or less normative for the Reformers, the theological analysis of faith split fairly clearly along sectarian lines. For Catholic theologians, faith was essentially an assent of the intellect to divine revelation and for the sake of theological clarity was sedulously distinguished from the other two theological virtues, hope and charity, which more fully conveyed the elements of will in the process of salvation. [43] For the Reformers, faith was to remain essentially an act of the will, of complete confidence in God, through assurance of personal salvation through the merits of Christ. [44] In point of fact, both Catholics and Protestants were talking about the same act, and both conceived it as an act of complete surrender to the revealing and loving God. Catholics conceived this surrender, however, as compounded of three acts, of faith, hope, and love; Protestants conceived it as a single act of faith, which had therefore necessarily to involve elements of will. The

---

[42] *Summarium Doctrinale de Actu Fidei* (Woodstock, Md., 1958), pp. 2–3. In much of the preceding paragraph I have followed the pattern of development given by A. R. Jonsen in his excellent article, "Faith: Patristic Tradition and Teaching of the Church," *New Catholic Encyclopedia* (New York, 1967), V, 796–797. For fuller treatment of the historical development of the conception of Faith during this period, see the classic study by Roger Aubert, *Le Problème de l'Acte de Foi*, 3rd ed. (Louvain, 1958), pp. 13–87.

[43] The Catholic viewpoint was codified in 1547 by the Council of Trent's Decree on Justification. See H. Denzinger and A. Schönmetzer, *Enchiridion Symbolorum Definitionum et Declarationum de Rebus Fidei et Morum*, ed. 33 (Freiburg im Breisgau, 1965), n. 1530–1531; hereafter this work will be referred to as Denzinger-Schönmetzer.

[44] Aubert summarizes this Protestant view as "confiance totale dans les promesses divines en général et surtout conviction absolue d'être personnellement justifié par les mérites du Christ." *Problème de l'Acte de Foi*, p. 73.

common note that brings them together is the implied admission that saving faith implies knowledge, but that knowledge alone is not enough. But the explication of this common note was destined not to be made until our own day, when the heat of sectarian controversy had begun to cool.

The Age of Rationalism, with its denial of the intellectual validity of revelation, had to be met in different ways according to one's own theological persuasion. Protestants who remained faithful to the Reformers' conception of faith were forced to retreat into it even further, the extreme result being perhaps Schleiermacher's analysis of faith as a living, quasi-mystical experience of God, devoid of true intellectual content.[45] Others, like Archdeacon Paley, tried to meet Rationalism on its own ground.[46] This is, too, the defense Catholic theologians decided to mount. If faith is essentially an act of intellect, then the intellect's power to achieve true religious knowledge must be defended.[47] But in order to meet Rationalists on their own ground, it was often necessary to prescind from theological data and to argue philosophically. One result was not infrequently an attempt to prove too much by the unaided reason. Another result was a separate analysis of what natural reason alone could achieve by way of religious knowledge and what could be known only by revelation, with an insistence on the distinction between the two acts, faith and reason.

Perhaps because he was relatively unburdened by the weight of sectarian controversy, Coleridge was able to come fresh to the subject. He was free to make what was, to a great extent, a psychological and epistemological analysis of his own religious experience. One crucial result was, as we have seen, a growing realization of the role of both intellect and will in his acceptance of religious knowledge. It was here that he brought together, wittingly or not, the two major strands, basically Protestant and Catholic, of the traditional analysis of faith.

Another result, equally important, of his analysis of his own reli-

---

[45] See Copleston, *History of Philosophy*, VII, part I, 183–193.

[46] This is especially true of Paley's *View of the Evidences of Christianity* (1794) and his *Natural Theology, or Evidences of the Existence and Attributes of the Deity collected from the Appearances of Nature* (1802).

[47] This concern culminated in the declaration of Vatican Council I in 1870 on the power of man's reason, even unaided by grace, to know God: "Eadem sancta mater Ecclesia tenet et docet, Deum, rerum omnium principium et finem, naturali humanae rationis lumine e rebus creatis certo cognosci posse." Denzinger-Schönmetzer, n. 3004.

gious experience, was his failure, or refusal, to distinguish between the acts by which he knows and accepts revelation and those by which he knows and accepts knowledge of spiritual realities achieved by his unaided intellect. The practical reason was capable of both. This is one of the chief difficulties that has often, in the past, stood in the way of recognizing that Coleridge ultimately had identified practical reason with faith: the fact that Coleridge was rarely, if ever, concerned with the traditional distinction between the natural and the supernatural.[48] Or, more accurately, he was concerned with the problem of "reason and revelation," that is, with the two *sources* of man's knowledge, what man learns by his unaided intellect and what he learns from revelation, but he did not postulate two distinct kinds of act by which knowledge of immaterial reality is achieved. He was far more interested in the continuity of such knowledge than in its discontinuity. Coleridge always saw man in his concrete situation, in a fallen but redeemed world, not in a hypothetical state of "pure nature." [49]

Ultimately the question must arise, to what extent is man's knowledge of religious ideas gratuitous for Coleridge, or in other words, is grace necessary for faith? Does man's action or God's have the priority?

At this point, several crucial questions come crowding in at once, each one dependent to some extent upon the answer to the others. For the sake of clarity, let us try to keep the questions distinct for the moment. The first is: what is the relationship of God's grace to the act of faith by which religious ideas are known? The second is: what is the role of the miraculous in the act of faith? The third is: what is the relationship of reason (in the non-Coleridgean sense) and revelation? This last question is the traditional problem of "faith and reason."

[48] That is to say, Coleridge did not distinguish natural and supernatural on the basis of their accessibility to man's powers, as, for example, theologians often distinguish between man's natural knowledge of God (that which he can attain by his unaided reason) and his supernatural knowledge of God (what he can attain only by revelation of God). He used the terms (and that only rarely) to distinguish material and spiritual, or, as he more often put it, nature and spirit. See, for example, *Aids*, 263; *LR*, 91–92. This distinction is, of course, quite consonant with the importance he attached to the distinction between understanding, the faculty of sense knowledge, and reason, the faculty of immaterial knowledge.

[49] One often disconcerting result of this continuity is that Coleridge came in time to speak indifferently of practical reason or of faith, leaving it to the reader to realize that it is only the *object* of knowledge which may differ for him, not the faculty nor the act of knowing.

The question of the gratuity of faith in Coleridge is not an overly difficult one. Coleridge's view, without exception, is that faith is a free gift given by God, a work of grace, which man is free to accept or reject. If Coleridge did not write often of this gratuity, it was no doubt precisely because it caused him so little difficulty.

As early as 1816, for example, writing of the reason/understanding distinction, Coleridge speaks of reason as "the source of principles, the true celestial influx and *porta Dei in hominem aeternum.*" He insists that in reason "there is and can be no *degree,*" assigning as the reason that *"Deus introit aut non introit."* [50] In 1819, in his lecture on the German philosophers, Coleridge sees the power of reason as essentially dependent upon, indeed a participation in, the eternal: "Must there not be some power, call IT with Lord Bacon the 'LUMEN SICCUM'; OR 'the pure light', with LORD HERBERT; CALL IT 'REASON', or call it the 'Faith of Reason' WITH KANT, must there not be some power that stands in human nature but in some participation of the eternal and the universal by which man is enabled to question, nay to contradict, the irresistible impressions of his own senses, NAY, the necessary deductions of his own understanding—to CHALLENGE and disqualify them, as partial and INCOMPETENT?" [51] In his marginal notes on John Donne's sermons, faith is "essentially an act, the fundamental work of the Spirit." [52] In the notes on *Pilgrim's Progress,* Coleridge objects to "the Arminians and other Pelagians," who "place . . . the saving virtue in the stream, with little or no reference to the source. But it is the faith acting in our poor imperfect deeds that alone saves us; and even this faith is not ours, but the faith of the Son of God in us." [53] A moving notebook entry of 1829 continues to insist on the dual authorship of the commitment to religious truth:

[50] *Letters of Samuel Taylor Coleridge,* ed. Ernest Hartley Coleridge, 2 vols. (London, 1895), II, 712–713; this collection will hereafter be referred to as *LSTC*. Even this early, be it noted, Coleridge uses the word reason when he could just as well have said faith. There is no discontinuity between them. As in Scholastic philosophy, the nature of a faculty is determined by its formal object. Whether Coleridge calls the faculty reason or faith, its object is always the same: spiritual reality. What discontinuity there is, is not between reason and faith, but only between understanding and reason. As Coleridge wrote in a letter of 1816, "From the understanding to the reason, there is no continuous *ascent* possible; it is a metabasis εἰς ἄλλο γένος even as from the air to the light. The true essential peculiarity of the human understanding consists in its capability of being irradiated by the reason, in its recipiency; and even this is *given* to it by the presence of a higher power than itself." *LSTC*, II, 713.
[51] *PL*, 374. The various enthusiastic emphases are Coleridge's.
[52] *LR*, 92.
[53] *LR*, 260–261.

May 4, 1829. More and more strenuously to impress on myself and render intelligible to others the great principle—that all truths of religion are *practical,* and by their *practicability* not their intellectual conceivability to be tried or judged of. Thus: I not only believe, that by Faith alone can I be justified, and that if I live at all, except the life-in-death under the curse of a most holy but for me impracticable Law, it is not I, but Christ that liveth in me (Gal. ch. [ii], 11–20) and that this faith is not *mine* but of Grace—the faith of the Son of God, Who communicates it to me, and whose righteousness is the alone righteousness by which I can be saved—and yet there must be an act of receiving on my part—but this very act is the effect of Grace—What shall I say then? Am I no longer responsible? God forbid! My Conscience would scream a *Lie* in my face if I but tried to think it. No!—but that I am applying the petty Logic of Cause & Effect, where they are utterly inapplicable. But does there exist any practical difficulty? Can I not with my whole heart abjure my own righteousness and feel that I must be transferred & transplanted to another *Ground* of my Individuality, a higher *Nature,* that is indeed above *Nature*—and can I not feel & know that however ardently I may desire this, I have no power to bring it about? [54]

Although Coleridge says clearly that "faith seems to me the co-adunation of the individual will with the reason, enforcing adherence alike of thought, act, and affection to the Universal Will, whether revealed in the conscience, or by the light of reason," he says no less clearly that "the corrupt will can not, without prevenient as well as auxiliary grace, be unitively subordinated to the reason, and again, without this union of the moral will the reason itself is latent." [55] In short, there is no separating out the role of man's will and the role of grace in the act of faith, for "all faith begins in a predisposition, analogous to instinct, inasmuch as the particular Will could not be awaked and realized into an actual Volition but by an impulse and communication from the universal Will. This latter is the vital air, which the particular Will breathes, but which must have entered & excited the faculty as the previous and enabling Condition of the first disposition to breathe, as well as the power of drawing the Breath.

---

[54] Notebook 40, ff. 25–25ᵛ. On the necessity of grace for faith, see also *LR,* 288, 479–480, and Notebook 3½, ff. 144–144ᵛ.

[55] *LR,* 106–107. What Coleridge calls prevenient and auxiliary grace seem to be equivalent to the Scholastic *gratia praeveniens,* which precedes and prepares for an act, and *gratia concomitans,* which is concomitant with the act itself.

It must be 'in us both to will and to do.' And not only at the beginning but thro' the whole Life do we need this *prevenient Grace*." [56]

It will perhaps be clear by this time that Coleridge sees the grace of God operating in the act of faith in two ways: as a light for the intellectual dimension of the act (the "pure light" of the passage cited from the 1819 lecture); and as a support to the volitional dimension (the "saving virtue in the stream"). Coleridge does not make much of the distinction, however, though he sometimes speaks of one or the other aspect, because he is more concerned with the conjoint action of reason and will as practical reason. Grace influences practical reason and so implicitly influences will as well as reason.

The second question we posed for ourselves, in the analysis of the relative roles of God and man in the process of faith, is that of the role of the miraculous in the act of faith. Both this and the following question, the problem of faith and reason, are closely linked with the nature of apologetics. [57]

Considered historically, the science of apologetics began with the great Apologists of the second and third centuries (Justin Martyr, Tertullian, and others), who viewed their task as the presentation to non-Christians of the case for Christianity. Before long, however, it took a distinctly defensive turn, and became a defense of orthodoxy

[56] Notebook 21½, f. 46ᵛ. This need for man's will, weakened by the Fall, to receive an influx of grace in order to make a saving act of Faith is summarized in a striking passage from Coleridge's philosophical lecture of January 25, 1819. "We hear [Christ] commanding us to be perfect even as our Heavenly Father is perfect, and yet declaring to men that they must perish—utterly perish—if they relied on themselves, or if they sought for a realization of that perfection . . . in aught but a reliance on a superior power: not a mere tame acquiescence in the truth of it, but in a total energy of their being with utter concentration of the soul to that our intense wish, a sense of its utter dependence which is entitled faith." Men have, he says later, "lost their Will." Still later, he goes on: "The eye gives you a power which enables you to see but you have not the hand to grasp, and you have not the wing to soar towards it, and what remains for you? This—and by this essentially are you distinguished from the desperate. You can ask . . . ask and it shall be given you . . . But the energy of the soul to act is by the divine grace made to be the very means of strength, made to be the very wing by which you are to fly and from which alone you can." *PL*, 222–225. In order for man to embrace the truth which he sees, his weakened will must be made whole again; it must be influenced by what the Scholastic theologians called "sanating grace," the grace which heals. Scholastic theologians also distinguish between sanating grace, which restores fallen nature to its pristine wholeness, and "elevating" grace, which gives man the power to perform a properly supernatural act. Coleridge, generally unconcerned with the natural/supernatural distinction, does not employ this elevating/sanating distinction.

[57] The essential source in any historical or theological study of miracles is the recent definitive study by the Flemish theologian Louis Monden, S.J., *Signs and Wonders: A Study of the Miraculous Element in Religion* (New York, 1966). For the relationship of the concept of miracle with the history of apologetics, see Monden, pp. 41–53.

against its attackers. Gradually the aim of apologetics came to be more and more, as it remains in many quarters even today, to demonstrate rationally the truth of Christianity; its history reaches from medieval scholastic "proof for the existence of God" through Butler's *Analogy of Religion* and Paley's *Evidences of Christianity* to countless modern Protestant and Catholic apologists. Within this context of thought, miracles tended to become part of the mechanism of apologetics: departures from the ordinary course of nature, which prove that God is master of His creation and testify that His revealed word is true. Hence miracles were taken to be directed more to unbelievers than to believers.

The rise of scientific discovery in the seventeenth and eighteenth centuries, however, shook apologetics profoundly, especially its treatment of miracles. It now began to appear that much of what had always been considered miraculous might be susceptible of natural explanation. The result was a wave of rejection of the possibility of miracles in such influential works as John Toland's *Tetradymus* (1720) and David Hume's "Essay upon Miracles" (1748).

The reaction of the Christian churches to these attacks was either to assume a posture of defense, invoking mystery for protection, or simply to yield the field to the enemy, conceding the impossibility of miracles but denying that they are necessary to Christian belief. It was a slow process for theologians to come to the realization that it was their very conception of miracle which was at fault. In England, Coleridge seems to have been one of the first of these.

Coleridge treats of miracles (and we confine our discussion to scriptural miracles, as Coleridge does) in only one of the works published during his lifetime,[58] and that only briefly, but he gave his attention to them fairly often in his marginalia, letters, and notebooks.[59] Three constant themes are repeated throughout this material: (1) the contravention of a law of nature is not of the essence of a miracle; (2) the essential significance of a miracle is its sign value; and (3) faith *precedes* the perception of a miracle, that is to

---

[58] *FR*, 393–394, 468.

[59] Besides the passages cited in the course of the following discussion, Coleridge discusses miracles in the following places: *PL*, 352; *LR*, 46, 60–61, 317–318, 427–429, 434–437, 543–544, 555–557; *NTPM*, 99; *TT*, 299; *CL*, IV, 799 (January 7, 1818); *Unpublished Letters of Samuel Taylor Coleridge* (hereafter cited as *UL*), ed. Earl Leslie Griggs, 2 vols. (London, 1932), II, 355–357 (July 1825); Notebooks 20 (ff. 25–26); 21½ (ff. 4ᵛ, 31–32); 33 (ff. 17–19); 45 (ff. 39ᵛ–40ᵛ); 51 ([f. 6ᵛ]).

say, recognition of a miracle as such is a result of faith rather than its cause.

Coleridge objects, always and everywhere, to the traditional definition of miracle: "Suspension of the laws of nature! suspension—laws —nature! Bless me! a chapter would be required for the explanation of each several word of this definition." [60] He prefers to begin with a philosophical definition: "An effect presented to the senses without any adequate antecedent, *ejusdem generis,* is a miracle in the philosophic sense. Thus: the corporeal ponderable hand and arm raised with no other known causative antecedent, but a thought, a pure act of an immaterial essentially invisible imponderable will, is a miracle for a reflecting mind. Add the words, *praeter experientiam:* and we have the definition of a miracle in the popular, practical, and appropriated sense." [61] This is indeed a necessary first step for Coleridge, because it bridges what he believed to be a false dichotomy between the natural sphere of the ordinary working of divine providence through secondary causes and the sphere of extraordinary supernatural action of God. For Coleridge, God can work miracles, that is, give striking divine signs, even through the working of natural causes: "If it be objected, that in nature, as distinguished from man, this intervention of particular laws is, or with the increase of science will be, resolvable into the universal laws which they had appeared to counterbalance, we will reply: Even so it may be in the case of miracles . . . But should that time arrive, the sole difference, that could result from such an enlargement of our view, would be this;— that what we now consider as miracles in opposition to ordinary experience, we should then reverence with a yet higher devotion as harmonious parts of one great complex miracle, when the antithesis between experience and belief would itself be taken up into unity of intuitive reason." [62]

[60] LR, 437.

[61] LR, 437. Coleridge gives much the same analysis in LR, 544–545 and in Notebook 21 ½, ff. 4ᵛ and 31–31ᵛ, where he makes it clear that *praeter experientiam* means beyond all previous experience.

[62] FR, 468. We might add to this several remarkable passages from Notebook 39 (c. 1826), the first of which we shall have occasion to refer to again shortly. Notebook 39, ff. 10–10ᵛ: "Do those Theologians, who define a miracle by a suspension of the Laws of Nature, consider that Nature *suffers* laws? That Nature is the Subject of Law, not a Lawgiver? That the Law which controls Nature, and gives her *Reality, yea,* which constitutes (what without its presence would be Chaos, Hades, blind, blank and void Multëity) Nature, is Reason? The *Word* aboriginal . . . self-subsistent, and living—to talk of the Suspension of which is the synthesis

Whether its cause be within or without the observed "laws of nature," the essential element of a miracle for Coleridge is that it be a divine sign, God's special means of speaking to man and drawing attention to His revelation. Coleridge remarks in Notebook 39 (c. 1826): "What other definition does the term, Miracle, require or admit than 'Acts, Incidents, Appearances calculated to excite awe and wonder'? And what more fitted to impress the mind with awe and wonder, than Law? The Effects are *always* admirable; but when they are such as to direct the Beholder's mind to the *Agent* while his attention is drawn to the Work—to make him recognize the presence of the Law itself shining thro' the Effects—then do these most rightfully claim the name of Signs and Wonders!" [63] In short, what is essential to a miracle is that it somehow reveal God and His truth. It

---

of Nonsense and Blasphemy? . . . What other definition does the term, Miracle, require or admit than 'Acts, Incidents, Appearances calculated to excite awe and wonder'? And what more fitted to impress the mind with awe and wonder, than Law?"

In Notebook 39, ff. 24–27ᵛ, Coleridge begins by speaking of the sensible miracles attendant on the apparition to St. Paul on the road to Damascus (Acts 9:1–22): "But if a Miracle be defined, as I have proposed, by its relation to a determinate Will, what difference would it make whether our Lord *produced* a thunder-storm at the time that he was working Subjectively in Paul—or had used a thunderstorm by the pre-established harmony of the moral & physical World coincident with that subjective operation? . . . I am sure, that a thinking mind will find a contradiction in the hypothesis of a *Will* acting immediately on a Stone. The Stone would cease to be a Stone—and any fair reply to this would end in destroying the objectivity, and with it the Subjectivity as its Correlate, & re-absorb both in the Absolute Subject—& the moment the imagination had re-created the world, and renewed the polarity, the impossibility would revive.

". . . They [the objectors] cannot pretend that it could not have been arranged in the vast knot of Causation, the evolution of which is the Life and History of the Universal with a foreknowledge of its coincidence with the Subjective Operation on the mind of the Apostle. Do they not admit, that the same Being was the Author & Ordainer of both.

". . . If I do not deceive myself, it is by no reluctance or indisposition to believe the exercise of a superhuman Power by our blessed Saviour that I am actuated—far rather, I find an a priori probability of this fully sufficient to supply the defect necessarily inherent in historic testimony of a Miracle—but by an earnest desire to produce in myself and in others that stedfast and lively Faith which can only exist with insight and a satisfied Reason—and by the consciousness of my inability to deny that the great majority of Miracles are clearly *subjective* —i.e. operation of mind on mind; and that in the apparent objective Miracles the Objective in so large a number is so capable of being resolved into providential co-incidence of natural causes, nay, the arguments for this being actually the matter of fact—ex.gr. the passage of the Red Sea, the Manna, the Quails &c, are so strong—that the very small remainder are as it were *extra-zodiacal*, out of the Character & Economy of the Divine Dispensations, and rank as Exceptions—the removal of which (if they could honestly and without trick or sophism or invalidation of the Sanity and integrity of the Apostles be removed) would, as far as I at present see, in no wise weaken or deteriorate the faith of a Christian nor the Reasons for the faith." On f. 14ᵛ of the same notebook, Coleridge had enumerated the most important "extra-zodiacal" miracles as the miracle at Cana, the feedings of the multitudes, the raising of Lazarus, and the Ascension of Christ.

[63] Notebook 39, ff. 10ᵛ–11.

is this, not any contravention of the laws of nature, which makes the miracle to be such: "Is it not that implication of doctrine in the miracle and of miracle in the doctrine, which is the bridge of communication between the senses and the soul;—that predisposing warmth which renders the understanding susceptible of the specific impression from the historic, and from all other outward, seals of testimony? Is not this the one infallible criterion of miracles, by which a man can know whether they be of God?" [64]

Finally, Coleridge sees miracles as part of the whole Christian revelation, and therefore as an object of the act of faith rather than as one of its causes: "The Miracles are *parts* of our Religion and Objects of our Belief, not the Grounds of it." [65] Miracles are directed not to unbelievers, but to believers. Coleridge comments on the miracle of Nathaniel under the fig tree (John 1:43-51) that "the *Faith* was there already. It existed *potentially* in the predisposition—and awaited only the perception of a corresponding Object to pass from potential into Actual. Now the miracle, simply as Miracle, will not of itself constitute even this correspondency—but, first, it would forcibly direct the attention of the predisposed Mind to it, as found in the person, manner, actions and doctrines of the Worker." [66] In another notebook entry Coleridge points out the harmony of this idea with "the demand of faith, as the condition sine qua non of the effectuation of the *Fiat,* in the miraculous Healings in the Gospel." [67] Finally, in a notebook entry of 1830, commenting on John 4:46-54, Coleridge says: "As a general *rule,* we may say—that without faith in the Patient the Miracle would not have been *symbolic*—or the outward sign of the yet more aweful Miracle worked by the indwelling Christ in the Soul. Faith was, as it were, the Bond or common term between the operation of Christ ab extra, and that of the indwelling Saviour." [68]

It is remarkable that although Coleridge deepened his understanding of the nature of miracles and their role in the Church, he never found reason to change the conviction expressed in a letter to Mary

---

[64] *FR,* 394.
[65] Notebook 38 (1829), f. 24.
[66] Notebook 47 (1830), [ff. 29-30ᵛ].
[67] Notebook 39 (c. 1826), f. 19.
[68] Notebook 48 (1830), [ff. 15-15ᵛ]. The necessity of faith for acceptance of miracles is also touched upon in *LR,* 552, and Notebook 22, f. 73.

Cruikshank in 1807: "My whole & sincere opinion is this: that Miracles are a condition & necessary accompaniment of the Christian Religion; but not it's specific & characteristic Proof. They were not so even to the first eye-witnesses; they cannot be so to us. I believe the Miracles, because many other evidences have made me believe in Christ; & thus, no doubt, the faith in miracles does then react on it's cause, & fills up & confirms my faith in Christ." [69] The miracles of Scripture are visible and striking signs of God's presence to man; belief in them flows from faith and then returns to nourish faith; and belief in them is inextricably bound up with belief in Christ Himself.[70]

The final problem we set for ourselves—that of faith and reason—might properly be distinguished into two distinct, albeit related, problems. The first focuses on man's faculties with respect to knowledge of religious truths; this will be referred to as the faith/reason problem. The second concerns the source of the data in religious knowledge, whether they are known from special revelation or by man's unaided study and reflection; this will be called the reason/revelation problem. Since confusion of the two problems has caused misunderstanding of Coleridge in the past, they will receive separate treatment here.

In a way, Coleridge's position on the faith/reason problem is implicit in much that has gone before. At any rate, premises have been established from which some conclusions may be deduced. First of all, we have seen Coleridge's subsumption of all knowledge of religious truth under the single power of reason. Secondly, we have seen, most recently in the treatment of miracles, his relative unconcern with the distinction between natural and supernatural. And yet the faith/reason distinction is most commonly expressed in precisely

---

[69] *CL*, III, 32–33 (September 1807).

[70] Coleridge's reflections on miracles are remarkably similar to the basic viewpoint of a modern theologian like Monden. In particular, Coleridge's admission of the possibility of miracles through the working of natural causes in a striking way is very close to Monden's statement that, once the theological sign-structure of an event has been established, there can be no objection to asserting that "a natural occurrence can express and signify more than its nature can account for. This surplus of meaning must be rooted in the divine intention which is the cause of the event." Monden goes on to suggest that since grace does not destroy nature, but rather "frees it, ennobles it, makes it divine," then a miraculous event which appears to be outside the known laws of nature may be only a speeding-up of the natural process (as, for example, in a miraculous cure), an elevation of the natural process to its true perfection, as fallen nature is for the moment "restored to its wholeness." Monden, *Signs and Wonders*, pp. 55–57.

these terms. It usually expresses the attempt to distinguish different powers in man, what he can do unaided and what he can do only with the help of grace. Coleridge does not find this distinction particularly meaningful or helpful.[71]

What does interest Coleridge—and this, too, we have seen in some detail—is the distinction between *kinds* of religious knowledge: the knowledge of religious truths which involves a man's will, and the kind which does not. He is concerned, that is to say, with the moral dimension of faith. As he wrote in a passage already cited, "Religion . . . must have a *moral* origin; so far at least, that the evidence of its doctrines could not, like the truths of abstract science, be wholly independent of the will." [72] Hence, we have seen, Coleridge distinguished two levels of reason: speculative reason, which may "reason" about immaterial reality, but does not involve the whole person; and practical reason, which—together with understanding, imagination, memory, and all the faculties of the person—is "co-adunated" with the will. This latter level is the higher reason, and it only is faith. Its object may be given by man's unaided intellect or by revelation; what is important is how a man acts upon it.

Thus, in a very real sense, the faith/reason problem in Coleridge evanesces, once his conception of reason has been properly understood. He so stresses the continuity of human knowledge above the sense level, as we have seen, that the discontinuity implicit in the usual formulation of the problem becomes impossible. To be sure, in

---

[71] This is not to say, obviously, that Coleridge did not admit a difference between religious truths given by special revelation and those achieved by reason apart from revelation. The data of revelation are known only because they are given by God, and so in a sense may be termed "supernatural." The faculty of reason, however, by which religious truths are known, is one and the same for all religious truths, no matter what their source. Coleridge wrote in his marginalia on Hooker: "That reason could have discovered these divine truths [the truths of Christian revelation] is one thing; that when discovered by revelation, it is capable of apprehending the beauty and excellence of the things revealed is another. I may believe the latter, while I utterly reject the former. That all these cognitions, together with the fealty or faithfulness in the will whereby the mind of the flesh is brought under captivity to the mind of the spirit (the sensuous understanding to the reason) are supernatural, I not only freely grant, but fervently contend. But why the very perfection of reason, namely, those ideas or truth-powers, in which both the spiritual light and the spiritual life are co-inherent and one, should be called super-rational, I do not see. For reason is practical as well as theoretical; or even though I should exclude the practical reason, and confine the term reason to the highest intellective power,—still I should think it more correct to describe the mysteries of faith as *plusquam rationalia* than super-rational." *LR*, 40.

[72] *BL*, I, 135. In his marginalia on Baxter's *Life of Himself*, Coleridge spoke of "the evils arising from the equivoque between faith and intellectual satisfaction or insight. The root of faith is in the will." *LR*, 319.

relating understanding (knowledge "in the forms of space and time") and reason (knowledge of nonmaterial reality) he stresses the discontinuity; to pass from one to the other is to pass, as he loved to say, εἰς ἄλλο γένος. However, in relating speculative reason and practical reason (reason "co-adunated" with the will, that is, faith), he stresses the continuity; there is one object for both, and it is an object outside the forms of space and time. It must be expressed in terms of images which are of space and time (hence the need for the concomitant exercise of the understanding and all that belongs to it, for example, memory), because it is only by such analogous expression that man can speak of spiritual realities; but the spiritual reality itself, the idea, requires the exercise of reason.

Coleridge himself saw clearly that in his terms the traditional distinction was not a fruitful one. One of his best statements of this is in a notebook entry of 1833:

> But the error of this & of much more in Hall & the inferiors of his class, has its source in opposing Faith to Reason, not only distinguishing but contra-distinguishing the former from the Latter. Had he seen, that Faith is the Synthesis of the Will and the Reason, that Will essentially is deeper than the Reason, and that it is the *Will finite* that by free self-subordination to the Reason as Universal, and even so, not exclusively as Reason, but as likewise the representative & ἐξήγησις of the Absolute Will, the only Absolute Good. Had he seen, I say, that Faith is the Co-adunation of the individual Will and the Universal Reason as the acknowledged *Word* and *Person* of the Absolute Will, he would have seen that Faith was more than the Reason because it *included* Reason, as one of its factors . . . Faith is more than Reason as being Reason + Will.[73]

Once again, as so often in Coleridge, it is unity which triumphs. With respect to man's knowledge of religious truths, there is one power which knows: reason. If it is not joined with the exercise of the will, it remains merely speculative; if it is "co-adunated" with the will, the union of the two becomes the practical reason. Whether the religious truth in question is learned from special revelation or from human reflection is irrelevant to Coleridge in this context; so, too, the natural/supernatural distinction is irrelevant. If the practical reason has been exercised, then—whether the truth came from reason

[73] Notebook 53, ff. [11–12].

or revelation—grace *has* been given, a supernatural act has been performed.

We are left now to relate the data of reason (in the non-Coleridgean sense) and the data of revelation, but in the light of what has been said already, Coleridge's position will not be difficult to ascertain.

Coleridge's approach to this question is above all an affirmation of the oneness of truth. As the Reverend James Marsh, editor of the first American edition of the *Aids to Reflection,* wrote in 1829, "it is in his view the proper business and duty of the Christian philosopher to remove all appearance of contradiction between the several manifestations of the one Divine Word, to reconcile reason with revelation, and thus to justify the ways of God to man." [74]

First of all, because truth is one, there can be no contradiction between truth learned from special revelation of God and truth learned by man's own study and reflection. The source of all truth is God, whether He reveals it through Sacred Scripture or through the revelation of nature; and this is ultimately the significance of Coleridge's often repeated dictum that "all religion is revealed religion." [75] Secondly, because man's reason is one, the faculty itself can cause no contradiction in the data: "How is it possible that Faith, which includes Reason, should contradict it?" [76] It is only the understanding, the "faculty which judges according to sense," which could deceive by going beyond its own evidence, and this must obviously be guarded against.

Most simply stated, the problem is, what is reason itself (in the Coleridgean sense) capable of with respect to religious truths, apart from what is given to it by revelation? Reason has three distinct capabilities.

Reason's first capability is simply the mind's own search for truth. It is natural theology, the philosophical study of God. It involves

[74] Preliminary Essay to *Aids,* 74. The passage goes on to say: "It may meet the prejudices of some to remark farther, that in philosophizing on the grounds of our faith he does not profess or aim to solve all mysteries, and to bring all truth within the comprehension of the understanding. A truth may be mysterious, and the primary ground of all truth and reality must be so. But though we may believe what *passeth all understanding,* we *can not* believe what is *absurd,* or contradictory to *reason.*" Italics in the original.

[75] See, for example, *TT,* 386 (March 31, 1832).

[76] Notebook 30 (1823–1824), f. 14ᵛ. The entry continues: "As well might the Sun be supposed to require the total extinction of Eye-sight, as the Supreme Mind to have demanded of us the Sacrifice of our Reason."

reflection and analysis of the order of the universe, of the nature of finite and infinite, of causality and finality, and the like. It is, in a sense, the philosophical propaedeutic to revelation by which the mind is opened up to certain of the possibilities of suprasensible knowledge. As Coleridge says in the *Stateman's Manual,* "all history seems to favor the persuasion I entertain, that in every age the speculative philosophy in general acceptance, the metaphysical opinions that happen to be predominant, will influence the theology of that age." [77] He is very aware of the limitations of such knowledge, to be sure. As D. G. James has said, "He is indeed willing to see confirmation of the idea [of God] in the order of the natural world; but nowhere does he with any urgency and confidence make that order a ground for argumentation; if he is ever tempted to do so he also shows that he is aware that any God thus 'proved' would be at best a God suitable for Deists." [78] This is precisely the point of Coleridge's quarrel with Paley and the Paleyites: they have given too much primacy to the merely speculative reason, instead of keeping it in its properly subordinate place as preparation for and confirmation of the practical reason. They have failed to take account of the "chasm, which the *Moral* Being only . . . can fill up or over-bridge." [79] Coleridge was in no such danger of losing his perspective. He endorsed the role of natural theology, but only on condition that it be kept within its proper limits.

Reason's second capability vis-à-vis religious truths is one of Coleridge's prime concerns: the negative task of assuring that there is no contradiction between basic philosophical principles and the data of revelation. As Coleridge wrote in Southey's *Omniana* of 1812, "whatever satirists may say, and sciolists imagine, the human mind has no predilection for absurdity." [80] Coleridge faced the question squarely in the *Aids to Reflection:*

[77] *SM*, Appendix E, 478.

[78] *The Romantic Comedy*, p. 185.

[79] "Opus Maximum," Victoria College MS. B₃, f. 39. The same passage appears also in *FR*, 471. There is a somewhat similar expression, much earlier, in Notebook 18 (1805; 1810–1811), f. 43.

[80] *NTPM*, 328. The same passage also appears in *FR*, 393. There is a similar formulation in Coleridge's marginal notes on the works of Robert Robinson: "Here is the gap in the evidence: and unless this be filled up, all the rest can but perplex the mind. Reason *can not* obtain evidence, that it is God who hath spoken, unless what is spoken is compatible with the co-existence (or, if I dared coin such a phrase, with the *sub-existence* at least) of Reason. As the groundwork therefore of all positive proof, the negative condition must be pre-monstrated, that the doctrine does not contradict, though it may and must transcend, the Reason; that it is incomprehensible but not absurd." *LR*, 536–537.

46

Do I then utterly exclude the speculative reason from theology? No! It is its office and rightful privilege to determine on the negative truth of whatever we are required to believe. The doctrine must not contradict any universal principle: for this would be a doctrine that contradicted itself. Or philosophy? No. It may be and has been the servant and pioneer of faith by convincing the mind that a doctrine is cogitable, that the soul can present the idea to itself; and that if we determine to contemplate, or think of, the subject at all, so and in no other form can this be effected. So far are both logic and philosophy to be received and trusted.[81]

Speculative reason may be trusted to render a judgment of noncontradiction on the data of revelation and to afford them forms of thought and expression. That function belongs to it—no mean function, be it noted—but nothing beyond.[82]

The third capability of reason with respect to revealed data is a positive one: to try to understand more and more about the data of revelation, the mysteries of faith. This third capability seems to fall within the ambit of practical reason, since it will be evident from the passages cited that such capacity is beyond the merely speculative reason. Although this capability of reason involves rational reflection on the revealed data, such reflection is done within the context of faith, for "in spiritual concernments to believe and to understand are not diverse things, but the same thing in different periods of its growth." [83]

---

[81] *Aids,* 222. The passage continues: "But the duty, and in some cases and for some persons even the right, of thinking on subjects beyond the bounds of sensible experience; the grounds of the real truth; the life, the substance, the hope, the love, in one word, the faith; —these are derivatives from the practical, moral, and spiritual nature and being of man" (222–223).

[82] Something like this seems to have been what Coleridge had in mind in the following passage: "They [the Epicureans and the Stoics] convinced men, and that too by arguments which have never been bestowed without success, that the human reason in and of itself can not go beyond the objects of the senses. It may hope, it may expect, it may pray, but of itself it cannot secure a point beyond that coincidence of external experience with the forms of the mind which constitutes what we ourselves call fact. All beyond that are forms; we can demonstrate that they are forms, not derived from accident, not originating in education or in prejudices, but necessarily evolved out of the human soul in a given state of cultivation; but still their reality remains unproved. I can demonstrate, for instance, that the mathematical circle and the different truths of geometry are all inherent in the human reason and in the forms of the mind itself but it would be in vain to seek for a proof of a perfect circle in nature, and as vain to attempt an explanation by an actual experiment on the measurement of a wooden circle. And if a man asked, 'Do you believe that there is such a thing as a circle, except as an idea?', you would be puzzled to give any other answer than the negative. Even so is it with all the great moral truths. They show a fitness in the human mind for religion, but the power of giving it is not in the reason; that must be given as all things are given from without, and it is that which we call a revelation." *PL,* 233.

[83] *Aids,* 228.

In his Preface to the *Aids to Reflection,* Coleridge makes a reverential bow to St. Augustine, citing the following passage written in the context of a discourse on "a high point of theology": *"Sic accipite, ut mereamini intelligere. Fides enim debet praecedere intellectum, ut sit intellectus fidei praemium."* And the bow is more than ceremonial, for Coleridge goes on to apply the words to himself, saying that "every author, who is competent to the office he has undertaken, may without arrogance repeat St. Augustine's words in his own right." [84] This third capability of reason is the classic *fides quaerens intellectum,* faith in search of understanding, summarizing the nature both of the science of theology and, within theology, of the science of apologetics for the believer. [85]

Coleridge was a firm believer in the meaningfulness of the distinction between comprehension and apprehension. He wrote in 1831: "Well may I *believe* what I do not *comprehend,* when there are so many things which I *know,* yet do not *comprehend;*—my life, for instance, my will, my rationality, &c. But let us be on our guard not to confound *com*prehending with *ap*prehending. I do not, even because I *can*not, believe what I do not *ap*prehend; *i.e.,* I cannot assent to the meaning of words to which I attach no meaning, though I may believe in the wisdom of the utterer." [86] This is only to say that while Coleridge was a firm believer in mystery, that the human mind cannot grasp completely the secret things of God even as they are revealed in the mysteries of faith, he believed none the less firmly in the obligation of the believer to understand the mysteries to the limit of his ability.

---

[84] *Aids,* 115.

[85] As we saw in our treatment of miracles, much of the traditional apologetics was directed to nonbelievers, trying to reason them toward faith or (to put the matter in a better light) to establish the "reasonableness" of the data of revelation, as a propaedeutic to the gift of faith. Today, many Christian thinkers have come to the realization that there must also be an apologetics for the believer, by which the believer studies, *post factum* as it were, the reasonableness of his faith as far as this can be done by the study of history, biblical exegesis, psychological analysis, philosophical principles, or any other human means at his disposal. There is a fine explanation of this conception by Avery Dulles, S.J., in his *Apologetics and the Biblical Christ* (Westminster, Maryland, 1963), Intro., pp. vii–xii. That Coleridge, unlike most apologists of his day, was aware of the need for a distinction between apologetics for the believer and for the unbeliever is evident from a remark pointing out "the expediency of separating the arguments addressed to, and valid for, a believer, from the proofs and vindications of Scripture intended to form the belief, or to convict the Infidel." *LR,* 507.

[86] *NPTM,* 169–170. Also see *LR,* 537. In Notebook L (1809–1818), ff. 12ᵛ–13ᵛ, there is an outline for a treatise (presumably never written) "Of Comprehension and Comprehensibility."

If acquiescence without insight; if warmth without light; if an immunity from doubt, given and guaranteed by a resolute ignorance; if the habit of taking for granted the words of a catechism, remembered or forgotten; if a mere sensation of positiveness substituted—I will not say for the sense of certainty, but—for that calm assurance, the very means and conditions of which it supersedes; if a belief that seeks the darkness, and yet strikes no root, immovable as the limpet from the rock, and, like the limpet, fixed there by mere force of adhesion:—if these suffice to make men Christians, in what sense could the Apostle affirm that believers receive, not indeed worldly wisdom, which comes to naught, but the wisdom of God, *that we might know and comprehend* the things that are freely given to us of God? On what grounds could he denounce the sincerest fervor of spirit as defective, where it does not likewise bring forth fruits in the understanding? [87]

In the *Stateman's Manual,* Coleridge attacks "mere acquiescence in truth, uncomprehended and unfathomed" and appeals to Scripture for authority, pointing out that knowledge is there "not only extolled as the crown and honor of a man, but to seek after it is again and again commanded us as one of our most sacred duties." [88] And again he states this belief in a brief note entitled "Evidences of Christianity": "The Christian, to whom, after a long profession of Christianity, the mysteries remain as much mysteries as before, is in the same state as a school-boy with regard to his arithmetic to whom the *facit* at the end of the examples in his ciphering book is the whole ground for his assuming that such and such figures amount to so and so." [89] In short, as Coleridge wrote in the *Stateman's Manual,* "it is impossible that the affections should be kept constant to an object which gives no employment to the understanding. The energies of the intellect, increase of insight, and enlarging views, are necessary to keep alive the substantial faith in the heart." [90]

Although the relationship of reason and faith in Coleridge now seems clear, it might be objected that we have not considered the

---

[87] *Aids,* 122. The same passage appears in the second *Lay Sermon* (as distinguished from the *Stateman's Manual,* which is the first "lay sermon"), ed. Henry Nelson Coleridge, in *The Complete Works,* ed. Shedd, VI, 185–186; this work will hereafter be cited as *LS.*

[88] *SM,* 449. The same passage also appears in *FR,* 100.

[89] *LR,* 556. The whole note is worth consulting in this context; see pp. 555–557.

[90] *LS,* 189; see also the passage from which this is taken, 185–190. It is evident from the context that the word "understanding" is used here in its generic sense of "intellect," not in Coleridge's consecrated use of it in distinction from reason.

relationship of the understanding to faith and the data of revelation. After all, was not this precisely the rock on which foundered the religious belief of nineteenth-century scientists like Darwin, Lyell, and Huxley? In the eyes of such men, science found no confirmation of the data of revelation. And yet is not Coleridge's answer, insofar as an answer can be given, already implicit in everything that has been said? This is precisely the function of the distinction between understanding and reason: to assert that there is a faculty higher than understanding (which can deal only with sense data), a faculty which is capable of suprasensible knowledge. A faculty which is capable of knowing and judging sense data alone is not competent to judge suprasensible realities. Where many scientists of the nineteenth century erred was in pushing the scientific judgment—a work of the understanding—beyond its proper sphere of activity. As we have insisted already, and as Coleridge never tired of insisting, it is only the understanding, the "faculty which judges according to sense," which can deceive—by going beyond its own proper evidence, the evidence of the senses. If one denies the existence of a faculty higher than understanding, there can be no knowledge of revelation or indeed of any nonmaterial reality.

This section on the relationship of the data of reason and revelation might properly close with a passage which links together again the two problems we distinguished at the outset: faith/reason and reason/revelation. The affirmation of the unity of man's faculty of religious knowledge is a reflection of the oneness of truth itself, for Coleridge sees "that the Scheme of Christianity, as taught in the Liturgy and Homilies of our Church, though not discoverable by human Reason, is yet in accordance with it; that link follows link by necessary consequence; that Religion passes out of the ken of Reason only where the eye of Reason has reached its own Horizon; and that Faith is then but its continuation: even as the Day softens away into the sweet Twilight, and Twilight, hushed and breathless, steals into the Darkness." [91]

In all this, Coleridge's was once again—as it so often was—a me-

---

[91] BL, II, 218. Besides the passages already cited, the following texts touch on the reason/ revelation problem: FR, 256–257; LS, 157, 200–201; PL, 111–112, 265–281 (passim); CCS, 132–134; LR, 39–40, 84, 327–328, 549–550; CL, III, 482, IV, 847–848.

diating role. The problem of reason and faith was clearly one of the central problems of the age, and it was being posed in a variety of different ways. Roughly at one pole were the Deists, the Paleyites, the Kantians and other German rationalists (Herder, Fichte, Schelling), and the Utilitarians, all of whom shared in matters of religion an enthusiasm for and commitment to what Coleridge considered the unbridled reason, which he would tend to equate (somewhat unjustly in certain cases) with the understanding. At the other pole were the Methodists, Evangelicals, Pietists, Quakers, and the like, who tended to refer their religious belief to a divinely given "inner light," over which man had no control. Between these two poles was Coleridge, who attempted constantly to keep in balance all the elements of man's religious faith: man's work and God's work in the process of faith; man's will and God's will; rational argumentation and divinely granted revelation; objective evidence and subjective religious experience. As so often, Coleridge was responding to the needs of his age, teetering and balancing between points of view any one of which seemed to him inadequate to the evidence at hand. As in poetry so in theology, a theological position was rich and meaningful for him in proportion to the variety of truths it held in balance. This is clearly the reason for the remarkable richness and depth of his analysis of faith.

There is one aspect of faith that has been, in a way, all-pervasive, and yet has seemed not to demand (or perhaps even to admit) separate treatment, precisely because it is all-pervasive: the relationship of faith to the Author of faith, of reason to the Supreme Reason. Coleridge's concern throughout has been man in his search for union with God. It is only within the context of this search that the urgency of Coleridge's complex analysis of faith can be appreciated. But with this in mind, together with the remembrance that Coleridge is always and everywhere the Christian Platonist, it is possible to appreciate what he accomplished. With some degree of success, he has taken the measure of man as the image of God by focusing his attention on the faculties of man which most properly make him an "image of God," his reason and his will. By fidelity to his own highest faculties, man can commit himself in faith and so achieve union with God, for "faith is the source and the sum, the energy and the principle of the fidelity of man to God, by the subordination of his human will, in all provinces of his nature to his reason, as the sum of spiritual truth, representing and manifesting the will Divine." [92]

[92] "Essay on Faith," *LR,* 565. In Notebook F, ff. 62ᵛ–64 (?1827), there is an interesting note on the Trinity as "light of the human mind" and the limitation of this light after the Fall.

❊ III. THE NATURE AND ROLE OF SACRED SCRIPTURE

The heart of Coleridge's views on the nature of Sacred Scripture is to be found in the slim volume called *Confessions of an Inquiring Spirit,* written about 1826 and published posthumously in 1840.[1] The *Confessions* are perhaps unique in the corpus of the discursive Coleridge as a more or less complete treatise on a single theological subject. He focuses clearly there on the problem of the nature and the relationship of scriptural inspiration and inerrancy, and we may perhaps best begin this chapter with the consideration of his approach to this problem.

Coleridge's views on the inspiration and inerrancy of Scripture, especially as they are found in this remarkable little book, have not been given the careful attention they deserve. To be sure, critics generally nod to his reverent but "liberal" approach to Scripture. There have even been, from time to time, encomia of Coleridge's

---

[1] The *Confessions of an Inquiring Spirit,* in the form of seven letters to an unidentified friend, gather together the main ideas of Coleridge's biblical criticism as it is found scattered in bits and pieces through many of his other writings. It is fairly clear from several notebook references to them that they were written during the period 1825–1827. In an undated note preserved by Mrs Gillman, Coleridge refers to the composition of the letters and to the reason for his postponement of publication. Speaking of the new higher criticism, Coleridge wrote: "I had long foreseen that this disclosure must take place, and that no *Cordon Salutaire* would exclude the infection; and from this conviction I wrote the letters on the Religious and Superstitious veneration of the Scriptures in the hope of preparing the minds of theological students for the discussion by showing that whatever the final result might be the *Truths* of *Christianity* stood on *foundations* of *adamant* . . . Anxious, however, that the momentous Truths and vindications of the mysteries of our faith from unscriptural perversions and distinctions, set forth in the 'Aids to Reflection' should have fair play, I suspended the publication of the Letters." This note was copied out by Mrs. Gillman for the never-completed second volume of her husband's "Life of S. T. Coleridge," and was finally published by her granddaughter, Mrs. Lucy Watson, in her *Coleridge at Highgate* (London, 1925), p. 102; I have not been able to find the original source of this note, which does not appear in the Victoria College copy of the notebooks. A notebook entry of September 1826 (Notebook 26, f. 98ᵛ) transcribes a proposed motto, not used in the published version, for "my Letters on the right and the superstitious veneration of the S.S.," and another entry of November 1827 (Notebook 36, f. 8ᵛ) refers to "Mss. Letters on the true and the superstitious Use and Estimation of the Bible" as seemingly recently composed.

The *Confessions of an Inquiring Spirit* was found in manuscript after the author's death; it was edited by his nephew Henry Nelson Coleridge and published six years after his uncle's death. References throughout will be to the Shedd edition, V, 569–623; it will be referred to hereafter as *Confessions.*

contribution to the liberalization of the concept of biblical inspiration in the face of modern historical criticism. John Tulloch, for example, in his St. Giles' Lectures for 1885, claimed that "to him belongs the honour of having first plainly and boldly announced that the Scriptures were to be read and studied, like any other literature, in the light of their continuous growth, and the adaptation of their parts to one another." [2] There has not been, however, a serious attempt to define the nature of Coleridge's theory of biblical inspiration nor to see it in relation to previous and subsequent theories.

Belief that the sacred books of Scripture are inspired by God has been a constant of the Judaeo-Christian tradition from the beginning.[3] Throughout biblical, patristic, and medieval times, there was little attempt, probably because there was little need, to work out a refined explanation of the nature and extent of biblical inspiration. Scripture was accepted as the inspired word of God and therefore as inerrant. God used men as instruments to convey his message to mankind, but he must necessarily have protected them from human weakness and error.[4]

---

[2] "Coleridge and His School," in *Movements of Religious Thought in Britain during the Nineteenth Century: St. Giles' Lectures* (London, 1885), p. 25. Vernon Storr, in *The Development of Theology in the Nineteenth Century* (London, 1913), also stresses the influence of Dr. Thomas Arnold on English thinking about Scripture: see pp. 191–193. For Arnold's treatment of inspiration, which is similar to Coleridge's, see his "Essay on the Right Interpretation and Understanding of the Scriptures" in his *Sermons,* 3rd ed., 3 vols. (London, 1844), II, 374–425.

[3] In the historical conspectus on the following pages, I have followed the broad lines of the excellent article on "Inspiration of the Bible" by Alfred Durand, in *The Catholic Encyclopedia* (New York, 1913), VIII, 45–50. See also J. T. Forestell's article "Bible, II (Inspiration)," in the *New Catholic Encyclopedia* (New York, 1967), II, 381–386.

Acceptance of the privileged position of the sacred books is, of course, characteristic of the Old Testament itself, together with the position of the prophet as a spokesman for Jahweh. Although it was not until Josephus (A.D. 37–95) that the word "inspiration" (ἐπίπνοια) appears in the Jewish tradition, the concept of Scripture as the word of God is a constant factor in the Old Testament. Christianity, from the very beginning, held firmly to belief in the Bible, both the Old and New Testaments, as the word of God. Although it is true that the New Testament does not assert its own inspiration, it is clear that it does lay the foundation for the belief of the Church in its inspired character: the New Testament consistently affirms itself at the same time to be in direct line of succession to the Old Testament, and to surpass it in dignity and importance. Hence its origin cannot be less exalted than that of the Old Testament.

[4] A favorite metaphor among the Fathers of the Church to express the notion of inspiration was that of the musician who plays beautiful music on a stringed instrument. In the more sophisticated medieval theologians, such as St. Thomas Aquinas, the philosophical notion of "instrumental causality" was applied, according to which the nature of the instrument (in this case, man as an "instrument" of a special kind, namely, endowed with free will) is taken into account, but even this notion was not elaborated or applied in detail. See also *Summa*

The Reformers, as a natural result of their insistence on *sola Scriptura*—Scripture as the sole rule of faith—began almost at once to work out more in detail the concepts of scriptural revelation and inspiration. Having rejected ecclesiastical control of Scripture, the Reformation soon found itself faced with the problem of linking belief more evidently with the word of God revealed in the Bible. In formulating an attitude toward Scripture, the almost inevitable result was that revelation was identified with inspiration. Everything in Scripture was inspired, they argued, and hence must have been revealed. In style as well as substance, it was generally thought to have been in some way "dictated" by God to man.[5]

Reacting to the Reformers, Catholic thinkers began to theorize about the nature and extent of biblical inspiration. The theorizing went on, but the Council of Trent (1545-1563) was content to define the traditional belief of the Church that all the books included in the Latin Vulgate are part of the sacred canon of Scripture.[6]

As the Reformation took stronger hold, opposing camps on the question of Scripture began to emerge. One camp, relying on the Reformation principle that each Christian is taught directly by the Holy Spirit, de-emphasized the "letter" of Scripture in the interests of a freer working of the Spirit; such, for example, were the Pietists of the seventeenth century. The other camp, arguing from the Reformation principle of individual interpretation, emphasized the "letter" of the Bible, and this tendency moved to the fore in the eighteenth

Theologica (Ottawa, 1953), pars II-II, qq. 171-174. An excellent commentary on St. Thomas' conception of the unique character of the instrumental causality found in inspiration is that of Paul Synave, O.P., and Pierre Benoit, O.P., *Prophecy and Inspiration,* transl. A. Dulles and T. Sheridan (New York, 1961), pp. 77-83, 94-95.

[5] Another result of the Reformers' emphasis on the words of the text as the *ipsissima verba* of God was Luther's rejection of certain parts of the canon of Scripture. This was due "not to any laxity in his doctrine of inspiration, but rather to a high doctrine of inspiration to which, in his opinion, certain books in the Canon, did not attain." R. A. Finlayson, "Contemporary Ideas of Inspiration," in *Revelation and the Bible: Contemporary Evangelical Thought,* ed. C. F. H. Henry (Grand Rapids, 1958), p. 232.

[6] It was not until Vatican Council I (1869-1870) that the Catholic Church defined the traditional belief of the Church that the books of the canon of Scripture (and all their parts) are inspired by God, that this inspiration is the action of the Holy Spirit, and that God is properly referred to as the "author of the Bible." See Denzinger-Schönmetzer, n. 3006: "Qui quidem Veteris et Novi Testamenti libri integri cum omnibus suis partibus, prout in eiusdem Concilii [Tridentini] decreto recensentur, et in veteri Vulgata latina editione habentur, pro sacris et canonicis suscipiendi sunt. Eos vero Ecclesia pro sacris et canonicis habet, non ideo, quod sola humana industria concinnati, sua deinde auctoritate sint approbati; nec ideo dumtaxat, quod revelationem sine errore contineant; sed propterea, quod Spiritu Sancto inspirante conscripti Deum habent auctorem, atque ut tales ipsi Ecclesiae traditi sunt." For the relevant decrees of the Council of Trent, see also Denzinger-Schönmetzer, n. 1502-1504.

century and joined forces with the historical and exegetical criticism which was just beginning to come into its own.[7] In summary, during the post-Reformation period, among both Catholics and Protestants, there was a growing appreciation of the human aspects of the Bible.

This new emphasis on the human aspects of Scripture had the healthy effect of weakening the view, which had been all too prevalent among both Protestants and Catholics, of Scripture as mechanically "dictated" by God—a view which had been encouraged by the simple identification of revelation and inspiration.[8] At the same time, rationalists of the eighteenth century saw the new textual and historical criticism of the Bible as an opportunity to undermine the divine element in Scripture. Their attacks brought about, in turn, doubts, queries, and sharp rejoinders.

The movement of "biblical rationalism" which preceded the age of Coleridge was not all of a piece by any means. There were those who tried to show how ridiculous it was to pretend that books which manifest all the weaknesses and defects of human writing could be of divine origin and authority.[9] There were others who, by using the literary techniques applicable to any human document, tried to distinguish what was sacred in the Bible from what was secular; only the sacred, they felt, need be upheld.[10] Still others turned to the

[7] The Oratorian Père Richard Simon (d. 1712) is sometimes said to be the founder of modern biblical exegesis.

[8] Hooker offers a classic expression of the "dictation" theory in a sermon on Jude 17–21. After quoting I Cor. 2:12–13, he says: "This is that which the Prophets mean by those books written full within and without . . . so often as He employed them in this heavenly work they neither spake nor wrote any word of their own, but uttered syllable by syllable as the Spirit put it into their mouths." *Works*, ed. J. Keble, 3 vols. (Oxford, 1836), III, 662. A homelier illustration of the dictation theory is found in an anecdote related about Coleridge's father, the Reverend John Coleridge, who was known as a Hebrew scholar. H. D. Traill preserves the story in his *Coleridge* volume in the English Men of Letters Series (New York, 1884), p. 2. After speaking of the Reverend Coleridge's "amiable simplicity and not unamiable pedantry," he goes on to illustrate these characteristics by "his practice of diversifying his sermons to his village flock with Hebrew quotations, which he always commended to their attention as 'the immediate language of the Holy Ghost'—a practice which exposed his successor, himself a learned man, to the complaint of his rustic parishioners, that for all his erudition no 'immediate language of the Holy Ghost' was ever to be heard from *him*."

[9] Such were, for example, naturalist philosophers like Hobbes and Spinoza; deists like John Toland and Matthew Tindal; rationalists like Reimarus, Lessing, and Voltaire.

[10] This was generally the approach of, for example, Johann Semler (who has been called "the father of biblical rationalism") and of J. G. Eichhorn. This is perhaps the place to note that Coleridge read the works of both these men, and that Eichhorn was probably the greatest single source in Coleridge's exegetical background. In 1819, Coleridge wrote to his son Derwent, recommending Eichhorn's introductions to the Old Testament (3 vols., 1780–1783), to the New Testament (2 vols., 1804–1818), and to the Apocrypha (1795), together with his commentary on the Apocalypse, remarking that "these will suffice for your *Biblical* Learning."

Reformation principle that the true and certain light comes to the individual through the enlightenment of the Holy Spirit; what was important was not the objective meaning of the biblical text itself, but the light of the Holy Spirit which it occasioned.[11]

As one reaches the age of Coleridge, two fairly distinct extremes are discernible. On the one hand, there was the influential work of men like Herder, who had been strongly influenced by the rationalistic criticism of the preceding century; on the other hand, there were the orthodox thinkers who strove to use the results of modern textual and historical criticism without either denying the inspired character of Scripture or admitting the possibility of error. One tendency emphasized the human aspect, the other the divine.

The human dimensions of Scripture, Herder felt, must be treated with careful attention. Whatever else it may be, Sacred Scripture is a literary work of art; each of its constituent parts is the product of a determinate time and place, culture and personality, geography and history. The Bible, like any other work of art, was not created in a vacuum. Herder did not call into doubt the inspiration of the Bible, but he saw it as a phenomenon more inherent in the writer than in the text; inspiration was for him essentially an exalted kind of religious enthusiasm. It is certainly true that Herder's historical biblical studies gave impetus to the researches of the nineteenth century, but his theological views on inspiration were just as important. His subjectivizing of the notion of inspiration helped to strengthen the already prevalent climate of Kantian Idealism, of Pietism and the like, whose end-product, perhaps inevitably, was Schleiermacher's radical subjectivization of Christianity itself.[12]

An outstanding example of the opposite tendency, the orthodox attempt to preserve the plenary inspiration and infallible inerrancy of Scripture, is the Anglican theologian William Lee, who delivered

---

CL, IV, 929. Other exegetes of whom Coleridge speaks with some familiarity are H. E. G. Paulus (d. 1851), Johannes Cocceius (d. 1669), and St. Jerome, whose commentary on the Bible he used; these are all mentioned, for example, in Notebook 44 (1830), where he also speaks of Eichhorn. In Notebook 45 (1830), he also speaks of the German philologist B. G. Niebuhr (d. 1831), as well as of Semler.

[11] This was basically the approach of the Pietists, of Wesley, and of the Quakers; its spirit is very much in accord with the Kantian philosophy with its stress on the moral dimension of religious experience and on conscience as its point of origin.

[12] For this view of Herder's approach to Scripture, I am indebted to G. F. Bromiley, "Church Doctrine of Inspiration," *Revelation and the Bible,* ed. C. F. H. Henry (Grand Rapids, 1958), pp. 215–216.

an important series of lectures on inspiration about a decade after the publication of Coleridge's *Confessions*.[13] Lee's lectures are one of the first significant attempts in English to work out a reasonable and consistent theory of inspiration, keeping in balance both the data of the theological tradition and the findings of modern historical research. Up to a point, he succeeds admirably.

Lee's first important principle is the insistence on a clear distinction between revelation and inspiration.[14] Revelation concerns the *matter* which comes to man from God in Scripture; it is the work of "the Eternal Word as the Divine Person who reveals." Inspiration concerns the *means* by which the Scriptures were composed; it is the work of "the Holy Spirit as the Divine Person who inspires" (p. 26). The distinction comes importantly into play in distinguishing what in Scripture is known only by supernatural revelation (for example, the Incarnation of Christ) and what is known by natural knowledge (for example, that there was a census ordered taken in the year of Christ's birth). It is clear, Lee says, "that the subject matter of many portions of Scripture must have been supernaturally revealed, while . . . other details of the sacred history have been derived from natural sources" (pp. 139–140). Everything in Scripture is inspired, that is, written under the guidance of the Spirit, but not everything is revealed by God.

The second principle in Lee's approach is his conception of the manner in which the Holy Spirit uses man as an instrument. The Holy Spirit does not use mechanical dictation but works in and through individual characteristics: the fiery Paul differs from the practical James; the matter-of-factness of the Chronicles differs from the sublimity of Job. "The actuation of the Spirit will not consist in the exclusion of the Human element, but rather in illuminating and exalting it, according to its several varieties, for the attainment of the end proposed" (p. 38).

Lee's third major principle is that of inerrancy. In his view, the Bible is protected from all possible error or inaccuracy not only in conveying matters supernaturally revealed by God but also in con-

---

[13] *The Inspiration of Scripture* (New York, 1857).

[14] The distinction was probably first expressly introduced by Melchior Cano (d. 1560) in his *De Locis Theologicis*.

veying matters learned by natural means: details of history, geography, chronology, etc. Lee summarizes under three headings the objections which are raised against the complete accuracy and infallibility of Scripture: (1) different books of the Bible contradict one another in details of chronology, numeration, etc.; (2) historical data are sometimes contrary to data discovered in profane sources; (3) elements of Scripture are occasionally contrary to the findings of modern science. According to Lee's principle, all these seeming errors cannot be so; it is only man's insufficient knowledge or understanding that makes them seem so. "If we fully and entirely believe in the Divine Origin of Holy Scripture, to assert that its statements do not harmonize is a contradiction in terms" (p. 346).

Lee's theory of inspiration is important not only for itself, but even more because it represents a systematization of the kind of view that was predominant at the time Coleridge was writing the *Confessions.* Writing in 1893 of such a "traditional theory" of inspiration, the liberal exegete William Sanday insists that "this was the view commonly held fifty years ago." [15] With this statement in mind, Lee's view—or one like it—is crucial for the understanding of the nature of Coleridge's achievement.

One is tempted to say that Coleridge's views on scriptural inspiration come mid-way between the two typical theories, Herder's and Lee's, which we have outlined. This would be true, in a sense, but a bit oversimplified. Coleridge's view is, to be sure, between the two, but he is in certain ways closer to the traditional viewpoint represented by Lee. At the same time, he differs from it in one important, indeed crucial, particular. As we shall see, Coleridge had learned an important lesson from Herder and the historians.

Because Coleridge's *Confessions* lacks the more or less systematic theological framework of a work like Lee's *Inspiration of Scripture,* it is necessary to formulate more explicitly the principles which often remain implicit in his treatment. It is perhaps the failure of critics to do this, that has led to a lack of recognition of the essential clarity, as well as the depth, of Coleridge's insight in the *Confessions.*

The principles of Coleridge's approach are three: (1) the distinc-

[15] *Inspiration* (London, 1893), p. 393.

tion between inspiration and revelation; (2) the unique instrumentality of the inspired author of Scripture; and (3) the special nature of scriptural inerrancy.

Coleridge was as insistent as Lee on the importance of a clear distinction between revelation and inspiration. The distinction is latent in his wording of the "Doctrine" which he sets out to investigate (and ultimately attack) in the essay: "that not only what finds me, but that all that exists in the sacred volume, and which I am bound to find therein, was—not alone inspired by, that is, composed by men under the actuating influence of, the Holy Spirit, but likewise—dictated by an Infallible Intelligence;—that the writers, each and all, were divinely informed as well as inspired" (Letter II, 582). The distinction does not remain merely implicit, however. As a key to Coleridge's thinking about Scripture, the distinction is made explicit several times, as when he distinguishes "the inspiration, the imbreathment, of the predisposing and assisting Spirit" from "the revelation of the informing Word" (Letter VI, 614). Indeed, the main error he finds in the above mentioned "Doctrine" consists in "the confounding of two distinct conceptions, revelation by the Eternal Word, and actuation of the Holy Spirit" (Letter VII, 619).[16]

The second principle which underlies Coleridge's investigation is his constant belief in the importance of the human "instrument," the inspired author. He is not an automaton, but an individual, rooted in time and place and in certain prejudices and thought-patterns. Coleridge finds that the commonly accepted belief that everything inspired is also revealed has led to the notion that "the men, whose names are prefixed to the several books or chapters, were in fact but as different pens in the hand of one and the same Writer, and the words the words of God himself;—and that on this account all notes and comments were superfluous, nay, presumptuous,—a profane mixing of human with divine" (Letter IV, 604). Actually, the reader

---

[16] An expression of this distinction is found during the same period in a notebook entry of December 12, 1823: "My views of Inspiration ($\asymp$ Revelation $::$ πνεῦμα: Λόγος) and the deduction of *degrees* in the excellency of Inspiration, become daily clearer and more distinct." Notebook 30, f. 29. The sign $\asymp$ here seems to mean "distinguished from." The distinction is usually implied rather than expressed, however, as, for example, in his notes on Jeremy Taylor, *LR*, 155–156, and in *TT*, 386–387 (March 31, 1832).

of the Bible should examine each passage "in reference to the circumstances of the Writer or Speaker, the dispensation under which he lived, the purpose of the particular passage, and the intent and object of the Scriptures at large" (Letter IV, 606). For, he asks, "is the grace of God so confined,—are the evidences of the present and actuating Spirit so dim and doubtful,—that to be assured of the same we must first take for granted that all the life and co-agency of our humanity is miraculously suspended?" (Letter VI, 612) [17]

Up to this point, Coleridge is in substantial agreement with the basic principles underlying the viewpoint typified by Lee. Lee insists as strongly as Coleridge on the importance of the inspiration/revelation distinction and on the relevance of the human elements of the inspired books. On the matter of inerrancy, however, they are far apart, and it is indeed here that Lee attacks Coleridge's *Confessions,* explicitly and vigorously.[18]

First of all, Coleridge does not accept the inerrancy of Scripture simply and without qualification. Rather, he attempts to establish criteria for its proper definition and application. Coleridge accepts as unquestionably revealed (and hence infallibly true) "whatever is referred by the sacred Penman to a direct communication from God, and wherever it is recorded that the Subject of the history had asserted himself to have received this or that command, this or that information or assurance, from a super-human Intelligence, or where

[17] Coleridge's wholehearted acceptance of the human contribution of the inspired authors may perhaps be indicated by several notebook entries. Notebook 26 (c. 1826), f. 7: "May I not truly characterize Paul's Epistle as a whole, by its universality of Spirit (and its Catholicity is the test of Inspiration—) because it contains a request to bring him his Cloak and Tablet, or a, give my love to this and that acquaintance—or a, my Fellow-prisoner, James, begs to be remembered to Mr. and Mrs. Trueheart? Or must I in defiance of common sense introduce a miraculous illumination of the Holy Spirit, and vi et armis impregnate the words with a sense of universal concernment, or aerate them by means of a Swedenborgian Forcing-Pump with a mystery?" Notebook 37 (1828), ff. 17–17ᵛ: "The Holy Spirit potenziating and glorifying his natural Genius and acquired Talents became for the Penman and his immediate Hearers the Spirit of the Penman, and partaking of his individualities, as a Man of that age, that country, composing under the influence of those particular events, views and motives; but the Spirit of the Penman has become the Holy Spirit for us, even the Spirit and Wisdom of the Most High —He has ascended on the fiery Chariot of Prophecy and let fall the Mantle of individual Humanity."

[18] Lee attacks Coleridge's concept of inerrancy in extensive footnotes on pp. 41, 53, 146, 218, 243, and 286 of his *Inspiration of Scripture*. Lee is generally accurate in his reading of Coleridge, and his antipathy springs not from misunderstanding but from a radical difference in principle on inerrancy. Once or twice, however, he badly misreads Coleridge, notably on p. 41, n. 1, where he seems to ignore Coleridge's clear distinction of revelation from inspiration.

the writer in his own person, and in the character of an historian, relates that the *Word of the Lord came* unto priest, prophet, chieftain, or other individual" (Letter III, 589).[19]

The traditional position that Coleridge inveighs against, however, goes far beyond this, to insist that "every sentence found in a canonical Book, rightly interpreted, contains the *dictum* of an infallible Mind" (Letter IV, 602), that there is no need to try to determine in Scripture "what parts are and what are not articles of Faith—all being such" (Letter IV, 601). Contrary to the clear evidence of historical inaccuracies of detail, of occasional discrepancies between one part and another of the Bible in minor matters, and of contradiction of modern scientific knowledge, the traditionalists insist on the complete infallibility of Scripture, whether in major or minor matters, whether in matters of religious teaching or of geography. The reason for this tenacious view is, to Coleridge, clearly fear—fear of shaking faith in the revealed character of Scripture by the admission of possible error or inaccuracy in non-religious details. As he sees it, this fear could be completely obviated simply by accepting the distinction between revelation and inspiration: every part of Scripture is inspired, that is, composed under the actuation of the Holy Spirit; but every part of Scripture is not revealed, that is, certain parts are communicated by God directly, while others depend on natural knowledge. "See here in these several writings one and the same Holy Spirit, now sanctifying a chosen vessel, and fitting it for the reception of heavenly truths proceeding immediately from the mouth of God, and elsewhere working in frail and fallible men like ourselves, and like ourselves instructed by God's word and laws" (Letter IV, 599).

It must be noted here, however, that Coleridge's use of the revelation/inspiration distinction is significantly different from that of Lee. It is here, in fact, that they definitively part company. Lee asserts the distinction but then fails completely to apply it to the aching problem of his age, the apparent discrepancies found in Scripture by modern textual and historical research. Coleridge posits the validity of the distinction but places it clearly in the context of a further distinction, that between inspiration and inerrancy. Lee, keeping inerrancy as a necessary characteristic of inspiration, is left in the position

---

[19] This criterion, however, taken *tout court,* would be considered quite uncritical by modern liberal exegetes.

that, if every part of Scripture is inspired, then every part of Scripture is infallibly inerrant. Coleridge saw, however, that, although inerrancy is a necessary characteristic of *revelation* (because it is directly given by God's infallible intelligence), it is not a necessary characteristic of *inspiration* (which deals not only with what is directly revealed but also with what is known by natural means).[20]

Coleridge, therefore, while believing in the plenary inspiration of the Bible, is left free to distinguish what is guaranteed by the charisma of inerrancy from what is not necessarily so guaranteed, for example, to distinguish the revelation of an important religious truth from the prophet's estimate of the number of men in Pharaoh's army.

What, then, is the criterion for distinguishing in the practical order what is revealed, and hence inerrant, from what is not revealed? The criterion is the intention of the sacred author, as that intention is manifested in his writing. That is precisely why the historical and literary criticism of the Scriptures is important. It is only by studying the contemporaneous literary forms, the prevailing thought-patterns, the history of the Hebrew people, the current liturgical practices, and so forth, that one can learn what is the true intent of any part of the Bible. It is for this reason that Coleridge attacks the practice of "bringing together into logical dependency detached sentences from books composed at the distance of centuries, nay, sometimes a *millennium,* from each other, under different dispensations, and for different objects," which are "detached from their context, and, contrary to the intention of the sacred writer, first raised into independent *theses,* and then brought together to produce or sanction some new *credendum*" (Letter IV, 599–600). On the contrary, as we have seen, each part must be examined "in reference to the circumstances of the Writer or Speaker, the dispensation under which he lived, the purpose of the particular passage" (Letter IV, 606). Only

---

20 "The distinction between the providential and the miraculous, between the divine Will working with the agency of natural causes, and the same Will supplying their place by a special *fiat*—this distinction has, I doubt not, many uses in speculative divinity. But its weightiest practical application is shown, when it is employed to free the souls of the unwary and weak in faith from the nets and snares, the insidious queries and captious objections, of the Infidel by calming the flutter of their spirits." *Confessions,* Letter VI, 614–615.

For examples of Coleridge's acceptance of the possibility of error in Scripture in nonrevealed matters, see also *NTPM,* 328–330; *LR,* 261; *NED,* I, 123–124. This subject is also touched on in the notebooks, for example, Notebook 42 (1829), ff. [35ᵛ–36].

by these means will we be able to discern what the inspired writer intends us to accept as revealed, that is, as asserted and declared by God Himself. Only then will we be able to see that while the inspired authors, and therefore God, intend to tell us that it is revealed that Jesus is the Son of God, they do not intend to tell us that it is revealed that there were 800,000 men in the army of Jeroboam.[21]

Despite the personal and discursive nature of Coleridge's *Confessions,* the underlying principles of his viewpoint on Scripture give it both structure and significance. It is remarkable how with these principles he has managed, without sacrificing the traditional belief of the Church that all Scripture is inspired by the Holy Spirit, to embrace the findings of the new literary and historical scholarship. Reverent and believing though he remains in his handling of the Bible, he has indeed learned an important lesson from the historical critics, many of whom could themselves have learned much from Coleridge.

---

[21] Coleridge wrote often of the importance of understanding differences of literary form, the nature of myth and allegory, the uses of symbolic language, historical background, etc., for a proper interpretation of scriptural passages. See, for example, *NTPM,* 138–139, 276–277, 287, 326–327; *Aids,* 234–235, 270 n.; *LR,* 127, 285, 299, 389, 399; *CL,* IV, 871 (August 5, 1818); *UL,* II, 327 (July 1824), 396–397 (1827). There are also two notes worth pointing out, which were written by Coleridge in Mrs. Gillman's Bible; they are quoted in full by Mrs. Lucy Watson in *Coleridge at Highgate,* pp. 113–116. There are innumerable applications of this principle in the later notebooks, of course, where Coleridge turned his attention more and more to commentary on Scripture. See especially Notebooks 26 (c. 1826), ff. 4ᵛ–7ᵛ; 33 (1827), passim; 35 (c. 1827), ff. 1–6; 36 (1827), passim; 37 (1828), passim, and especially ff. 17–18ᵛ; 38 (1829), passim; 41–54 (1829–1833), passim. A random sampling of these applications is enlightening. Speaking of the proper interpretation of the infancy narratives in Matt. 1–2, Coleridge asks: "Is it possible, that at a very early period, as early as A.D. 80 or 90 a poetic Romance, allegorico-cabalistic, a Christopaedia, could have been written?" Notebook 30 (1823–1824), ff. 29–29ᵛ. Of the Epistle of Jude, Coleridge writes: "Of Jude's Epistle I think far more favorably than Luther did—but yet I cannot deny that it consists of coarser materials than one wishes to find in the writing of a Brother of the Lord according to the Flesh. And the reference to fabulous and apocryphal Legends doubtless offended Luther, as it has since put meaner minds to their shifts, the τοὺς πολλοὺς, I mean, who mistake inspired writings for words miraculously dictated. I confess, these allusions in Jude offend my *taste* rather than my judgement. They are evidently introduced as mere *illustrations,* & not for their own sake as facts. I read them in the same spirit as if the writer had reminded his Flock of what the Wolf said to the Lamb—or to any other well-known & familiar Apologue." Notebook 41 (1829–1830), f. [34ᵛ].

In his commentary on the first ten chapters of Genesis, Coleridge writes: "I am not satisfied that a physical Fire-Flood is a doctrine of Revelation—for surely, every allusion to a popular tradition or current notion in a letter addressed by an Apostle to his Countrymen is not of necessity to be taken as a revealed truth. A catastrophe of this kind is not as far as we know impossible . . . I find it difficult not to suspect, that the Xth Chapter . . . affords a safer ground for our knowledge of the state and extent of Geographical Science, in the age of the Compiler in writing of the Book of Genesis, than of the actual Heraldry & Geneology of the different Tribes and Nations here enumerated." Notebook 42 (1829), ff. [31ᵛ–33].

Remarkable, too, is the basic similarity between Coleridge's approach to inspiration and inerrancy and that of certain modern theologians and biblical scholars.

Three modern approaches, representative but not necessarily all-inclusive, can be distinguished. One is that of the Evangelical writers, who generally hold firmly to the conservative tradition represented by Lee and deny the possibility of error, on any level, in the inspired writings.[22]

Another approach effectively reduces the question of inspiration to an investigation of psychological and historical aspects of prophetic "possession" and the like, on the grounds that "it is not their *words* that are inspired . . . it is the *men* who are inspired." [23] The problem of inerrancy is solved by simply denying its existence: "Inspiration does not carry inerrancy, nor is it inerrancy that gives authority." [24] There is here no attempt to distinguish scriptural material which is inerrant from that which is not necessarily so. The charisma of inerrancy is reduced to a fiction.

The third approach attempts to keep in balance the various elements of Scripture: revelation, inspiration, inerrancy, as well as the "human" elements. Although it is expressed in more technical and systematic terms, the essential balance is the same one reached by Coleridge, and the distinctions it employs are essentially the same.[25] Like Coleridge's *Confessions,* this approach builds upon the following foundation: all Scripture is *inspired* by (written under the guidance of) the Holy Spirit; [26] *revelation* is not necessarily coter-

---

[22] An extensive cross-section of Evangelical thought on Scripture may be found in *Revelation and the Bible,* ed. C. F. H. Henry (previously cited).

[23] C. H. Dodd, *The Authority of the Bible* (London, 1928), p. 30.

[24] *Ibid.,* p. 129.

[25] One of the best expositions of this approach to the problem is that of Paul Synave and Pierre Benoit in *Prophecy and Inspiration* (see above, n. 4). Other important treatments are Augustin Bea, S.J., *De Sacrae Scripturae Inspiratione* (Rome, 1935); Pierre Benoit, "L'Inspiration," in *Initiation Biblique,* 3rd ed., ed. A. Robert and A. Tricot (Tournai, 1954), pp. 6–45; and Jean Levie, *La Bible, Parole Humaine et Message de Dieu* (Paris, 1958).

[26] The treatment of the nature of inspiration in theologians like Synave and Benoit will obviously be far more nuanced and sophisticated than the treatment of Coleridge in the *Confessions.* For example, in elaborating the Thomistic approach of the *Summa Theologica,* pars II–II, qq. 171–174, they distinguish: Revelation ("a gift of supernatural knowledge to the mind by way of *infused species*"); Cognitive Inspiration ("a light which illuminates the *speculative judgment* and raises it to a supernatural mode of knowledge"); Scriptural Inspiration ("a supernatural impulse which stimulates the will and directs the *practical judgment* with a view to the composition of a book which is to produce a certain effect"). See *Prophecy and Inspiration,* p. 110. In Scripture, any or all of these may be operative at any given point.

minous with inspiration; *inerrancy* is necessarily coterminous with revelation but not with inspiration.

The treatment of inerrancy by Paul Synave and Pierre Benoit is sharper and more clearly stated, but it is very similar to Coleridge's in its insistence on the different values of the inspired word; on Scripture's charisma of inerrancy as the infallible guarantee of its truth when it does intend to assert the truth of matters relevant to the teaching willed by God; and on the fact that Scripture does not always, and in every context, intend to speak formally as teacher.

Inerrancy is not the purpose of inspiration; it is its result—or better, it is one among several of its results. It would be its only result if God's sole purpose in enlightening his messenger was to have him teach truths. Now this is not the case. Instruction is only one of the aims proposed to the practical reason of the inspired subject; there are other ends which belong especially to the affective order, such as to encourage, console, reprimand, etc. Truth will then be one of the qualities of the inspired word, but not the only one . . .

Inerrancy, then, does not come into play as often as inspiration, or at least not in the same way. There is no doubt that, when God teaches and insofar as he teaches, he can neither be deceived nor deceive us; his word is necessarily exempt from all error. This is what is called the privilege of "inerrancy." But God is not always teaching and, when he has his interpreter speak without vouching for the truth of his statement, inspiration operates without entailing inerrancy; or, more exactly, in such a case inerrancy consists precisely in preventing the interpreter from vouching for the truth of matters which are not pertinent to the teaching willed by God.[27]

Let there be no mistake about it. Coleridge was not a trained theologian, nor did he make any pretense of being one. He might,

---

The distinction helps, among other things, to explain the seeming preponderance of either the divine or the human element in one or another part of the Bible, and to resolve the problem of human error.

[27] *Prophecy and Inspiration*, pp. 132–133. There is an excellent note which reflects this view in *The Documents of Vatican II*, ed. Walter M. Abbott, S.J. (New York, 1966), p. 119, n. 31. It might be well to point out, as the above-cited note insists, that "this is not a quantitative distinction, as though some sections treated of salvation (and were inerrant), while others gave merely natural knowledge (and were fallible). It is formal, and applies to the whole text. The latter is authoritative and inerrant in what it affirms about the revelation of God and the history of salvation. According to the intentions of its authors, divine and human, it makes no other affirmations." Coleridge's statement is not so nuanced, to be sure, but this seems to me consistent with his point of view.

in fact, legitimately be accused of several theological blunders in his treatise on inspiration. For one thing, he seems to have fallen at one point into the fallacy of confusing his distinction between inspiration and revelation—both of which are supernatural gifts—with the traditional distinction between the providential and the miraculous, which is meant precisely to distinguish the natural and the supernatural.[28] Again, in linking the inspiration of the Scriptures with the influence of the Holy Spirit on all the faithful,[29] he runs the risk of not protecting sufficiently the privileged character of the charisma of scriptural inspiration. Besides, recent theological thought on the question has already moved beyond Benoit (to whose approach Coleridge's bears such striking resemblances), to insights Coleridge never achieved. Theologians in the Benoit tradition have more recently found room for views which would make revelation less objectivist and propositional, and which would therefore make the distinction between revelation and inspiration less important than it was for Coleridge.[30]

At the same time, Coleridge's achievement here was no mean one. In an age when intellectual equilibrium was only precariously maintained, he managed to keep a delicate balance between his belief in the inspired character of the Scriptures and his clear realization that they were historical documents properly subject to the investigation of modern scholarship. Once again Coleridge was the mediator, balancing between traditional fundamentalism and the rationalistic danger he saw lurking in Germany. The remarkable resemblance between the basic approach of the *Confessions of an Inquiring Spirit* and some of the notable modern theological thinking on inspiration should not be taken as a sign of a lack of progress in theological

[28] *Confessions*, Letter VI, 614. See above, n. 20. This confusion may be to some extent deliberate, however, in view of the tendency we have seen in Coleridge to break down the natural/supernatural distinction.

[29] *Confessions*, Letter VII, 619. There is an interesting parallel here with the recent work of the celebrated German theologian Karl Rahner on inspiration. He sees the Scriptures as an essential and constitutive element of the Apostolic Church, and their inspiration as simply one part of the activity of the Holy Spirit in establishing the Church as the guardian of the *depositum fidei*. Scriptural inspiration is thereby linked with the other "charismata" of the Apostolic Church. Of course, Rahner is careful to point out the privileged character of these charismata of the nascent Church. See Karl Rahner, S.J., *Inspiration in the Bible*, transl. Charles H. Henkey (New York, 1961), pp. 39–80.

[30] See, for example, Luis Alonso Schökel's *The Inspired Word: Scripture in the Light of Language and Literature*, transl. F. Martin (New York, 1965); his approach is, through careful study of the literary "modes" of the Bible, to broaden the conception of literary truth.

thought during the past hundred years. On the contrary, it is rather an indication that Coleridge's thinking, though often only in germinal form, was frequently far ahead of the majority of his contemporaries.[31]

Another question which is of some importance in this context is that of the relative roles of "objective" and "subjective" in belief in Scripture. Although it is touched on only by way of appendix in the *Confessions,* Coleridge makes it quite clear that there must be a balance between the objective ("or historical and ecclesiastical") and the subjective ("or spiritual and individual") poles of religion.[32] This is as true of Scripture as it is true of the Christian religion as a whole; we found it to be true in the discussion of faith in the last chapter, particularly in the relationship of miracles and evidences of Christianity to the act of faith, and it remains true in the context of the *Confessions.* Christianity must not be allowed to decline to the state "into which the Latin Church sank deeper and deeper from the sixth to the fourteenth century; during which time religion was likewise merely objective and superstitious, a letter proudly emblazoned and illuminated, but yet a dead letter that was to be read by its own outward glories without the light of the Spirit in the mind of the believer." Such a religion is wholly objective "to the exclusion of all its correspondent subjective." It is "altogether historical, an *opus operatum*" (Letter VII, 620). The object of the present age must be "to restore what ought never to have been removed—the correspondent subjective, that is, the assent and confirmation of the Spirit promised to all true believers," for "Revealed Religion (and I know of no religion not revealed) is in its highest contemplation the unity,

---

[31] How far ahead of his time Coleridge was on the question may be seen in the fact that even the sympathetic Professor Shedd, in his 1853 introductory essay to the *Complete Works,* almost twenty years after Coleridge's death, felt constrained to take very strong exception to Coleridge's views on inspiration. See Shedd, I, 55–61. Shedd insists, for example, that "we regard it as an error in him . . . that the Canon is not contemplated as a complete whole in and by itself, having a *common* origin in the Divine Mind, in such sense, that as a body of information it is infallibly correct on all the subjects that come within its scope and purpose. There must be truth somewhere, in regard to all, even the most unimportant particulars of history, biography, and geography, that enter into the subject matter of the Sacred Canon, and it seems to us altogether the most rational . . . to presume and assume that it lies in the Canon itself—in the outward Revelation considered as a finished whole, and an infallible unit and unity." Shedd, I, 57.

[32] See *Confessions,* Letter VII, 620–622. One of the few discussions of this matter is in the rather thin treatment of Coleridge on Scripture by H. D. McDonald in *Ideas of Revelation: An Historical Study, A.D. 1700 to A.D. 1860* (London, 1959), pp. 171–179, which considerably overstresses the role of the subjective in Coleridge's view of revelation.

that is, the identity or co-inherence, of Subjective and Objective. It is in itself, and irrelatively, at once inward Life and Truth, and outward Fact and Luminary. But as all Power manifests itself in the harmony of correspondent Opposites, each supposing and supporting the other, —so has Religion its objective, or historic and ecclesiastical pole, and its subjective, or spiritual and individual pole" (Letter VII, 621). There is in man's contact with Scripture a mutual fitness of man for the word of God and of God's word for man and, flowing from this, a kind of mutual causality:

> . . . no man, I say, can recognize his own inward experiences in such Writings, and not find an objectiveness, a confirming and assuring outwardness, and all the main characters of reality, reflected therefrom on the spirit, working in himself and in his own thoughts, emotions, and aspirations—warring against sin, and the motions of sin. The unsubstantial, insulated Self passes away as a stream; but these are the shadows and reflections of the Rock of Ages, and of the Tree of Life that starts forth from its side.

On the other hand, as much of reality, as much of objective truth, as the Scriptures communicate to the subjective experiences of the Believer, so much of present life, of living and effective import, do these experiences give to the letter of these Scriptures. In the one *the Spirit itself beareth witness with our spirit,* that we have received the *spirit of adoption;* in the other our spirit bears witness to the power of the Word, that it is indeed the Spirit that proceedeth from God. (Letter VII, 622)[33]

[33] Here again, Professor Shedd seems doubtful about Coleridge's respect for the objective validity of Scripture. See Introductory Essay, Shedd, I, 55–57. He is afraid, at first, that Coleridge might have adopted the subjectivist principle of a philosophy like Fichte's ("in which the truth is laid in the Subject wholly") that "the Subjective Reason . . . is placed first, as the fixed and absolute norm or rule to which the Objective Reason is to be brought up and conformed" (56). In the last analysis, however, Shedd admits that "Coleridge believed that the Scriptures are, as matter of fact, true on all primary points, and that those Christian doctrines which he, in common with the Christian Church, regarded as *vital* to human salvation, are all plainly revealed in them" (56–57), and that Coleridge "ultimately adopted the views of the Critical philosophy, substantially those of all theistic systems, which explains the possibility of knowledge, by a preconformity of the Subject to the Object, instead of an identity of substance between them. On this system there is a dualism between the Object and the Subject. Of the two, the former is the unlimited and the universal, and stands over against the latter as the limited and particular. It is the *Objective,* therefore, which possesses the fixed and uniform character (in this instance, the infallibility) to which the Subjective comes up with its pre-conformed powers of apprehension, and the function of the latter consequently, is a recipient instead of an originant or creative one" (56).

Shedd's initial doubt occasionally seems justified, but only because Coleridge is sometimes careless or incomplete in making his position clear, as when he writes in a letter to Dr. Green (March 29, 1832): "If I lose my faith in *Reason,* as the perpetual Revelation, I lose my faith altogether. I must deduce the objective from the subjective Revelation or it is no longer a

The problem of the relationship between the objective and the subjective is, of course, one that troubled and fascinated Coleridge all his life in a variety of contexts. One thinks, for example, of his discussions of the question of how Shakespeare creates character: by meditation (subjective) or by observation (objective). His conclusion, as in so many other contexts, is that there is a "co-adunation" of the two poles; Shakespeare's characters are "at once true to nature, and fragments of the divine mind that drew them." [34] Or one thinks of his distinction between copy and imitation: a copy is a mere waxen image of reality, or a mirrored reflection; an imitation involves a profound interrelationship of objective and subjective. In the imitation involved in true poetry, "we take the purest parts [of nature] and combine them with our own minds, with our own hopes, with our own inward yearnings after perfection, and, being frail and imperfect, we wish to have a shadow, a sort of prophetic existence present to us, which tells us what we are not, but yet, blending in us much that we are, promises great things of what we may be." [35] Translating this latter distinction into religious terms, the copy would be a merely inert or superstitious assent to Scripture; the imitation would be the objective meaning caught up into the subjective reading of it, the "co-adunation" of the two. Although written much earlier and in another context, Coleridge's remark to Southey in a letter of 1803 falls nicely to the point: "Believe me, Southey! a metaphysical Solution, that does not instantly *tell* [?you] something in the Heart, is grievously to be suspected as apocryphal." [36] As in poetry so in religion—whether in his analysis of the act of faith, or

revelation, but a beastly fear and superstition." *UL*, II, 442. See also Notebook F, f. 64 (?1827). Coleridge's more careful statements, however, make it clear that Shedd's final analysis is the correct one, that Coleridge never lost the balance between subjective and objective revelation. In addition to the passages already cited from the *Confessions*, witness the following comment on the nature of belief in scriptural miracles, in a note on Samuel Noble's *Appeal* (1827): "There is so much of truth in all this reasoning on miracles, that I feel pain in the thought that the result is false,—because it was not the whole truth . . . they overlook the distinction between congruity with reason, truth of consistency, or internal possibility of this or that being objectively real, and the objective reality as fact. Miracles, *quoad* miracles, can never supply the place of subjective evidence, that is, of insight. But neither can subjective insight supply the place of objective sight. The certainty of the truth of a mathematical arch can never prove the fact of its existence." *LR*, 525. For other expressions of this point of view see, for example, *PL*, 233; *LR*, 317–318; Notebooks 21½, f. 68ᵛ, and 42, ff. [35ᵛ–36]; and Notebook F, f. 26 (1826), ff. 67–68 (1827).

[34] *Shakespearean Criticism*, ed. T. M. Raysor, 2 vols. (London, 1960), II, 85.

[35] *Shakespearean Criticism*, II, 53.

[36] *CL*, II, 961 (August 7, 1803).

of the nature of the Church, or of Redemption, or of Scripture itself—
we find (as in the passage cited above from the *Confessions*) that
religion has "its objective, or historic and ecclesiastical pole, and its
subjective, or spiritual and individual pole" (Letter VII, 621).

Beyond the central statement of his position on the nature of Scripture in the *Confessions of an Inquiring Spirit,* other questions relating to Scripture found treatment elsewhere. One matter frequently
discussed, either theoretically or by way of application to particular
passages, was the problematic one of the different "senses" of Scripture.

Interpretation of different senses, or levels of meaning, in Sacred
Scripture was a staple of patristic and medieval theology, as indeed it
had already been in a more limited way in the New Testament itself
with its interpretation of Old Testament texts.[37] Though emphasis
on the variety of levels of meaning became somewhat less marked
in succeeding ages of theology, this tradition of interpretation has
continued. The most important of these find their place in Coleridge:
the literal sense, the so-called accommodated sense, the typical sense,
and what has come to be known today as the *sensus plenior* ("fuller
sense") or "sense of the Spirit."

Coleridge's profound respect for the literal sense of the Bible has
already been sufficiently indicated. It is manifest everywhere in his
treatment of scriptural passages: his concern for historical and geographical background; the literary forms employed; the nature of
language, symbol, and myth. The literal sense, the sense intended
by the writer in his use of the words, is necessarily the foundation of

---

[37] Besides the literal, accommodated, and typical senses, there were several other senses of
Scripture which were of importance in medieval exegesis. The most notable of them found
their classic codification in a distich of the fourteenth-century ecclesiastical writer Nicholas
of Lyre.

> Littera gesta docet, quid credas allegoria,
> Moralis quid agas, quo tendas anagogia.

The lines are preserved in the *Patrologia Latina,* ed. J. P. Migne, 217 vols. (Paris, 1844–1855),
CXIII, col. 28. The literal sense gives the facts, the allegorical sense refers to some mystery of
faith; the moral sense is the moral teaching which flows from the mystery; the anagogical
is the eschatological sense, referring to the last things, the "end time." Walter Burghardt
points to Jerusalem as the "classic, all-inclusive example"; it refers to "(a) the historical city
of the Jews, (b) the Church, (c) the Christian soul, and (d) the heavenly Jerusalem, the
Church triumphant." "On Early Christian Exegesis," *Theological Studies,* XI (1950), 104.
For an excellent explanation and commentary on medieval exegesis, see Supplement IV in
William F. Lynch, S.J., *Christ and Apollo: The Dimensions of the Literary Imagination* (New
York, 1960), pp. 227–267.

all the rest. Unless the "sense of the letter" has been carefully determined by thorough study of text and context, there is danger that the "sense of the Spirit" may be interpreted arbitrarily. Coleridge would agree with St. Augustine's insistence that "whoever understands in the Sacred Scriptures something other than the writer had in mind, is deceived." [38] Coleridge warns specifically against "the *gnosis,* that is, the science of detecting the mysteries of faith in the simplest texts of the Old Testament history, to the contempt or neglect of the literal and contextual sense." [39]

The other senses of Scripture used by Coleridge are all, in one way or another, spiritual senses. Since Coleridge does not use them with complete consistency or perfect distinction from one another, it may be well to explain the distinctions as they are normally used by theologians.[40] The so-called "accommodated" sense is not really a sense of Scripture; it is an accommodation, an application of a text to another meaning which it merely suggests, and which was in no way the intention of the original text. Such would be, for example, to use Christ's miracle of the raising of Lazarus as a text to preach on the "raising" of a sinful soul to the new life of grace.

The typical sense involves the reference of a person, object, or event in Scripture prophetically to some other person, object, or event, as, for example, Adam is seen not only in terms of his immediate role in Genesis but also as a type or figure of Christ (Rom. 5:14). Theologians generally teach that a typical sense can only be known if it is clearly indicated as such in Scripture itself, as, for example, Christ clearly uses Jonah as a type of His own Resurrection from the dead (Matt. 12:38–41).

[38] *Christian Instruction ("De Doctrina Christiana"),* transl. John J. Gavigan, O.S.A., in *The Fathers of the Church* collection (New York, 1947), II, 57. Coleridge's devotion to the primary, literal sense may be seen in the following observation of Henry Nelson Coleridge on his uncle's reading of the Psalms: "During many of his latter years he used to read ten or twelve verses every evening, ascertaining (for his knowledge of Hebrew was enough for that) the exact visual image or first radical meaning of every noun substantive; and he repeatedly expressed to me his surprise and pleasure at finding that in nine cases out of ten the bare primary sense, if literally rendered, threw great additional light on the text." The note goes on to say that "he was not disposed to allow the prophetic or allusive character so largely as is done by Horne and others; but he acknowledged it in some instances in the fullest manner." *TT,* 323 n.

[39] *LR,* 86.

[40] There is an excellent treatment of the senses of Scripture, together with principles of interpretation, in Dom Celestin Charlier's *The Christian Approach to the Bible,* transl. H. J. Richards and B. Peters (London, 1958), pp. 255–273.

The *sensus plenior* has perhaps been best defined as "that additional, deeper meaning, intended by God but not clearly intended by the human author, which is seen to exist in the words of a biblical text (or group of texts, or even a whole book) when they are studied in the light of further revelation or development in the understanding of revelation," [41] that is, when seen in the light of the whole Bible as a part of God's developing plan. An instance of this sense of Scripture would be to interpret the "breath of Yahweh" which moved over the waters in the first chapter of Genesis as being, in the light of the full revelation of both Testaments, the Holy Spirit. The human author of Genesis was not conscious of this fuller meaning, but the divine Author was conscious of it and intended it, and Christians, who see the context of the whole Bible, can become aware of it. This sense of Scripture is clearly similar to the typical sense in that the human author is not, at least fully, conscious of it. It differs from the typical sense, however, in that it does not depend on its spiritual meaning being pointed out specifically, but its meaning is mediated by the whole context of the two Testaments in their developing revelation.[42]

That Coleridge was aware of the use of accommodations of Scripture and that he approved of them on the condition that they be admitted to be such, is evident from a notebook entry (one of several on the subject) of 1833. In this entry he speaks of "a justifiable *accommodation* of the Texts of Scripture, if not given or pretended as the *interpretation*—as the supposed sense or intention of the Sacred Writer, neither the primary nor any (*consciously* intended) secondary sense; but simply as expressing the thoughts which the words were fitted to suggest . . ." So far, so good. What follows, however, betrays a confusion between an accommodation and the properly spiritual senses, for he continues: ". . . but which, *if* truths & truths of vital interest and import, it may be no presumption to believe, under *this* condition, to have been comprized in the intention of that Holy Spirit, present no less tho' with less manifestation of Power in

---

[41] Raymond Brown, S.S., *The Sensus Plenior of Sacred Scripture* (Baltimore, 1955), p. 92. This is the most complete work to date on the *sensus plenior*, but also see the splendid treatment by Pierre Benoit, "La plénitude de sens des Livres Saints," *Revue Biblique*, LXVII (1960), 161–196.

[42] The *sensus plenior* is also said to differ from the typical sense in that the meaning is in the words, rather than in a specific person, object, or event.

the faithful spiritually-minded Reader of [?this] age, as *to* the Inspired Teachers, two thousand years or more ago." [43] This last quotation sounds like what we have called the *sensus plenior.*

With respect to the typical sense, Coleridge was not unaware of its inherent dangers, particularly the danger of invoking its use in any particular case without specific warrant of Scripture itself. As he wrote in the *Stateman's Manual:* "It is too notorious into what strange fancies (not always at safe distance from dangerous errors) the oldest uninspired writers of the Christian Church were seduced by this passion of transmuting without Scriptural authority incidents, names, and even mere sounds of the Hebrew Scriptures, into Evangelical types and correspondences." [44] When, however, Coleridge found a typology indicated by Scripture itself, he welcomed it with enthusiasm. Witness, for example, what he says of David: "David is a complex type—now of the Church as the mystic Body of Christ in all her different states, and now of Christ himself as the Head and Indwelling Principium Vitae of the Mystic Body." [45] Or witness his interpretation of the messianic Psalm 22 in the light of Christ's attribution of it to Himself on the Cross: " 'My God! my God! Why hast thou forsaken me' . . . the most decisive of all the Scriptural Proofs that the prophetic import of the passages in the Old Testament generally received as Messianic, and which the Church has since interpreted of Christ, was the true sense & intention of the sacred Writer—at all events, was the Mind of the Spirit, by whose inspiration the passages were written. Here Christ in the most solemn and aweful moment distinctly appropriates to himself, and as partly fulfilled, & therefore at the due time to be wholly fulfilled, the prophecies in the 22nd Psalm." [46]

It will perhaps be evident from this last quotation that for Coleridge the lines between the typical sense and the broader scriptural sense which we have called the *sensus plenior* are not clearly drawn. This will be even more evident in the following passage from Cole-

---

[43] Notebook 54, f. [19ᵛ]. There is an application of the accommodated sense in Notebook 46 (1830), f. [21ᵛ].

[44] *SM*, Appendix C, 474.

[45] Notebook 36 (1827), ff. 51–50ᵛ. Where the folio reference is given in reverse order, Coleridge has written that section of the notebook from back to front.

[46] Notebook 50 (1831–1832), f. [31]. This typology, one of Coleridge's favorites, is also discussed in his notes on Jeremy Taylor, *LR*, 159–160, and in *TT*, 323–324 n.

ridge's notes on Donne, where he is clearly speaking of a broader spiritual sense (our *sensus plenior*) but calls it by the more restricted term "typical."

If this were meant to the exclusion or neglect of the primary sense,—if we are required to believe that the sacred writers themselves had such thoughts present to their minds,—it would, doubtless, throw the doors wide open to every variety of folly and fanaticism. But it may admit of a safe, sound, and profitable use, if we consider the Bible as one work, intended by the Holy Spirit for the edification of the Church in all ages, and having, as such, all its parts synoptically interpreted, the eldest by the latest, the last by the first, and the middle by both. Moses, or David, or Jeremiah (we might in this view affirm) meant so and so, according to the context, and the light under which, and the immediate or proximate purposes for which, he wrote: but we, who command the whole scheme of the great dispensation, may see a higher and deeper sense, of which the literal meaning was a symbol or a type; and this we may justifiably call the sense of the spirit.[47]

Terminology apart, this is precisely what theologians mean by the *sensus plenior*.

Though Coleridge never lost sight of the individuality of the many human authors of the books of Sacred Scripture—their differences in period, place, background, purpose, and personality—on the deepest level he saw the Bible as a single Book whose Author is the Holy Spirit. The human elements of Scripture become there, as Coleridge wrote in the *Statesman's Manual,* "a system of symbols, harmonious in themselves, and consubstantial with the truths of which they are the conductors . . . Its contents present to us the stream of time continuous as life and a symbol of eternity." These symbols are characterized not only by the "translucence of the special in the individual, or of the general in the special, or of the universal in the general," but "above all by the translucence of the eternal through and in the temporal." [48] Hence there is often a deeper meaning, a "fuller sense," than even the human author himself understood; God intends it, and Christians who see the Bible as a whole can read it. "As a transparency on some night of public rejoicing, seen by common day, with

[47] *LR,* 86–87.
[48] *SM,* 436–437.

the lamps from within removed—even such would the Psalms be to me uninterpreted by the Gospel." [49] But with this light, this "lamp from within," Coleridge can read the organic relationship between the two Testaments and can see (looking backward from his vantage point of the Gospel) that the doctrine of the Trinity, for example, had been, not yet announced, to be sure, but at least adumbrated in the Old Testament. Within this "fuller sense," he could see the revelation of Christ "proceeding from dim dawn to full noontide." [50]

While Coleridge did not write with the precision of a theologian on the senses of Scripture, the main lines of his approach are clear and strong. The literal sense is the anchor of all, and the spiritual senses must be made fast to it. If they are securely anchored in the text, however, the divine Author can speak in senses broader than an isolated passage, taken *in vacuo,* would allow. There is an Old Covenant and there is a New Covenant, but the book of their revelation is one, because the Word of God is One.

Other scriptural problems involve matters of the text itself rather than its interpretation. Coleridge discusses, at one time or another, the most important of these: authorship; authenticity (or genuinity), which means that the work in question is what it purports to be, for example, that it belongs to the apostolic age; and canonicity, which involves the determination of what books actually belong to the canon of inspired books and therefore constitute the rule of faith.

The first two of these, authorship and authenticity, are questions of provenance and are frequently treated as one by Coleridge, although he distinguishes them where distinction seems necessary. And distinction is, in fact, found to be necessary, when the actual authorship of a book of Scripture is called into question; a book may be authentic even though its reputed authorship is in doubt. Coleridge wrote, for example, of the Apocalypse (the Book of Revelation): "I myself believe the Evangelist John to have been the author of the Apocalypse; but still in controversy I should content myself with demonstrating it's Apostolic *Age.*" [51] Coleridge's treatment of the

---

[49] Notes on the Book of Common Prayer, *LR*, 28.

[50] *NTPM*, 136. This sense of Scripture is discussed and applications made of it in *LR*, 25–28; *TT*, 478; and *CL*, IV, 582 (August 2, 1815).

[51] *CL*, IV, 803 (January 10, 1818). Coleridge wrote several times on the authenticity of the

Epistle to the Hebrews is another case in point: "It seems to me, as it did to Luther, incomparably more probable that the eloquent treatise, entitled an Epistle to the Hebrews, was written by Apollos than by Paul; and what though it was written by neither? It is demonstrable that it was composed before the siege of Jerusalem and the destruction of the Temple; and scarcely less satisfactory is the internal evidence that it was composed by an Alexandrian. These two *data* are sufficient to establish the fact, that the Pauline doctrine at large was common to all Christians at that early period, and therefore the faith delivered by Christ. And this is all I want." [52] On a passage of the Reverend Philip Skelton to the effect that "every book of the New Testament can be proved to have been written by him whose name it hath all along borne," Coleridge commented in 1825: "This is true to the full extent that the defence of the divinity of our religion needs, or perhaps permits, and I see no advantage gained by asserting more." [53] Clearly, what was most important for Coleridge was not the authorship of a book but the assurance that it represented the true teaching of the Apostolic Age.[54]

It does not seem that canonicity was ever any great problem for Coleridge, nor did he write often about it. In accepting the Thirty-Nine Articles, he accepted the determination by the Church of England of the canon of inspired books as set down in Article VI. This canon differs from the Roman Catholic canon by excluding those Old Testament books which were not found in the Hebrew Bible and from that of at least some of the Reformers by not taking a stand against the canonicity of several books called into doubt by Luther

---

Apocalypse, with several changes of mind about it. In 1827, in his lengthy notes on a newly translated book on the Second Coming of Christ by a Spanish Jesuit, Coleridge expresses strong doubts about the authenticity of the Apocalypse. *LR*, 512–521, passim. The same doubt is expressed in an undated note in Henry More's *Theological Works*, *LR*, 115. In 1830, however, he finds himself "without the least sympathy with Luther's suspicions on this head, but on the contrary receiving this sublime poem as the undoubted work of the Apostolic age." *CCS*, 113 n.

[52] *LR*, 162–163. This passage is dated 1819. For the same sentiment, see *TT*, 264. Coleridge's (and Luther's) belief that the Epistle to the Hebrews was not written by St. Paul is today the generally accepted one. See, for example, F. F. Bruce's commentary on Hebrews in *Peake's Commentary on the Bible*, ed. Matthew Black and H. H. Rowley (London, 1962), p. 1008.

[53] *LR*, 445.

[54] For other discussions of authorship and authenticity, in the context of one or another book of Scripture (Ecclesiastes, the infancy narratives of Matthew and Luke, the Epistles of Peter, etc.), see *LR*, 79, 421–422, 450–454, 518–519, 532; and *TT*, 280. There is a more general discussion of the authenticity of Scripture in Notebook F, ff. 27^v–29^v (1826).

and others.[55] Coleridge's clearest statement of this acceptance of the Church's authority to determine the canonical books is found in the second Lay Sermon. Speaking of the writings of Sacred Scripture, he says that to them "I should be tempted with Burke to annex that treasure of prudential wisdom, the Ecclesiasticus. I not only yield, however, to the authority of our Church, but reverence the judgment of its founders in separating this work from the list of the canonical books, and in refusing to apply it to the establishment of any doctrine, while they caused it to be 'read for example of life and instruction of manners.' " [56]

The canon of the Old Testament was clearly defined for Coleridge by Article VI, but as for the New Testament books which were left in question (Hebrews, James, etc.), Coleridge was left, along with the rest of the Church of England, to decide for himself their proper place. This he was ready to do, and he did so on the basis of their authenticity and their conformity to Christian doctrine.

We have already touched upon Coleridge's criteria of authenticity, and it remains to say a word about the role of "catholicity," faithfulness to the letter and spirit of Christian teaching, as a criterion of canonicity. It appears in Coleridge in two different contexts. First of all, even where the canonicity of a book had already been determined for him, Coleridge wanted to see what criteria the Church herself had used in the formation of the canon. The principle, he found, was this: "The truth is, the ancient church was not guided by the mere

[55] Article VI of the Anglican Articles of Religion, in enumerating the books of the Old Testament, distinguishes between the canonical books and those which "the Church doth read for example of life and instruction of manners," the Apocrypha. The latter are III and IV Esdras, Tobias, Judith, "the rest of the Book of Esther," Wisdom, Jesus the Son of Sirach (Ecclesiasticus), Baruch, the Song of the Three Children, Susanna, Bel and the Dragon, the Prayer of Manasses, I and II Maccabees. The Apocrypha are also excluded from the Canon by the Protestant churches, but most of them (all except III and IV Esdras, the Song of the Three Children, Bel and the Dragon, and the Prayer of Manasses) have been included in the Roman Catholic Canon since the first official formulation of the Canon at the Council of Rome in 382; see Denzinger-Schönmetzer, n. 179, 186, 213, 1335, 1502. On the development of the Old Testament Canon in the early Church, see Albert C. Sundberg, Jr., *The Old Testament of the Early Church,* Harvard Theological Studies, XX (Cambridge, Mass., 1964).

Of the New Testament, Article VI says: "All the books of the New Testament, as they are commonly received, we do receive and account them for canonical." Since several books of the New Testament were in dispute at the time of the composition of the Articles in 1553 (including Hebrews, Jude, James, and the Apocalypse, all of which were omitted from the Canon by Luther), the statement of Article VI is ambiguous. Whether or not it was deliberately so, is discussed by E. C. S. Gibson in his study of *The Thirty-Nine Articles of the Church of England,* 2 vols. (London, 1896), I, 271–274.

[56] *LS,* 151 n.

fact of the genuineness of a writing in pronouncing it canonical;—its catholicity was the test . . ." [57] Second, where a disputed New Testament work was at issue, Coleridge followed the lead of the early Church in joining catholicity with authenticity as a test of whether or not the book belongs to the canon of inspired writings. Witness, for example, his rejection of the so-called Epistle of Barnabas: "I have not the smallest doubt that the epistle of Barnabas is genuine; but it is not catholic; it is full of the γνῶσις, though of the most simple and pleasing sort." [58]

This reliance on the Church and on faithfulness to Christian teaching seems at bottom not very different from the standard Anglican procedure outlined, for example, by E. C. S. Gibson in his commentary on the Articles: "The Church of England appeals to the historical evidence of reception by the visible Church, which, as Article XX. states, is 'a witness and keeper of Holy Writ.' This method of determining the canonicity of the books is in complete accordance with the general appeal which the Church of England makes to antiquity. It stands in sharp contrast to the method adopted by most of the Protestant communities in the sixteenth century, who preferred to base their acceptance of the books of Scripture on the 'inner witness of the Spirit.'" [59] If Coleridge does not appeal strongly to antiquity as a criterion, it is only to highlight other objective criteria of canonicity: the authority of the Church, authenticity, and fidelity to Christian revelation. Once again, if he does not always speak with the theologian's precision, the main thrust of his appeal is clear.

In approaching Coleridge on the validity of the principle of *sola Scriptura,* the sufficiency of Scripture alone as the rule of faith, there is a distinct temptation simply to define him as soundly Protestant.[60]

[57] *TT,* 387 (March 31, 1832). For much the same statement, see *TT,* 330 (June 6, 1830).

[58] *TT,* 387 (March 31, 1832). See, on the other hand, his assertion of the catholicity of the Epistle to the Hebrews, *TT,* 264 (January 6, 1823). In at least one notebook entry, Coleridge appeals also to acceptance through the ages by "men of taste" as a criterion of catholicity and hence of canonicity; see Notebook F, ff. 40ᵛ–41 (1826).

[59] *The Thirty-Nine Articles,* I, 250. It should be noted that several times Coleridge seems to shift almost imperceptibly into a more Protestant position, with more reliance on the direct light of the Spirit, as, for example, when he seems to use as an evidence of inspiration (or authenticity?) "that *Lumen Dei,* that spiritual Lustre resting on the inspired Scripture, like that on the Face of Moses, when he came forth from the Presence of Jehovah." Notebook 54 (1833), f. [9]. See also *LR,* 157, 297, 374–375.

[60] In addition to the passages cited below, see also *NTPM,* 69, and *LR,* 237, where Coleridge insists that all the truths necessary for salvation are found in Scripture. This belief is

After all, he does professedly "agree with Taylor against the Romanists, that the Bible is for us the only rule of faith." [61] He did express his belief, when asked in 1827 what form of recantation should be administered to a Roman Catholic who becomes a Protestant, that "no other Recantation ought to be required, than a declaration that he admitted no outward Authority superior to, or co-ordinate with, the Canonical Scriptures, and no Interpreter that superseded or stood in the place of, the Holy Spirit enlightening the mind of the each [sic] true Believer according to his individual needs." [62]

All of this accords well with Article VI of the Articles of Religion, which says: "Holy Scripture containeth all things necessary to salvation: so that whatsoever is not read therein, nor may be proved thereby, is not to be required of any man, that it should be believed as an article of the faith, or be thought requisite necessary [sic] to salvation." It accords well with Article VI, too, in that both are asserted with the same adversary in view: Rome. Both are set clearly against the Roman Catholic concept of Tradition as it was then understood.[63] Tradition was understood to be another source of revelation. According to common Roman Catholic belief of the time, other truths had been revealed by God to the Apostles besides those which had been written down and finally collected in the New Testament. There was an oral Tradition which preceded the composition of the New Testament, and this oral Tradition perdured in the Church even after part of it had been committed to writing. The Church is the custodian and interpreter of these two sources of revelation, Scripture and Tradition.

---

also shared, of course, by Catholics, who believe that although there are revealed truths of faith preserved by the tradition of the Church which are not found in Scripture, all the truths absolutely necessary for salvation are contained in Scripture.

[61] Notes on Jeremy Taylor, LR, 240.

[62] Notebook 26, ff. 58ᵛ–59.

[63] Theological reflection since Coleridge's day, including the work of such nineteenth-century theologians as J. A. Möhler, Cardinal Newman, and Cardinal Franzelin, has led the Roman Catholic Church to emphasize more strongly the unity of revelation. As the Catholic theologian Gabriel Moran wrote recently, "it is neither the book nor the oral teaching that transmits revelation but Scripture and tradition linked inseparably in the Church." *Scripture and Tradition: A Survey of the Controversy* (New York, 1963), p. 85. See also George H. Tavard, *Holy Writ or Holy Church: The Crisis of the Protestant Reformation* (New York, 1959), esp. pp. 244–247. This change of emphasis was dramatized in the drafting of Vatican Council II's dogmatic constitution on Revelation; the original first chapter, entitled "Two Sources of Revelation" (namely, Scripture and tradition) was changed to two chapters entitled "Revelation Itself" and "The Transmission of Divine Revelation." See *The Documents of Vatican II*, ed. Abbott, pp. 112–118, especially chap. ii, art. 10; see also the introductory note to the constitution, p. 107.

Against such a concept of Tradition, Coleridge, with the Articles, stood firm.[64] It was for precisely this reason that Coleridge rejected the "apostolic" denomination of the Apostles' Creed.[65] "If you put the Creed as in fact, and not by courtesy, Apostolic, and on a parity with Scripture, having, namely, its authority in itself, and a direct inspiration of the framers, inspired *ad id tempus et ad eam rem,* on what ground is this to be done, without admitting the binding power of tradition in the very sense of the term in which the Church of Rome uses it, and the Protestant Churches reject it?" [66] There is one Christian revelation, Coleridge held, and that revelation is found in the New Testament.

At the same time, however, despite Coleridge's very Protestant stand against Tradition, we find him Anglican rather than Protestant in his insistence on the need for the Church in the understanding of Scripture. Although we nowhere find him appealing explicitly to the Articles on this issue, what he says is in accord with Article XX, which asserts the Church's authority as "keeper of holy Writ." [67] As early as 1812, Coleridge wrote that "the co-ordinate authority of the Word, the Spirit and the Church, I believe to be the true Apostolic and Catholic doctrine," for he cannot bring himself to believe "that from the mere perusal of the New Testament a man might have sketched out by anticipation the constitution, discipline, creeds, and sacramental ritual of the Episcopal Reformed Church of England, or that it is not a true and orthodox Church, because this is incredible." [68] As he wrote in the margin of one of Skelton's works, "Whatever God has given, we ought to think necessary;—the Scriptures, the Church, the Spirit. Why disjoin them?" [69] A conversation preserved in the *Table Talk* puts his position even more clearly: "It is

---

[64] There are other remarks in much the same vein in *LR,* 70–71, and in Notebook 52 (1833), f. [8ᵛ].

[65] See *LR,* 56, 168–171, 185–186, 300, 421, 518, 554–555. For further references to the Apostles' Creed, see below, Chap. IV, n. 50.

[66] *LR,* 353.

[67] It should be pointed out, however, that at least once Coleridge speaks very slightingly of Articles XIX ("Of the Church") and XX ("Of the Authority of the Church"). He seems to imply that the Church has been defined entirely in terms of its relationship with Scripture, rather than for its own sake, with the result that the Church's role is virtually nullified. "The Romanists sacrifice the Scripture to the Church, virtually annulling the former: the Protestants reversed this practically, and even in theory (see the above-mentioned Articles), annulling the latter." *LR,* 248.

[68] *LR,* 237. Fourteen years later, in 1826, Coleridge returned to this passage and commented: "I still agree with the preceding note."

[69] *LR,* 429.

now twenty years since I read Chillingworth's book; but certainly it seemed to me that his main position, that the mere text of the Bible is the sole and exclusive ground of Christian faith and practice, is quite untenable against the Romanists. It entirely destroys the conditions of a church, of an authority residing in a religious community, and all that holy sense of brotherhood which is so sublime and consolatory to a meditative Christian. Had I been a Papist, I should not have wished for a more vanquishable opponent in controversy." [70]

Coleridge seems to have known fairly precisely where he stood in this Protestant-Romanist controversy: he stood in the middle. Having seen the extremes to which both sides were often led,[71] Coleridge believed the truth to be that Scripture and Church are of equal dignity and importance, for both speak the Word of God. "It has been my conviction that in respect of the theory of the Faith . . . the Papal and the Protestant communions are equi-distant from the true idea of the Gospel Institute, though erring from opposite directions. The Romanists sacrifice the Scripture to the Church, virtually annulling the former: the Protestants reversed this practically, and even in theory (see the above-mentioned Articles), annulling the latter." [72] Coleridge was quite aware that he was departing from the majority of his fellow Protestants on this issue. In his marginal notes on a sermon of Donne's which asserted that "we have a clearer, that is, a

[70] *TT*, 361 (July 25, 1831). The work of William Chillingworth to which Coleridge refers is his *Religion of Protestants, a Safe Way to Salvation* (1638), a work of controversy written in reply to the arguments of a Jesuit, Father Knott.

[71] The following two quotations will give some idea of what Coleridge saw as the extremes. The first extreme is the "unscriptural": on the assertion that it is heresy to believe "that Mary ceased to be a virgin when she had borne Christ," Coleridge comments that it is "mere unscriptural, nay, anti-scriptural gossiping . . . as to Mary's private history after the conception and birth of Christ, we neither know nor care about it." *LR*, 62–63. On the other hand are the "bibliolatrists": "In the reign of Edward VI., the Reformers feared to admit almost any thing on human authority alone. They had seen and felt the abuses consequent on the Popish theory of Christianity; and I doubt not they wished and intended to reconstruct the religion and the church, as far as was possible, upon the plan of the primitive ages. But the Puritans pushed this bias to an absolute bibliolatry. They would not put on a cornplaster without scraping a text over it." *TT*, 330 (June 4, 1830). The latter passage continues: "Men of learning, however, soon felt that this was wrong in the other extreme, and indeed united itself to the very abuse it seemed to shun. They saw that a knowledge of the Fathers, and of early tradition, was absolutely necessary; and unhappily, in many instances, the excess of the Puritans drove the men of learning into the old Popish extreme of denying the Scriptures to be capable of affording a rule of faith without the dogmas of the church. Taylor is a striking instance how far a Protestant might be driven in this direction."

[72] *LR*, 248. The "above-mentioned Articles" referred to are Articles XIX and XX of the Thirty-Nine Articles. See above, n. 67.

nearer light than the written Gospel, that is, the Church," Coleridge remarked: "True; yet he who should now venture to assert this truth, or even contend for a co-ordinateness of the Church and the Written Word, must bear to be thought a semi-Papist, an *ultra* high-Churchman. Still the truth is the truth." [73]

As is so often the case, Coleridge saw the problem of the relationship of Scripture to the Church ultimately in practical terms, as it affects the lives of individuals. In the *Aids to Reflection,* he approached the question in terms of the classic Protestant assertion of the right of private judgment, which he thought to be—if taken by itself—disastrous. "Where private interpretation is every thing, and the Church nothing—there the mystery of Original Sin will be either rejected, or evaded, or perverted . . . ; in the mystery of Redemption metaphors will be obtruded for the reality; and in the mysterious appurtenants and symbols of Redemption (regeneration, grace, the Eucharist, and spiritual communion) the realities will be evaporated into metaphors." But he will not allow himself to be accused of Romanism, for he continues in a note:

The Author of the Statesman's Manual must be the most inconsistent of men, if he can be justly suspected of a leaning to the Romish Church; or if it be necessary for him to repeat his fervent Amen to the wish and prayer of our late good old king, that 'every adult in the British Empire should be able to read his Bible, and have a Bible to read!' Nevertheless, it may not be superfluous to declare, that in thus protesting against the license of private interpretation, I do not mean to condemn the exercise or deny the right of individual judgment. I condemn only the pretended right of every individual, competent and incompetent, to interpret Scripture in a sense of his own, in opposition to the judgment of the Church, without knowledge of the originals or of the languages, the history, customs, opinions and controversies of the age and country in which they were written; and where the interpreter judges in ignorance or in contempt of uninterrupted tradition, the unanimous consent of Fathers and Councils, and the universal faith of the Church in all ages. It is not the attempt to form a judgment, which is here called in question; but the grounds, or rather the no-grounds on which the judgment is formed and relied on.

---

[73] *LR,* 88. There are other references to the Scripture/Tradition problem in *LR,* 40–41, 148–149, 176, 239, 241–242, 298–299, 482; *TT,* 387; and Notebooks 18 (f. 21), 24 (f. 23), 29 (ff. 104–107ᵛ), 35 (ff. 33ᵛ–34), 47 (f. [26ᵛ–27]), 53 (f. [5]).

My fixed principle is: that a Christianity without a Church exercising spiritual authority is vanity and delusion.[74]

Finally, there is need not only of "spiritual authority" to guide the Christian in his reading of Scripture but also of divine grace. "As I can not think that it detracts from a dial that in order to tell the time the sun must shine upon it; so neither does it detract from the Scriptures, that though the best and holiest they are yet Scripture, and require a pure heart and the consequent assistances of God's enlightening grace in order to understand them to edification." [75] The reader of the Bible must have "those inward means of grace, without which the language of the Scriptures, in the most faithful translation and in the purest and plainest English, must nevertheless continue to be a dead language,—a sun-dial by moonlight." [76]

Perhaps it might be said, by way of summary, that Coleridge's most important contribution to the understanding of the nature and role of Scripture is his acceptance of the place of man's humanity in it all.[77] His theory of inspiration and inerrancy took into account the human dimensions of its composition and hence the importance of these human elements in the right understanding of the Bible. His views on the polarity of objective and subjective and on the senses of Scripture also brought the human elements into balance with the divine. His reflections on authorship and authenticity manifested his willingness to do the "human homework" necessary in the treatment of the books of Scripture as historical documents. Finally, his ultimate reliance on the Church for the determination of the canon and for guidance in the interpretation of Scripture marks the humility of the Christian who realizes man's weakness as well as his strength. As always, Coleridge shows himself to be the Christian who remains, for all his faith in God, profoundly and beautifully conscious of his humanity.

[74] *Aids,* 294–295, and note.
[75] *LR,* 237–238. Although this passage was written in 1812, when Coleridge reviewed it in 1826 he found nothing to change.
[76] *SM,* Appendix A, 456. Also see *LR,* 69–70, 154–155; and Notebook F, ff. 32–33ᵛ (1826).
[77] To what has already been discussed we might add another very human dimension, Coleridge's use of the Bible as a guide to political action, especially in the *Stateman's Manual,* which is subtitled "The Bible the Best Guide to Political Skill and Foresight." See also *LS,* 151–154.

❈ IV. THE ONE AND TRIUNE GOD

There was a well-nigh unassailable tradition in Coleridge's day that God must be spoken of as if he were two. There was the God of reason and there was the God of revelation; the God who is one and the God who is triune. There was the God who manifests himself in the world of nature, and the God of Scripture who revealed himself as Father, Son, and Holy Spirit. This division had reached something of a climax during the eighteenth century, when churchmen either retreated in horror from the "God of reason" proposed by rationalists and deists, or, like Paley, went out to meet the rationalists on their own ground. Generally speaking, even by Coleridge's day, few seemed to think of the possibility of trying to find common ground.

Coleridge, stressing as always the continuity between reason and faith and between natural and supernatural, tried to break down this dichotomy. All religion is revealed, he insisted, and so whatever is known of God is revealed. It seemed obvious to Coleridge that God's revelation of himself is one, whether it be mediated through the natural world or through Sacred Scripture. Even by the unaided reason, without the help of the special revelation of Scripture, man can come to an idea of the God who is both one and three; even the mystery of the Trinity can be glimpsed, however distantly and dimly, by the thinking man. By the unaided reason man can come at least to intimations of the triune God; in Scripture he finds a fuller revelation of the same mystery. The one knowledge leads, in God's providence, toward the other, and is continuous with it.

If distinctions are to be made in this matter, it will be safer to make them according to Coleridge's own pattern of thought. The implicit distinction which Coleridge uses (without, however, expressly articulating it) is a distinction between the "idea of God" and his actual existence.[1] We shall find that for Coleridge the formation of the idea of God will be the work both of the unaided intellect in its reflection

[1] It is only in the present chapter and the next that we need insist upon this distinction between the order of intelligibility and the order of existence, because the only important

on itself and the world and of the special revelation of the Bible. Belief in the actual existence of God must, as we have seen, also bring into play man's moral being and hence necessarily involves an act of faith.

We begin, then, in the order of conception. What is Coleridge's idea of God? First of all, it must be borne in mind that Coleridge was writing in reaction to the eighteenth-century rationalist tradition, that of rationalist philosophers like Hume, as well as that of their Christian counterparts in the mold of Archdeacon Paley. As C. R. Sanders has very properly pointed out, "Coleridge's teachings about the nature of God were to a great extent motivated by his dislike of some eighteenth-century conceptions of God, particularly of a purely mechanistic God and of an absentee God." [2] He was, in fact, dissatisfied with any conception of God which distorted reality or any which he found radically incomplete. "Without rejecting the Enlightenment's God of intelligence and the Calvinist's God of supreme power, he yearned for a God who would be manifested in his fullness, in whom the clear light of truth would be united with the infinite strength of a Creator, a Governor, a Protector, and with the warm charity of a Father." [3] It was this last attribute of God which most haunted Coleridge.

In view of what Coleridge believed about the "consubstantiality"

areas in which Coleridge indulges in prolonged theological speculation apart from doctrinal considerations are those of the nature of God (including the Trinity), the Creation, and Sin.

[2] *Coleridge and the Broad Church Movement* (Durham, North Carolina, 1942), p. 77. In a letter of 1817, Coleridge attacks those who substitute "the Lockian and Newtonian [conception]—From God we *had* our Being—for the Pauline—*In* whom we move and live and *have* our Being. The moderns take the 'Ο θεός as an hypothetical Watch-maker, and degrade the τὸ θεῖον into a piece of Clock-Work—they live without God in the world." *CL*, IV, 768. See also *CL*, IV, 760, and Coleridge's footnote in *BL*, II, 59.

[3] Sanders, p. 78. It was probably a yearning for just such a God which prompted one of Coleridge's rare reflections on the genesis of the idea of God in the soul. In a passage in the Opus Maximum manuscript, Coleridge sees the idea of God originating in the child's relationship with his parents, his instinctive reaching out toward something that is not himself. "Why have Men a Faith in God? There is but one answer, the Man & the Man alone has a Father & a Mother." Even before the infant has achieved a sense of its own self, it becomes aware of another with whom the feelings of warmth and comfort are linked. But this is more than mere animal instinct. It involves an exchange of human smiles, the dawning of love. "Beyond the beasts, yea and above the Nature of which they are the inmates, Man possesses love & faith & the sense of the permanent," because he is "irradiated by a higher power, the power namely of seeking what it can no where behold & finding that which itself has first transfused—the permanent, that which in the endless flux of sensible things can alone be known, which is indeed in all but exists for the reason alone, for it is Reason." MS. B₃, ff. 67–68.

of all being, it is clear that what man knows of spiritual reality may properly be expressed in terms of material reality; what he knows of the divine may be expressed in terms of the human. As long as the differences of degree are kept clearly in mind, attributes and powers belonging to one level of being may be predicated of another level of being. In the "great chain of being" man reaches the higher by means of the lower. Bearing this in mind, then, and bearing in mind Coleridge's insistence on the primacy of will in man, one is hardly surprised to find Coleridge's central definition of God to be "Absolute Will." His reflections on the nature of God led him to conclude "that *Deus est ens super ens,* the ground of all being, but therein likewise absolute Being, in that he is the eternal self-affirmant, the I Am in that I Am; and that the key of this mystery is given to us in the pure idea of the will, as the alone *Causa Sui.*" [4]

At first thought, it may seem strange to affirm the priority of will to being in God. How can there be will before there is existence? Does not "willing" presuppose the existence of the one who wills? This is precisely the difficulty Coleridge poses for himself in one section of the Opus Maximum manuscript.[5] First of all, Coleridge takes pains to make clear that the priority he asserts for the Absolute Will is in the logical order, that is, in the order of conception. "The most cloudy gnostic could not have been ignorant that the existence of a Will anterior to that of being in that sense of the term anterior in which a moment is supposed during which the one is while the other is not is a gross absurdity." [6] He begins, therefore, with the position that "in the order of necessary thought the Will must be conceived as anterior to all or that which supports the being." [7]

Next, Coleridge goes on to show that this priority of the Absolute

---

An undated note in Notebook 29 (f. 55) describes beautifully the dawning of the idea of God in the mind: "Did you *deduce* your own being? Even that is less absurd than the conceit of deducing the Divine Being. Never would you have had the notion, had you not had the Idea—rather, had not the Idea worked in you, like the Memory of a Name which we cannot recollect and yet feel that we have, and which reveals its' existence in the mind only by a restless anticipation & proves its' prior actuality by the almost explosive instantaneity with which it is welcomed & recognized on its' re-emersion [sic] out of the Cloud, or its' re-ascent above the horizon of Consciousness."

[4] *LR,* 103. See also *FR,* 465 n. 2 (dated 1829); *LR,* 61–62, 87, 89; *TT,* 517 (June 23, 1834); *UL,* II, 387 (October 25, 1826).

[5] Victoria College MS. B₃, ff. 235–242.

[6] MS. B₃, ff. 235–236. Coleridge discusses the inapplicability of temporal sequence to God in Notebook L (1809–1818), ff. 38–38ᵛ.

[7] MS. B₃, f. 239.

Will in the order of conception comes from the nature of the will itself. The complex course of Coleridge's argumentation on this point has been admirably summarized by J. H. Muirhead: "Temporal relations, he insists, are inapplicable to the Absolute. Even though we conceive of will as a cause, causality itself transcends time, seeing that it merges . . . in the idea of interaction, in which cause and effect must be conceived of as contemporaneous. Attributed to the Supreme Reality, causality must therefore mean co-eternity. But he adds that it is a co-eternity in which will must be conceived of as the more fundamental factor, seeing that its very essence is to be causative of reality; to reverse this and make it a product is to destroy it as will. On the other hand, there is nothing in the conception of being which is exclusive of that of product." [8] Thus, to return to Coleridge's own words, his "first idea" is "an absolute Will, which therefore is essentially causative of reality and therefore *in origine* causative of its own reality, the essential causativeness, however, abiding undiminished and undiminishable." [9]

The perfection of will on the human level, however, involves something further. It involves the self-containment, or better the self-realization, which we call personality. We often think of personality in terms of its limitations: self-concern and exclusiveness. Its perfection, however, involves not merely self-containment but also a relationship of sympathy toward others who are not oneself. "Self-realization" (the term is Coleridge's [10]) involves self-containment together with openness to the reality outside.[11]

In applying this conception to God, Coleridge insists that self-realization be seen in its perfection. In order to make it quite clear that it is being used of God in an eminently perfect way, without the human limitations of self-seeking and exclusiveness, Coleridge prefers to use another term for it: Personeity. "If then personeity, by which term I mean the source of personality, be necessarily contained

---

[8] *Coleridge as Philosopher*, p. 112. Muirhead does not give the folio references, but it is clear that he is summarizing MS. B₃, ff. 236–242.

[9] MS. B₃, f. 242. As elsewhere in quotations from the Opus Maximum manuscript, I have normalized the punctuation.

[10] MS. B₃, f. 243.

[11] Muirhead refers to Coleridge's interpretation of the meaning of personality as "a circumference continually expanding through sympathy and understanding, rather than as an exclusive centre of self-feeling, and consequently of the meaning of individuality and uniqueness as something to be won." *Coleridge as Philosopher*, p. 229. See also pp. 227–230.

in the idea of the perfect Will, how is it possible that personality should not be an essential attribute of this Will, contemplated as self-realized . . . ? The Will therefore as being, and because a Will therefore a personal being, having the *causa sui* or ground and principle of its being in its own inexhaustible causative might:—this is our second idea." [12]

From this point the argumentation leads directly to consideration of the triune God, and this long section of the Opus Maximum remains Coleridge's fullest and most satisfactory account of his speculations on the Trinity.[13]

We have seen that, as Will, God is "essentially causative of reality and therefore *in origine* causative of [his] own reality," and at the same time that, as Personeity, he is necessarily other-directed. The next step must be some kind of action or movement, necessarily causative, toward reality other than the Self. Coleridge continues: "The causativeness hath not ceased, and what shall the product be? All power and all reality are already present . . . What then remains to be communicated? It must in some high sense be other and yet it must be a Self. For there is no other than Self . . . We must . . . proceed as if we substantiated Alterity itself . . . The alterity must have some distinctive from the original absolute identity or how could it be contemplated as other, and yet this distinctive must be such as not to contradict the other co-essential term. It must remain in some sense the Self, though another Self." [14] The same process is expressed as "an infinite fulness poured into an infinite capacity"; it is "a Self wholly and adequately repeated, yet so that the very repetition contains the distinction from the primary act, a Self which in both is self-subsistent, but which yet is not the same because the one only is self-originated" (f. 251).

In his search for an analogy for this process, after first rejecting "any production of thing from thing, or propagation of image from image," Coleridge turns to the working of the human mind and the classic analogy of the production of thought and word.[15] The Alterity

[12] MS. B₃, ff. 243–244.
[13] MS. B₃, ff. 244–283.
[14] MS. B₃, ff. 242–246.
[15] Besides the passages to be cited below on the psychological analogy, see also *LR*, 108–110, and *CL*, IV, 632–633 (April 14, 1816). There is an ingenious but unconvincing use of another analogy, that of the relationship of mind and body, in a letter of Coleridge to his friend Joseph Cottle; see *CL*, III, 483–486 (April 1814).

is thus "the word itself, or adequate expression of the paternal per-soneity" (f. 253), and since the "absolute mind" is "from all eternity personal, therefore from all eternity Father Almighty," the word "in and to whom the mind passeth forth or is uttered" is "personal and the only begotten Son of God" (ff. 253-254). Here Coleridge has (again, in the classical tradition of Christian theology) joined the analogy of human intellection with the scriptural analogy of sonship. "A supreme self-originated being hath communicated himself with-out withholding, and for this act, no recipient being conceived previously thereto, the nearest analogy, and at all events the least inappropriate term and conception that human knowledge and hu-man language contain, is that of *begetting,* and the most expressive relation that of *Father* and *Son.*" [16]

God's idea of himself is, it must be remembered, an adequate idea; hence it must be consubstantial with the reality which it expresses. "If then we designate what we have named in imitation of the Jewish Philosopher, the *Deus idem et alter,* and for the convenience of reasoning the infinite product of the infinite causality, God's co-eternal idea of himself, we recollect that it is the adequate idea, and that if it be not real it cannot express the reality and therefore is not adequate. To be the adequate idea of the Father it must be first substantial as the Father, and consubstantial or of the same substance with the Father." [17]

The term idea is a useful tool here, but it is not an appropriate image to express the relationship of the Father and the Son. For the images which he chooses to express the analogies of his Trinitarian theology, Coleridge has clearly stayed within traditional bounds. "In-asmuch as the term Idea does not in itself necessarily involve relation, it becomes comparatively a less fit exponent of the truth which it is meant to convey, than those which were used both before and after the Christian aera in the works of philosophy as well as in the pages of Scripture—the Son, the Word, or even than the term substituted

[16] MS. B₃, f. 259. The passage continues: "The Father hath communicated himself ab-solutely, not therefore a shadow of himself, and it would be as gross an absurdity in reason as it would border on blasphemy in religion, to represent the infinite product of an infinite causality as standing in the same relation as the reflex thought of a thing to the thing itself in the hypothetical processes of a finite understanding" (ff. 259-260). On the notion of genera-tion applied to the Trinity, see also *LR,* 408.

[17] MS. B₃, ff.263-264. The "Jewish Philosopher" is Philo Judaeus.

for Idea by the Apostle, the *Icon* . . . , i.e. a perfect likeness, which is yet for that reason not the same and yet its adequate and consequently self-subsistent and living representative." [18]

This relational aspect of the generation of the Son by the Father brings to the fore the importance of reciprocity; relationship is a two-way matter. The act by which the Son is generated is, to be sure, "the act of the Father in the generation and contemplation of the Son, and directed toward the Son." "But it is likewise and simultaneously, as it were, the act of the Son in referring himself and in him the plenitude of divine forms to the Father, and thus directed towards the Father. By what other term can we designate this act, but by affirming that it is an eternal proceeding from the Father to the Son and from the Son to the Father, but such procession being in its nature circular, at once ever refluent and ever profluent, the Greek Fathers have entitled the περιχώρησις or the primary, absolute, co-eternal intercirculation of Deity." [19]

But the process is not yet complete; there remains the act by which the Father and the Son are one. Here again the analogy Coleridge uses is the classic one: the "wind" by which air manifests itself "in the form of action" and which, appropriated to animals and men as breath or "spirit," symbolizes life.[20] Applied to the Godhead, this act is seen as "the Holy Spirit, that which proceedeth from the Father to the Son, and that which is returned from the Son to the Father, and which in this circulation constitutes the eternal unity in the eternal alterity and distinction, the life of Deity *in actu purissimo.* This is truly the Breath of Life indeed" (f. 276/260ᵛ). The Spirit is "the act, in which the Father and the Son are One," and thus we have "the Idem, the Alter and the Copula by which both are one and the Copula one with them" (f. 277/259ᵛ).

Ultimately, this Spirit by whom (for the Spirit is personal, being "one with them") the Father and the Son are one is a Spirit of Love. "Himself being all, he communicated himself to another as to a Self: but such communication is Love, and in what is the re-attribution of

---

[18] MS. B₃, ff. 264–265. For St. Paul's use of the term εἰκών, see, for example, Col. 1:15.

[19] MS. B₃, ff. 267–268. Theologians commonly translate the Greek word περιχώρησις by the latinate term "circumincession." See also *LR*, 62.

[20] MS. B₃, f. 275. This page is actually f. 261ᵛ, but has also been given separate pagination. Hereafter this will be indicated as follows: f. 275/261ᵛ.

that Self to the Communicator but Love. This too is Love, filial Love. Love is the Spirit of God, and God is Love" (f. 278/258^v).

At least in the order of conception, then, the matter seems to be fairly well settled. "We have the Absolute under three distinct ideas, and the essential inseparability of these, without interference with their no less essential interdistinction, is the Divine Idea" (ff. 278–279/258^v–257^v).[21]

There is one further matter which merits attention, however, before we move out of the order of speculation. Up to this point, Coleridge's speculations on the nature of the triune God have been, in their essential lines, strongly traditional. His "psychological theory" of the Trinity is in no significant way different from the analysis given by St. Augustine in his *De Trinitate,* in which he uses the human analogies of self-reflection and self-love to express the processes of the Trinitarian life. This theory, further developed by medieval Scholastic theologians, notably by St. Thomas Aquinas, became part of the theological tradition of the Western Church.[22] To be sure, the the Scholastic theologians began with the assumption that they could not have begun to speculate on the nature of the Trinity had its existence not been revealed by Scripture, while Coleridge's speculations began, at least methodologically, with no such revelation; all of which is only to say that Coleridge believed that knowledge of the Trinity is to some extent accessible to the unaided intellect. In almost all other respects, however, Coleridge's theorizing remains that of the Scholastic tradition of the Western Church.

There remains one significant departure from this tradition. In both eastern and western theology, the Trinity has been conceived in terms of a "triad": the Father, Son, and Holy Spirit eternally co-existing, and co-existing as well in the order of conception—the Father eternally begetting the Son, the Spirit eternally proceeding from both. The conception is at the same time dynamic and scrupu-

---

[21] There is a strikingly similar entry in Notebook 35 (c. 1827), f. 45: "I affirm that the man is a Tritheist, who *in such a way* thinks of Jesus Christ as true and entire God, that his mind is not under the necessity of thinking at the same time of the Father and of the H. [sic] Spirit. The Tri-unity is intelligently confessed only where the Idea, God, contains *distinct* ideas of the Father, of the Son, and of the Spirit, yet such that being distinct they are at the same time inseparable, and after [?some] determinate and immutable order."

[22] For examples of the use of the psychological analogy for the Trinity by several modern theologians, see Bernard J. F. Lonergan, *Divinarum Personarum Conceptio Analogica,* 2nd ed. (Rome, 1959), and Leonard Hodgson, *The Doctrine of the Trinity* (Digswell Place, England, 1943), especially pp. 85–112.

lously faithful to belief in the equality and eternity of the three Persons. This triad is, however, also a "monad." Hence it is possible to conceive of it as "a Trinity *in* Unity and a Unity *in* Trinity." [23] Coleridge felt, on the other hand, that he must find a "ground" for the Trinity which is logically prior to it. Thus he conceived the Trinity rather in terms of a "tetractys," which Professor Shedd very well summarizes as "the scheme namely of a Monad logically anterior to, and other than, the Triad—of a Monad which originally *is* not a Triad, but *becomes* one—whereby four factors are introduced into the problem." [24]

Although the Trinity is conceived in the Opus Maximum manuscript as "the venerable Tetractys of the most ancient philosophy" [25] (of which the four elements are "the absolute or the prothesis, the Idem, the Alter and the Copula"), there are clearer expressions of it elsewhere; all of them, it might be noted, date from 1820 and after. The clearest of all, however, is Coleridge's "Formula Fidei de Sanctissima Trinitate" of 1830; it is worth quoting at length:

THE IDENTITY.

The absolute subjectivity, whose only attribute is the Good; whose only definition is—that which is essentially causative of all possible true being; the ground; the absolute will; the adorable πρόπρωτον, which, whatever is assumed as the first, must be presumed as its antecedent . . .

But that which is essentially causative of all being must be causative of its own,—*causa sui,* αὐτοπάτωρ. Thence

THE IPSEITY.

The eternally self-affirmant self-affirmed; the "I Am in that I Am," or the "I shall be that I will to be;" the Father; the relatively subjective, whose attribute is, the Holy One; whose definition is, the essential finific in the form of the infinite; *dat sibi fines.*

But the absolute will, the absolute good, in the eternal act of self-affirmation, the Good as the Holy One, co-eternally begets

THE ALTERITY.

The supreme being; ὁ ὄντως ὤν; the supreme reason; the Jehovah; the Son; the Word; whose attribute is the True (the truth, the light, the *fiat*); and whose definition is the *pleroma* of being, whose essential poles are

---

[23] See Shedd's Introductory Essay to Coleridge's *Works,* I, 44.
[24] *Ibid.*
[25] MS. B₃, f. 277/259ᵛ.

unity and distinctity; or the essential infinite in the form of the finite;—lastly, the relatively objective, *deitas objectiva* in relation to the I Am as the *deitas subjectiva;* the divine objectivity . . .

But with the relatively subjective and the relatively objective, the great idea needs only for its completion a co-eternal which is both, that is, relatively objective to the subjective, relatively subjective to the objective. Hence

THE COMMUNITY.

The eternal life, which is love; the Spirit; relatively to the Father, the Spirit of Holiness, the Holy Spirit; relatively to the Son, the Spirit of truth, whose attribute is Wisdom; *sancta sophia;* the Good in the reality of the True, in the form of actual Life.[26]

At this point Professor Shedd enters a gentle demurrer, pointing to what is probably the weakest part of Coleridge's theoretical superstructure. The problematic factor is the "assumption of an aboriginal Unity existing primarily by itself, and in the order of nature, *before* a Trinity—of a *ground* for the Trinity, or, in Coleridge's phrase a *prothesis,* which is not in its own nature either triune or personal, but is merely the impersonal base from which the Trinity proper is evolved."[27] Shedd believes that this introduces into the Godhead "a process of development . . . which is incompatible with its immutable perfection, and with that golden position of the schoolmen that God is *actus purissimus sine ulla potentialitate*"—a dictum, by the way, to which Coleridge strongly subscribed and which he loved to repeat. Shedd saw in this an unfortunate influence of pantheism, introducing unawares an element of potentiality into God, in place of "the theistic conception of self-completeness."[28] It is difficult to see how Coleridge's theoretical application of the conception of the tetractys to God can be defended from the charge of modalism

---

[26] *LR,* 18–19. Much the same formula appears in Notebooks 48 (1830), 52 (1833), and 55 (1834). In Notebook 47 (1830), f. [33], Coleridge refers to the four elements of the tetractys as θεός, ὁ θεός, ὁ υἱὸς θεοῦ, τὸ πνεῦμα. In a *Table Talk* entry of 1827, Coleridge expresses the same division as Prothesis (God, "the absolute Will or Identity"), Thesis (the Father), Antithesis (the Son), Synthesis (the Spirit). See *TT,* 289–290. Further references to the tetractys in the context of Trinitarian discussions are found in Coleridge's notes on Baxter (1820) in *LR,* 355–356, and in his undated marginal notes on Daniel Waterland in *LR,* 404, 416, 426.
[27] Introductory Essay, *Works,* I, 44.
[28] *Ibid.*

levelled by Shedd, but one may in any event join with Shedd's charitable and very proper judgment that "we are far from believing that Coleridge's practical faith as a Christian in the Trinity, was in the least affected by this tendency to modalism in his speculative construction of the doctrine." [29]

It should perhaps be made clear at this point just what has been done. For the sake of clarity, we have divided our consideration of God (as Coleridge does, though often only implicitly) into the realm of conception and the realm of existence. This is not to say that this is always or necessarily the order in which Coleridge, or anyone else, approaches them. One may begin, for example, with reflection on the idea of God—omniscience and omnipresence, the analogous attribution of human qualities, the intelligibility of the Trinity, and the like—quite apart from any position on the existence of God; one may then perhaps move toward an affirmation of the existence of these ideas as realities. The process may, on the other hand, be quite the reverse. One may begin with an affirmation of faith in the existence of God, or of the Trinity, or of some attribute of God, and only then initiate a process of reflection on its deeper intelligibility. In other words, the affirmation of existence and the reflective search for intelligibility are two distinct moments in the theological endeavor. Both are necessary in the properly human acceptance of religious truth. The search for intelligibility may precede or may follow the affirmation of existence. Often enough it will do both, as when an unbeliever, by philosophical and theological reflection, disposes himself for an affirmation of faith, which is then followed by further reflection on the deeper intelligibility of his faith. It is, once again, St. Augustine's *fides quaerens intellectum,* faith in search of understanding.

Coleridge's aim is clearly to explain the intelligibility of his faith in the triune God, "to prove the possibility and ideal truth of the dogmas common to the churches of Christendom." [30] His method, however, at least here in his speculations on the Trinity, is to prescind from the reality or non-reality of the ideas he discusses, to act as if he had not made his affirmation of faith: "For . . . my present purpose and profession is wholly and exclusively to prove that it is pos-

29 *Ibid.*
30 MS. B₈, f. 255

sible to form an idea self-consistent and consistent with all other truths respecting the Godhead." [31]

With this in mind, we may move at last from the order of conception to the order of existence. Speculation alone is clearly not enough. "The Trinity of persons in the Unity of the [sic] God would have been a necessary idea of my speculative reason, deduced from the necessary postulate of an intelligent creator . . . But this would only have been a speculative idea, like those of circles and other mathematical figures, to which we are not authorized by the practical reason to attribute reality." [32] What can one know, according to Coleridge, of the actual existence of God without the aid of revelation?

First of all, knowing that much of what Coleridge wrote concerning rational knowledge of God's existence was written in reaction to Paleyan attempts to prove the existence of God by merely rational arguments, one should not be surprised to find him often asserting that "proof" for the existence of God is impossible. In his philosophical lecture of January 4, 1819, Coleridge spoke of the "Chubbs and Morgans" of the preceding century, pointing out that "it is astonishing with what coolness they proceeded to give demonstrative proofs, which no man could reject, of the being and attributes of God and a future state." [33] In a later lecture that month he insisted that "by the mere power of reasoning no man ever yet arrived at God, at that Being given by his conscience and his moral being. Then his intellect, his senses, and all the objects of both intellect and senses, are one continued book forever calling it forth, forever reminding him of it, forever bringing it into distinction and comparison. But those who think it easy to demonstrate the being of a deity are mistaken." [34] And in a *Table Talk* entry of 1834 he says: "Assume the existence of God,—and then the harmony and fitness of the physical creation may be shown to correspond with and support such an assumption; —but to set about *proving* the existence of a God by such means is a

---

[31] MS. B₃, ff. 257–258.

[32] "Confessio Fidei" (November 3, 1810) in *LR*, 17. Although this "Confessio Fidei" is commonly dated 1816, it was actually written in 1810. The text appears in Notebook M (1810), ff. 2–7ᵛ, and the 'o' of the 1810 date on f. 2 could easily be mistaken for a '6.'

[33] *PL*, 126. Thomas Chubb and Thomas Morgan were early eighteenth-century deists.

[34] *PL*, 209 (January 25, 1819).

mere circle, a delusion. It can be no proof to a good reasoner, unless he violates all syllogistic logic, and presumes his conclusion." [35]

Of course, let it be said that the God of whom Coleridge speaks in such a context, whose actual existence cannot be known apart from revelation, is the God in whom Coleridge actually does believe, the personal God of Christianity. Coleridge is willing to admit—and it is the most he will admit—that the unaided human mind can come to a knowledge of a God in the attenuated sense of an impersonal force. Indeed, "no man in his senses can deny *God* in some sense or other, as *anima mundi, causa causarum,* &c., but it is the *personal, living, self-conscious* God, which it is so difficult, except by faith of the Trinity, to combine with an infinite being infinitely and irresistibly causative. Τὸ ἓν καὶ πᾶν [the One and All] is the first dictate of mere human philosophy." [36] A *personal* God is the point at issue, and Coleridge was firmly convinced that the existence of a personal God could be known only by special revelation. In point of historical fact, "the Personality of God, the living I AM, was the distinctive privilege of the Hebrew Faith." [37]

What then of the Trinity? First of all, we have already seen from Coleridge's speculations in the Opus Maximum manuscript that the Trinity as an idea is to some extent accessible to the unaided human mind, which is to say that the very idea of a personal God involves the idea of the Trinity. He even wrote of its "self-evidence . . . as a universal of the reason,—as the reason itself—as a light which revealed itself by its own essence as light," [38] while to young James Gillman Jr. he wrote in 1827: "I have never heard an argument against the Trinity that did not apply with equal force against the existence of a Supreme Being in any form." [39] An intelligent and personal God can be conceived only as a triune God.[40] But the question remains, can the actual existence of such a personal and triune God be asserted by the unaided human reason? Coleridge wrote in one of his note-

---

[35] *TT*, 502 (February 22, 1834). See also *PL*, 277–278; *Aids*, 221–222; *LR*, 267; *CL*, IV, 766 (1817). There are also notebook entries on this subject in, for example, Notebook 23. For a somewhat more sympathetic view, however, see *NTPM*, 264 (1820).

[36] *NED*, II, 6–7.

[37] *UL*, II, 401 (1827). See also *SM*, 439; *PL*, 125; and Notebook F, ff. 83–86ᵛ (1832).

[38] *LR*, 408.

[39] From a previously unpublished note included by Mrs. Lucy Watson in her *Coleridge at Highgate*, p. 127. For other assertions of the accessibility of the Trinity to reason, see *BL*, I, 136–137; *LR*, 404–405, 441; *CL*, III, 283–284 (1810), IV, 894–895 (1818).

[40] See *LR*, 36.

books in 1830: "Most important it is that you should observe the *personality* of this infinite Mind is an article of *faith,* not less dependent on a Revelation or at least of a Moral Assumption, than the doctrine of a trinity or Tri-personality—which indeed is the legitimate & necessary consequence of the former."[41] Once Coleridge begins to speak of the actual existence of a personal, and therefore for him necessarily triune, God, he has passed into the realm of his characteristic practical Christianity. There is once again the chasm, which man's "moral being only" can overleap.

For a longer look at this "practical" view of the Trinity we must turn to the *Aids to Reflection.*[42] In a sense, the splendid pages on the Trinity in the *Aids* form a summary of much that we have seen already, with the addition of the crucial moral dimension.

Coleridge begins with the enunciation of two principles we have already seen: that the idea of the Trinity is necessarily involved in the very idea of God; and that, apart from special revelation, this idea could not have been verified in reality "though it might have been a legitimate contemplation for a speculative philosopher, a theorem in metaphysics valid in the Schools" (p. 216). Once the idea has been established and clarified in the mind (pp. 217–218), by reflection, reading, discussion with others, then the two poles of all religious experience come into play. The objective pole offers the scriptural revelation, the "historical assurance" of "the actual existence of this Divine Being" (p. 218); concomitantly with it, the subjective pole (including will and conscience) impels the person to see the doctrine as personally and immediately significant, for "it must concern me, as a moral and responsible being" (p. 220). As in any act of faith, both poles are necessary: "Revelation must have assured it, my conscience required it" (p. 220).[43] As so often in Coleridge, we come back to the crucial importance of the moral aspect of faith, to the role of the will. "It is not enough, the Deist might justly say,

---

[41] Notebook 48, ff. [30ᵛ-31].

[42] The doctrine of the Trinity is treated in *Aids,* 216-222.

[43] An example of the presence of the subjective pole without the objective may be seen in Coleridge's lengthy discussion of the natural desire for God in the Greeks before the coming of Christ. He speaks of their "imperative voice," for "with the most piercing of all invocations, that of inward prayer to the Unknown Being, unknown yet wished for, did it call, till He who alone could give the answer to it appeared in his Son and introduced the decision by the voice of revealed religion." *PL,* 149–150. See also pp. 149-157.

that there is no cogent reason why I should *not* believe the Trinity; you must show me some cogent reason why I should" (p. 222).

Rather obviously, this is not, as we have already insisted, to exclude the role of the speculative reason. "It is its office and rightful privilege to determine on the negative truth of whatever we are required to believe," to assure that the doctrine does not "contradict any universal principle" (p. 222), while philosophy is "the servant and pioneer of faith by convincing the mind that a doctrine is cogitable, that the soul can present the idea to itself; and that if we determine to contemplate, or think of, the subject at all, so and in no other form can this be effected" (p. 222). This is precisely what we found Coleridge to be doing in the Trinitarian speculations of the Opus Maximum. But to go beyond this to the actual reality of the idea is to appeal to the moral nature of man, for "the grounds of the real truth; the life, the substance, the hope, the love, in one word, the faith;—these are derivatives from the practical, moral, and spiritual nature and being of man" (p. 223). This is the realm of the practical reason.

Besides what we have seen of the revelation of the personality of God in the Old Testament ("the distinctive privilege of the Hebrew Faith"), the actual revelation of the Trinity which Coleridge finds in Scripture is quite consonant with his views of the nature of the Bible itself: it is gradual and evolving, sometimes fragmentary, always in forms of imagery and expression which are adapted to its immediate human context. In particular, the Old Testament pointed toward and adumbrated the New Testament; it foretold, often only dimly, what would be more fully revealed in the coming of Christ. Hence Coleridge asks: "Why is it *necessary,* on what grounds of psychology is it *rational,* to demand an answer to the question, in what distinct conceptions the more spiritual Israelites under the Law, and of the Prophetic Aera presented to themselves the *idea* of the Word of God, that *was* (*i.e.* was not a mere verbal abstraction) and yet was not a creature contradistinguished from God? The great *idea* possessed all the faithful, but before the coming of Jesus, few, perhaps not one, possessed the idea." The idea was rather "a sacred tradition, a treasured prophecy—a mysterious cypher in which all treasures of all knowledge were contained, but by involution." The doctrine of the

99

Trinity is "a *Prophecy,* . . . like the great Prophecy of the Redemption, proceeding from dim dawn to full noontide." [44]

Similarly within the New Testament itself, the revelation of the Trinity is not given everywhere with the same clarity. Coleridge asks, for example, in a note on Daniel Waterland's treatise on the Trinity: "Is it clear that the distinct *hypostasis* of the Holy Spirit, in the same sense as the only-begotten Son is hypostatically distinguished from the Father, was a truth that formed an immediate object or intention of St. John? That it is a truth implied in, and fairly deducible from, many texts, both in his Gospel and Epistles, I do not, indeed I can not, doubt;—but only whether this article of our faith he was commissioned to declare explicitly?" [45] For all its fragmentary and evolutional character, however, the Trinitarian revelation of the New Testament is abundantly clear in its main lines, in that "the Word and the Spirit are spoken of everywhere in Scripture as individuals, each distinct from the other, and both from the Father: that of both all the divine attributes are predicated, except self-origination; that the Spirit is God, and the Word is God, and that they with the Father are the one God." [46]

Coleridge found no great problem with the articulation between Scripture and the early Councils on this matter. [47] The doctrine of both is the same. "*All* Scripture from Genesis to the Apocalypse declares, there is but one God. In the New Testament three distinct Agents are spoken of, the Father, the Son, and the Paraclete or Holy Ghost . . . To each of these the name, names, and incommunicable attributes of the Supreme Being are given. Ergo, there are three, and these Three are One.—This is the Scripture Trinity; and what other is contained in the Nicene Creed?" [48] At the same time, Coleridge does seem to have a sense of the importance of the passage from the scriptural mode of expression to a conciliar mode—more dogmatic, more metaphysical, more precise—by means of which misinterpre-

---

[44] From a note on Jahn's *Appendix Hermeneuticae, NTPM,* 136.

[45] *LR,* 423–424.

[46] Notes on Jeremy Taylor, *LR,* 229. This clarity of expression on the Trinity in the New Testament is called into question in a single notebook entry of 1826, although Coleridge firmly maintains even there that the doctrine of the Trinity may be "legitimately deduced from very many passages of the New Testament—nay rather, from the whole Canon"; see Notebook F, f. 39ᵛ.

[47] Coleridge speaks frequently of the Council of Nicea and, like many Anglicans, generally gives authority to at least the first four ecumenical councils: Nicea (325), Constantinople I (381), Ephesus (431), and Chalcedon (451).

[48] *LR,* 536.

THE ONE AND TRIUNE GOD

tations of Scripture are corrected. As he wrote of the "Nicene Form of the Trinity," although it is "not so good for a positive apprehension of the Truth," it is "valuable as precluding dangerous error in the conception of this Mystery." [49]

The seriousness with which Coleridge treated credal formulae may be illustrated by the difference between his attitudes toward the Nicene Creed and the so-called Athanasian Creed, a Latin creed from about the end of the fourth century, which is still part of the liturgy of the Church of England.[50] Coleridge accepted the Nicene Creed without reserve: "My outward Creed is the Apostles' as expanded in the Nicene." [51] The Athanasian Creed, on the other hand, Coleridge was never able wholly to accept. At one time, he calls it "not false, but imperfect," for "this Creed truly expresses the equality of Attributes and the Identity of the Godhead; but does not confess the subordination of the Persons." [52] At another time he goes so far as to call it "heretical in the omission, or implicit denial, of the Filial subordination in the Godhead, which is the doctrine of the Nicene Creed." [53] In any event, whatever qualification he gave to his anathema, he felt that there were "weighty reasons" for removing it

[49] Notebook 36 (1827), f. 60ᵛ. There is a much earlier note (probably 1809) in Notebook 17, f. 84, on the precision of conciliar language: "An important mistake in Theology, the not distinguishing between expressions apparently favoring any particular opinion in writers prior to the controversy concerning that opinion, & the same or similar in writers during & after that controversy.—Thus the most Arian passages in Fathers prior to the Nicene Council are no proof that the writers were *Arians*—i.e. that if the two opinions had been accurately stated & proposed to them, they would not have at once converted their language."

[50] The Athanasian Creed, often called the "Quicunque" from its opening word, was attributed to St. Athanasius (died c. 373) until the seventeenth century. Since then this attribution has been abandoned, and its authorship is now uncertain; it may, in fact, be a compilation of material by various hands. See the article by L. G. Owens, "Athanasian Creed," *New Catholic Encyclopedia* (New York, 1967), I, 995–996. For the text of the Athanasian Creed see Denzinger-Schönmetzer, n. 75–76; the text of the Nicene Creed (the creed of the Council of Nicea) is in n. 125. A sound modern treatment of the creeds is J. N. D. Kelly's *Early Christian Creeds* (New York, 1950). There is a helpful discussion of the Apostles', Nicene, and Athanasian Creeds, especially the history of their use in the Church of England, in Gibson, *The Thirty-Nine Articles*, I, 296–355. The use of the three creeds is sanctioned by Article VIII of the Thirty-Nine Articles.

Even when he expresses it in his own words, Coleridge's creed is always founded on the Nicene Creed—and on the Apostles' Creed of which the Nicene is a development. As he wrote in Notebook 20 (f. 32): "My inward Creed, as a Christian, remains without subtraction or addition as it stands in the Aids to Reflection . . . My outward Creed is the Apostles' as expanded in the Nicene." See, for example, his "Confessio Fidei" of 1810 in *The Complete Works*, ed. Shedd, V, 15–18; *Aids*, 229–230; his "Letter to His Godchild" in *LR*, 565–567; Notebook 29, ff. 32–32ᵛ. On the development of the Apostles' Creed and Coleridge's doubts about its apostolic origin, see *LR*, 56, 168–171, 185–186, 300, 353–354, 421, 518, 554–555. On Coleridge's view of the need of creeds, see *LR*, 385–386.

[51] Notebook 20, f. 32 (c. 1825).

[52] Notes on Burnet's *History of the Reformation*, NTPM, 69–70 (dated 1823).

[53] TT, 290 (July 8, 1827). See also Coleridge's notes on Skelton, *LR*, 427.

from the liturgy, since, unless it be interpreted laxly, "it could not be cleared of a very dangerous approach to Tritheism in its omission of the Subordination of the Son to the Father, not as Man merely, but as the Eternal Logos." [54]

Even the clarifications of as late a council as the Council of Lyons (the "Filioque" council of 1274, which defined the procession of the Holy Spirit from both the Father and the Son) could win Coleridge's approval. He admits: "There can, I think, be no doubt that the Latin Church were [sic] *philosophically* justified in asserting & insisting on the procession of the Holy Ghost from the Father and the Son (i.e. from the Father thro' the Son)," though he adds the qualification, "however culpable in seeking to impose the interpolated *'filioque,'* on the Eastern Churches, as . . . one of those *confessed and expressed* articles of Belief, which were semper, ubique et ab omnibus." The added clarity brought by the conciliar statement is helpful, since "the sublime Idea of the Tri-unity may be *totally inferred* from the Scriptures, but is only partially expressed, and there is . . . no direct assertion to be found in the New Testament of the Procession of the Holy Ghost from the Son." [55]

Much as Coleridge appreciated the value of conciliar and credal formulae in making scriptural revelation more precise (and in the process, it is to be hoped, more clear), he seems occasionally to have caviled at what seemed to him an overinsistence on a particular word of the formulation. We have already noticed his objection to the mystique of the word "filioque," much as he sympathized with its purpose. Another was the famous and controverted word ὁμοούσιος, the battle-cry of the Council of Nicea, by which the Council defined the Son to be "consubstantial" with the Father. After pointing out the essential identity of doctrine between the Council of Nicea (A.D. 325)

---

[54] *CL,* IV, 686 (September 25, 1816). For other pejorative comments on the Athanasian Creed, see *LR,* 385–386 and 427. It is difficult to see that Coleridge's fear was justified, since the creed clearly states: "Pater a nullo est factus nec creatus nec genitus; Filius a Patre solo est, non factus nec creatus, sed genitus; Spiritus Sanctus a Patre et Filio, non factus nec creatus nec genitus, sed procedens." Denzinger-Schönmetzer, n. 75. It is interesting to note that Coleridge's disciple F. D. Maurice saw no contradiction between the two creeds, the Nicene and the Athanasian, on the matter of the Son's subordination to the Father. See Maurice's *Theological Essays* (London, 1871), p. 482, and the comment by C. R. Sanders in *Coleridge and the Broad Church Movement,* pp. 252–253.

[55] Notebook 47 (1830), f. [39–39ᵛ]. In Notebook 53 (1833), he confesses that "the controversy between the Greek and the Latin Church, respecting the insertion by the latter of 'a filioque', begins to appear to me of more importance, less a matter of words, than I once thought" (f. [19]). See also *LR,* 242–243.

and the (nonecumenical) Council of Rimini, which met in 359 to heal the wounds left by Nicea, Coleridge goes on: "This was the confession of the great Council at Rimini: and how the mere omission for peace sake [sic] of the unscriptural term, ὁμοούσιος, could cause it to be denounced as heretical, only the Fever-heat of Party can account for.—Give up ὁμοούσιος, the dear lucky ὁμοούσιος, that had set all Christendom by the ears? It was not to be thought of!" [56]

For Coleridge, what was important was the statement of the essential faith in the Trinity. As long as precision and clarity were achieved in different formulations of the doctrine, it remained quite possible that the somewhat different lights might complement one another. On the same two councils, Nicea and Rimini (here called by its Latin name, Ariminum), Coleridge wrote in another note that he could discover no essential difference between them. But "if there be a difference between the Councils of Nicea and Ariminum, it perhaps consists in this;—that the Nicene was the more anxious to assert the equal Divinity in the Filial subordination; the Ariminian to maintain the Filial subordination in the equal Divinity. In both there are three self-subsistent and only one self-originated:—which is the substance of the idea of the Trinity, as faithfully worded as is compatible with the necessary inadequacy of words to the expression of ideas, that is, spiritual truths that can only be spiritually discerned." [57]

In all this discussion of "the one and triune God," it will no doubt be noticed how little stress there has been on development in Coleridge's ideas in this area, in sharp contrast to the gradual evolution we saw in his views on the nature of faith. The fact seems to be, on the speculative side, that once Coleridge turned his mind to the problem of the Trinity in the 1820's (notably in the Opus Maximum), his "system" was well and fairly completely established as we have outlined it. From then on, when he turned his attention to it, it was only to deepen his understanding without changing his basic positions or insights. From the doctrinal point of view, after his early Unitarian adventure Coleridge embraced completely the doctrine of the Trinity and never departed from it. His deepening understand-

[56] Notebook 35 (c. 1827), f. 43. The same view is expressed in Coleridge's notes on Jeremy Taylor, LR, 173–174.
[57] Note in Coleridge's copy of Luther's Table Talk (dated August 18, 1826), LR, 296. For other comments on conciliar statements on the Trinity, see Coleridge's marginal notes on William Sherlock's Vindication of the Doctrine of the Holy and ever Blessed Trinity and the Incarnation of the Son of God (1690), LR, 381–404, passim.

ing of the doctrine came from his theological speculations, together with a growing knowledge of the history of its conciliar formulations and an ever-deeper knowledge of its scriptural foundations.

This chapter might appropriately close with the remark that once again, the will has come to the fore. The triune God is, above all, Absolute Will; and it is only with the aid of his own will, in the exercise of practical reason, that man can come to a knowledge of the actual existence of this triune God. And this exercise of practical Christianity was, after all, what was of highest importance in the view of one than whom "few minds in the whole history of the Christian Church . . . have had more awful and adoring views of the Triune God, or have bowed down in more absolute and lowly worship before the Father, Son, and Holy Ghost." [58]

[58] Shedd, Introductory Essay, *Works,* I, 45.

❄ V. CREATION AND SINFUL MAN

Intimately linked with Coleridge's analysis of the Trinity, in fact flowing directly from his treatment of God's Absolute Will, is his analysis of Creation and the Fall of Man. Once again we shall find Coleridge playing his recurring themes on the nature of will in God and man.

Here again, as in the last chapter, it will be convenient to divide the consideration, as Coleridge does, into the order of speculation and the order of existence. We begin, then, in the a priori order of conception.

The broad lines of Coleridge's speculation on Creation and Sin are fairly clear in the Opus Maximum manuscript, which we have already seen in the context of his discussion of the Absolute Will. If this material is taken together with some of the notebooks of about the same period (the early and middle 1820's), a fairly clear understanding of Coleridge's speculative stance emerges.

The key is Coleridge's notion of Alterity, for on this depends Coleridge's speculative understanding of two basic Christian ideas: the existence of a finite created world, and its Redemption. Discussion of the Redemption will be reserved for the following chapter.

The significance of Coleridge's discussion of the Trinity goes far beyond mere speculative understanding of the Trinitarian doctrine itself. We have already made it clear, I hope, that Coleridge considered his defense of the Trinity a defense of religion itself, in that the concept of the Trinity is bound up with the very idea of God. "There is, there can be, no *medium* between the Catholic Faith of Trinal Unity, and Atheism disguised in the self-contradicting term, Pantheism."[1] In particular, we may look at his view of the relationship between Ipseity and Alterity in the Godhead, for, as James Boulger has pointed out, "on the validity of the 'distinctity' granted to the Logos or Alterity within the greater unity of Identity hinges the

[1] *LR*, 406.

strength of a philosophical dualism of Creator and created, Absolute and individual will, God and created finite substance." [2]

We have already seen that the Alterity or Logos is the Ipseity's perfect image of itself, perfectly expressed and perfectly known. At the same time, they are not identical. Existence is attributed to each in a different way, the former as knowing, the latter as known; the one as generating, the other as generated; the one as Father, the other as Son. But this is not all. Bearing in mind Coleridge's acceptance of the "consubstantiality of all being," we may expect to find a similar attribution, *mutatis mutandis,* on other levels of being as well. This distinction within the divine being itself becomes "the ground and transcendent analogue for the phenomenon of creation," [3] the pattern for distinction of finite beings from the infinite and of finite beings among themselves: "As soon as the duplication [the distinction of Alterity from Ipseity] is presented to the mind, and with it the form of alterity, we have only to learn that in this other all others are included, that in this first substantial and intelligible distinction (= ὁ Λόγος) all other distinctions that can subsist in the indivisible unity (Λόγοι θεῖοι) or contain it, are included." [4] It is, in short, the

---

[2] *Coleridge as Religious Thinker* (New Haven, 1961), p. 138. One's judgment as to whether or not this "greater unity of Identity" is compatible with a Christian conception of the Trinity will depend, of course, on how much weight one gives to Professor Shedd's kind of reading of the implications of Coleridge's "Tetractys." See above, pp. 92–95.

[3] Boulger, *Coleridge as Religious Thinker,* p. 148.

[4] Opus Maximum, Victoria College MS. B₃, ff. 270/266ᵛ–271/265ᵛ. Whatever these finite beings may be which are created, Coleridge sees no compelling evidence for including angels among them, at least as a separate class of beings. He says, for example, in Notebook Q (1833–1834): "The existence of superhuman Spirits, forming a class or different *kind* of personal Beings, between God, and Man made perfect, may be a defensible assumption; but not revealed in Scripture with sufficient distinctness, with sufficient means given us confidently to say, where the term, Angel, is used simply as Messenger, employe; where symbolically; & where (if any where) positively, as a contra-distinguished Order of Beings; to be legitimately imposed as an article of Faith—tho' it may be a pious, a probable opinion, and a blameless *Belief.* If apparently *implied* in sundry passages of Holy Writ, it is no where made the immediate Subject of a positive affirmation for its' own sake. And the reason is evident—it has no necessary *moral* interest" (p. 29; I follow here the pagination, presumably Coleridge's, in the original notebook). The same reason for this exclusion is given somewhat more clearly in Coleridge's marginal notes written in 1827 in a book by Reverend John Oxlee: "Surely it is not presuming too much of a Clergyman of the Church of England to expect that he would measure the importance of a theological tenet by its bearings on our moral and spiritual duties, by its practical tendencies. What is it to us whether angels are the spirits of just men made perfect, or a distinct class of moral and rational creatures? Augustine has well and wisely observed that reason recognizes only three essential kinds;—God, man, beast. Try as long as you will, you can never make an Angel any thing but a man with wings on his shoulders"; *LR,* 461. In his notes on Hooker, after referring to this same dictum of St. Augustine, Coleridge adds: "Were our bodies transparent to our souls, we should be angels"; *LR,* 37. For much the same view, see also *LR,* 124–125. For a view (probably earlier) which seems to accept the existence of angels, see *NTPM,* 364.

classic conception of the Divine Ideas, which had its beginning in Plato and was developed and perpetuated within the tradition of Scholastic theology.

Coleridge defines Divine Ideas in the Opus Maximum as the "Omnipresence or Omnipotence represented intelligentially in some one of the possible forms which are the plenitude of the divine Intelligence, the Logos or substantial adequate Idea of the Supreme Mind." These Ideas are "necessarily immutable, inasmuch as they are One with the Eternal Act, by which the absolute Will self-realized begets its Idea as the other Self." [5] The argument in favor of their existence is exceptionally lucid: "To suppose God without Ideas, or the realizing knowledge of all the particular forms potentially involved in the absolute causativeness, would destroy the very conception of God. It amounts indeed to knowing, and yet not knowing, since it would be vain to pretend that the supreme mind contemplated the one idea of its own absoluteness." Again, the reasons are clear. "For either the absoluteness contains in itself the possibility of being in the whole plenitude, or it does not. If not, in what sense is the absoluteness essentially causative of reality? But if it does the point is conceded. To say that God knows the universal only without knowing at the same time whatever is contained in the universal, whether as arising out of himself, or out of the relations which the involved realities must form and represent to each other, would be, if possible, more absurd than to attribute to a man perfect insight into a genus with an entire ignorance of its species, i.e. well acquainted with the genus, only not knowing what it meant." [6]

But for all his emphasis on the role of the Logos as the pattern and *locus* of the Divine Ideas—and hence on the intellective aspect of the Godhead—it must not be forgotten that in Coleridge's conception, God is first of all the Absolute Will. While it remains true that all created things are known eternally in the Divine Ideas, it is perhaps even more important that they are willed to exist as such by the Di-

---

[5] Opus Maximum, Huntington MS. on the Divine Ideas, p. 31. At this point the Opus Maximum MS. in the Victoria College Library is incomplete and must be supplemented with a chapter from the same manuscript which (with another chapter on Neo-Platonism, Indian philosophy, etc.) somehow became separated from the rest and is now in the Henry E. Huntington Library in San Marino, California. These manuscript chapters are clearly from the same work and, like the rest, are in Dr. Green's hand with occasional emendations by Coleridge.

[6] Opus Maximum, Huntington MS., pp. 33-35.

vine Will. In the words which Coleridge puts in the mouth of God: "The whole host of heaven and earth from the mote in the sunbeam to the archangel before the throne of glory owe their existence to a Will not their own, but my own Will is the ground and sufficient cause of my own existence; what I will to be I eternally am, and my Will is the being, in which all that move and live, live and move and *have* their being." [7]

At this point it will be helpful to distinguish two relationships that are involved here: one is that between the Creator and the creature, the other is that between the Absolute Will and the individual will. As James Boulger has very well pointed out, the first is in the order of being and is conceived of by Coleridge as a more or less static relationship; the other is a dynamic relationship in the order of will. [8]

Of the first relationship Coleridge says relatively little beyond what we have seen already: the creature is entirely dependent upon the Creator for his very being; the distinction in God between the Ipseity and the Alterity is a transcendent analogue for the distinction between Creator and creature; the Divine Ideas are the eternal patterns for individual finite existents.

Coleridge's main concern, not surprisingly, is with the second relationship, the relationship in the order of will. If it is true that for Coleridge God is above all the Absolute Will, it is also true that the focus of his interest on the human level is the finite will of man. And his most important question about that finite will involves, inevitably, its relationship to the Absolute Will. Therefore, Coleridge's conception of the nature of Creation is primarily moral, and its main purpose is to lay the intelligible groundwork for a properly Christian view of the relationship between God and man.

Two of Coleridge's basic positions have already been made sufficiently clear, that God is Absolute Will and that for man "a responsible Will is not only the postulate of all religion, but the necessary datum incapable from its very nature of any direct proof." [9] In accordance with Coleridge's belief in the "consubstantiality of all being," he sees the attribution of the conception of will to both of them as perfectly proper. At the same time he makes the predication anal-

[7] Opus Maximum, MS. B₃, ff. 225–226.
[8] *Coleridge as Religious Thinker*, p. 153.
[9] Opus Maximum, MS. B₂, ff. 52–53.

ogously, and the differences are made explicit and apparent. The essential difference between the attribution of Will to God and to man lies in the different relationship of each to the Universal Reason: in God, the Absolute Will and the Universal Reason are identified; in man, they are at best only brought into a more or less viable conformity or synthesis. "The identity of the absolute Will and the universal Reason is peculiar to the idea of God. In man therefore we must be able to discover a substitute or analogon for *identity* and likewise for *absolute,* these being peculiar to the divine idea. This we find in one instance in the conception of synthesis, and in the other by the substitution of individual: so that what in God is the identity or necessary co-inherence of the absolute Will and the Reason subsists in man as the possible, either realized or realizable, synthesis [?with] the common or universal reason by the subordination of the former to the latter." [10] A passage which follows this stresses the relationship between universal and individual which is involved in this subordination. In God, universal and individual "pre-exist each in the other, a perfect One, as Prothesis: in man the analogous factors appear severally as Thesis and Antithesis, and he himself is to compleat the analogon by uniting them in a Synthesis, which . . . he can effect only by a continued act of subordinating the one to the other." [11]

Clearly the foundation has been laid for the possibility of a failure of conformity between the individual will and the Absolute Will.

Reason itself obliges us to conclude that God-likeness, or to be the image of God, must be the proper character of man; that however as this likeness is not self-existent or necessary, but the product of the individual Will, then if it existed originally in man it must have been given by some other Will as the inceptive momentum or condition, in order to the commencement and continuance of the act by the individual Will; that therefore the proper character may be lost, and that if it should be lost, which like all other facts, i.e. results of the individual Will, is determinable only by history, that is, the fact itself, the restoration to this his proper character must be the proper duty, the moral destination, of man.[12]

At this point we are brought full circle, in a sense, to Coleridge's

[10] Opus Maximum, MS. B₃, f. 2.
[11] Opus Maximum, MS. B₃, f. 3.
[12] Opus Maximum, MS. B₃, ff. 5-6.

conception of conscience, which is here again defined as "the specific witnessing respecting the unity or harmony of the will with the reason effected by the self-subordination of the individual will, as representing the self to the reason, as the representative of the will of God," [13] and to faith, which is "the source and the sum, the energy and the principle, of the fidelity of man to God by the subordination of his human Will to his Reason as to the sum of all spiritual truths representing and manifesting the Will divine." [14]

At the same time, in the theoretical possibility of a failure of conformity of man's will with the divine Will, we are brought face to face with the problem of moral evil. We are immediately in the realm not merely of will in the abstract, but of man's very concrete, and very problematic, free will. Since the analysis in the Opus Maximum is incomplete at this point, we must turn to the notebooks, particularly to Notebook 26, most of whose entries are probably from the period about 1825–1826.

One may begin with the relationship of will to reason, much as we have seen it already. "Reason contemplated severally and distinctly is a Law that supposes a Will as its subject. It cannot therefore be coercive for it requires obedience, and obedience can be required only where disobedience is possible." But the question immediately arises, is freedom compatible with disobedience to reason and hence to the Absolute Will?

Generally, Freedom is employed as a mere synonime [sic] of Will . . . But there is another, less common but far more correct Sense of the word, according to which Freedom expresses that highest perfection of a finite Will, which it attains by its perfect self-determined Subordination to Reason, "whose service is perfect Freedom." A will therefore may cease to be free and yet remain responsible: because its unfreedom has originated in its' own act. A will cannot be *free* to choose evil—for in the very act it forfeits its' freedom, and so far becomes a corrupt Nature, self-enslaved. It is sufficient to say, that a Will *can* choose evil, but in the moment of such choice ceases to be a *free* will. [15]

This remarkable passage makes clear that Coleridge's conception of freedom is, whatever its source, profoundly Augustinian: man is

[13] Opus Maximum, MS. B₃, f. 7.
[14] Opus Maximum, MS. B₃, f. 22.
[15] Notebook 26, ff. 31–31ᵛ.

free only when he chooses the good.[16] This is confirmed by Coleridge's insistence in the Opus Maximum manuscript that "the *Will* has to struggle upward into *Free-Will*." It must strive to attain "that Freedom which is impossible except as it becomes One with the Will of God . . . and which Man possesses not indeed, but yet is beginning to possess in the effort of emancipating himself from the bonds that prevent it." Man begins with a responsible will and must endeavor to make it a free will, that is, to conform with the Absolute Will. "In Man the Will, as Will, first appears. Enough for him that he hath a Will at all; for this is the condition of his responsibility, of his humanity; in the possession of a responsible Will his creator has placed him, with all means and aidances to boot, to its growth and evolution: with these, in the possession of a Free Will he is to place himself." [17]

The question remains, however, how is it possible for a finite will, which is created precisely as an image of the Absolute Will, not to be in conformity with that Absolute Will? In other words, how is moral evil possible? Coleridge's best statement of his answer to this question is found in a long section of the Opus Maximum manuscript.[18] Although the argument is long and tortuous, what Coleridge is saying is in reality fairly straightforward. Since—as we saw in treating of the Trinity—the essence of personal individuality is the will, it is of the nature of the will to assert its own individual existence. But it must do so honestly, that is, according to its own nature. The nature of the finite will is to be an image of the Absolute Will. If, however, the finite will asserts its own individuality for its own self-realization alone, "under the predominance of the particular," instead of willing the particular "solely as the glory and representation of the plenitude of the universal," then it becomes a "separated finite." To do so is to contradict one's own being. To do so is to bring moral evil, sin, into the world.

With this explanation, the following long passage from the Opus

[16] An excellent summary of the Augustinian conception of freedom may be found in an article of Alexandre Durand, S.J., "La Liberté du Christ dans son Rapport à l'Impeccabilité," *Nouvelle Revue Théologique*, LXX (1948), 811–822. In this conception, liberty is found in its perfection only in Christ, who is impeccable precisely because he is perfectly free. The imperfection of liberty, as found in man, involves also the possibility of choosing evil. The perfect liberty of Christ is "une liberté sans option."

[17] Opus Maximum, MS. B₃, f. 119. See also *Aids*, 207.

[18] Opus Maximum, Huntington MS., pp. 10–43.

Maximum manuscript, offering Coleridge's "principle of solution" for the problem of evil, should stand out in sharper relief.

The solution is this. To God the idea is real, inasmuch as it is one with that will, which, as we see in its definition, is verily *Idem et Alter;* but to itself the idea is absolutely real, in so far only as its particular will affirms, and in affirming constitutes its particular reality to have no true being except as a form of the universal, and one with the universal Will. This, however, is the affirmation of a will, and of a particular will. It must, therefore, contain the potentiality, that is, the power of possibly *not* affirming the identity of its reality with the reality of God, which is actual absolutely *(Actus purissimus sine ullâ potentialitate)*; or of willing to be, yet not willing to be only because God is, and in the being of God alone. In other words, if the essence of its being be will, and this will under a particular form, there must be a possibility of willing the universal or absolute under the predominance of the particular, instead of willing the particular solely as the glory and presentation of the plenitude of the universal. As long as this act remains wholly potential, i.e. implied in the holy will as its opposite, necessarily possible because, being a holy will, it is a will, and a particular will, so long is it compatible with God, and so long therefore hath it an actual reality as one of the eternal, immutable ideas of God. But in the will to actualize this potentiality, or as in common language we should say, in the will to convert this possibility into a reality it necessarily makes —*it*self! shall I say? or rather *a* self that is not God, and hence by its own act becomes alien from God . . . What could follow but a world of contradictions, when the first self-constituting act is in its essence a contradiction? [19]

Sin, then, is clearly the finite will's deliberate refusal to acknowledge its essential dependence on the Absolute Will.[20]

With Coleridge's a priori treatment of Creation and sinful man fairly well in hand, we may perhaps move with greater assurance

---

[19] Opus Maximum, Huntington MS., pp. 39–43. There is relevant material also on pp. 137–145 of this manuscript. Muirhead's discussion of the nature and origin of evil, based on Coleridge's discussion in the manuscript just cited, is extremely helpful; see *Coleridge as Philosopher,* pp. 236–244. James Boulger also discusses this problem, but instead of the Huntington Library manuscript (which was not available to him) he turns to Notebook 26, whose argument seems to me far less clear and cogent; see *Coleridge as Religious Thinker,* pp. 150–159. The relevant notebook passages are in Notebook 26, ff. 1–125, some of which are transcribed in Boulger's Appendix I.

[20] Coleridge also attempts to express the same idea in terms of a relationship of act and potency. He speaks, for example, of "this idea of the reality of the potential and the necessity . . . of predicating both the actual and the potential of one and the same subject,

into the a posteriori order which will find its focus in the data of revelation.

Not surprisingly, there is relatively little further to be said here on the subject of Creation, beyond the confirmation in reality of Coleridge's speculations. Occasionally Coleridge stresses that revelation makes it clear that Creation took place in time, as when in Notebook 26 he insists (on the basis of the revelation of Genesis) that "the Universe of Finite Existences began, & is not a co-eternal Effect of an Eternal Ground & Cause, a creation, not an emanation." [21] Again, in a commentary on Genesis 1:1, Coleridge finds clearly revealed the absoluteness of Creation's dependence on the Creator: "God the absolute Beginner of all things—not of their form, and relations alone, but of their very *Being* . . . This Verse precludes the systems of Cosmotheism, Pantheism, and a primal Element—in short, every possible form of the eternity (i.e. unbeginningness) of the World or any part of the World . . . all that has been, is, or will be, had, have, and will have, a Beginning, save God alone." [22] And again, Coleridge often refers to the scriptural name of God, "I Am," and to Christ as the mediator of all Creation; such references are a confirmation of his speculations on God the Father as the ground of all reality and on the role of the Alterity in Creation. The most striking of these references is found in what are said to be Coleridge's last words, reported by J. A. Heraud in an oration at the Russell Institu-

---

namely, that its being is actual as far as it is in the being of God and potential in relation to itself as particular existence." Opus Maximum, Huntington MS., pp. 61–63. At first glance this might be taken to mean much the same as the Scholastic use of act and potency in the context of the problem of finitude: act the metaphysical principle of perfection, of existence; potency the principle of limitation. In context, however, and as Coleridge uses the terms elsewhere (in Notebook 26, for example), it becomes clear that they shift considerably, to the extent that one can scarcely rely on them in determining the pattern of Coleridge's thought. In the present context, Coleridge uses potency itself in a double sense, distinguishing between positive and negative potency. In God's plan, man's individual will was destined never to be actualized, since only God is "Act"; God is in fact *"Actus purissimus."* See Notebook 26, ff. 124^v–125. As James Boulger summarizes the argument of a section of Notebook 26: "The individual will in harmony with the Absolute Will was in positive potency, while the negative potency or possibility of evil lay in its ability to act for itself . . . But the will realized the negative potency, willed itself individual, and fell into apostasy and Original Sin." Boulger, *Coleridge as Religious Thinker,* pp. 157–158. On pp. 154–157, Boulger transcribes the lengthy passage from Notebook 26 whose argument he summarizes.

What Coleridge has done here is to reverse the ordinary meanings of act and potency. At bottom, "he is saying . . . that the function (or action) of the individual will in harmony with the Absolute Will is not to act." Boulger, pp. 158–159.

[21] Notebook 26 (c. 1826), f. 24.
[22] Notebook 27 (c. 1818), ff. 11^v–12.

tion, and presumably told him by Dr. Green, who was (with Dr. Gillman) present at Coleridge's death bed. "And be thou sure in whatever may be published of my posthumous works to remember that, first of all is the Absolute Good whose self-affirmation is the 'I am,' as the eternal reality in itself, and the ground and source of all other reality. And next, that in this idea nevertheless a distinctivity is to be carefully preserved, as manifested in the person of the Logos by whom that reality is communicated to all other beings." [23] Beyond this, there is little else. [24] Creation is for Coleridge ultimately a mystery, to be grasped as well as can be, by reflection and speculation, but in the last analysis to be accepted with reverence and love.

The actuality of sin, however, is quite another matter. Here the revelation is fuller, and both the fact and the consequences of sin are evident and insistent. One begins most properly with the doctrine of Original Sin, in which Coleridge finds confirmed his speculative assertion about the possibility of the defection of a finite will from the Absolute Will. He wrote in 1810 in his "Confessio Fidei": "I believe, and hold it as the fundamental article of Christianity, that I am a fallen creature; that I am of myself capable of moral evil, but not of myself capable of moral good, and that an evil ground existed in my will, previously to any given act, or assignable moment of time, in my consciousness. I am born a child of wrath. This fearful mystery I pretend not to understand. I can not even conceive the possibility of it,—but I know that it is so. My conscience the sole fountain of certainty, commands me to believe it, and would itself be a contradiction, were it not so—and what is real must be possible." [25]

Although there are frequent comments on the doctrine elsewhere, Coleridge's only extended discussion of Original Sin is in the *Aids to Reflection*. [26] He places the discussion, quite deliberately, in the context of an attack on the teaching of the seventeenth-century Anglican divine, Bishop Jeremy Taylor, whose *Unum Necessarium* (1655), a treatise on repentance, was a center of controversy in the seven-

[23] Recorded by Mrs. Lucy Watson in *Coleridge at Highgate*, p. 158.

[24] There is a section of the Opus Maximum which attempts, very abstrusely, to link Creation with the law of gravity, the physical forces of attraction and repulsion, and the like. This was a fairly frequent preoccupation of Coleridge's middle and even later years and invites further study. See Victoria College MS. B Supplement, chaps. 16–20; the Supplement is a group of unbound pages which belong to the manuscript volume B₁.

[25] "Confessio Fidei," *LR*, 16.

[26] See *Aids*, 267–290.

teenth century for its unorthodox teaching on Original Sin.[27] Taylor is selected for discussion precisely because he is "the ablest and most formidable antagonist of this doctrine" (p. 267).

Coleridge prefaces his treatment of Taylor with a brief exegesis of the second and third chapters of Genesis. He concludes that the narrative there, properly interpreted according to its allegorical genre, offers "a just and faithful exposition of the birth and parentage and successive moments of phenomenal sin (*peccatum phaenomenon* [sic]; *crimen primarium et commune*), that is, of sin as it reveals itself in time, and is an immediate object of consciousness. And in this sense most truly does the Apostle assert, that in Adam we all fell. The first human sinner is the adequate representative of all his successors. And with no less truth may it be said, that it is the same Adam that falls in every man, and from the same reluctance to abandon the too dear and undivorceable Eve" (p. 269 n.). Just what Coleridge means by this remains to be seen.

Coleridge insists, as he often does, on his own definitions of even the most consecrated terms. Since a sin is "an evil which has its ground or origin in the agent, and not in the compulsion of circumstances" (p. 271), the term "original sin" is a pleonasm, "the epithet not adding to the thought, but only enforcing it" (p. 274). All sins are "original sins." On the other hand, the traditional acceptation of Original Sin as it is found in mankind after Adam is not sin at all: "A state or act, that has not its origin in the will, may be calamity, deformity, disease, or mischief; but a sin it can not be" (p. 274).

But Coleridge is willing to waive this objection and will "suppose the Bishop to comprise under the term Sin, the evil accompanying or consequent on human actions and purposes" (p. 276). Thus, says Coleridge, Taylor conceives Original Sin as "a calamity, which being common to all men must be supposed to result from their common nature;—in other words, the universal calamity of human nature" (pp. 276–277). Accepting this conception of Original Sin, then, Coleridge goes on to ally himself strongly with Taylor's attack on the

[27] See *Unum Necessarium, or The Doctrine and Practice of Repentance*, in *The Whole Works of the Right Rev. Jeremy Taylor, D.D.*, ed. R. Heber, 15 vols. (London, 1822), VIII, 233–532. For a skillful summary of Taylor's views on Original Sin, see John Hunt, *Religious Thought in England from the Reformation to the End of the Last Century*, 3 vols. (London, 1870–1873), I, 341–345. Coleridge's marginal notes on Taylor's *Unum Necessarium*, including his views on Original Sin, are in *LR*, 195–218.

belief that "this calamity, so dire in itself, should appear to the All-merciful God a rightful cause and motive for inflicting on the wretched sufferers a calamity infinitely more tremendous;—nay, that it should be incompatible with Divine Justice not to punish it by everlasting torment." Particularly objectionable are the "pretended justifications of God grounded on flimsy analogies drawn from the imperfections of human ordinances and human justice-courts" (p. 277).[28] So far Coleridge and Bishop Taylor are in agreement. The merciful God cannot punish all men for a guilt that belongs only to their first parents; the sins of the father may not be visited upon his offspring, simply that some hypothetical order of justice may be served.

The two soon part company, however, when Coleridge objects strongly to the doctrine Taylor puts in place of the one rejected. Coleridge's summary of Taylor's position is succinct and accurate: "God, he tells us, required of Adam a perfect obedience, and made it possible by endowing him 'with perfect rectitude and supernatural heights of grace' proportionate to the obedience which he required. As a consequence of his disobedience, Adam lost this rectitude, this perfect sanity and proportionateness of his intellectual, moral and corporeal state, powers and impulses; and as the penalty of his crime, he was deprived of all supernatural aids and graces. The death, with whatever is comprised in the Scriptural sense of the word, death, began from that moment to work in him, and this consequence he conveyed to his offspring, and through them to all his posterity, that is, to all mankind. They were born diseased in mind, body and will" (p. 279).[29] Such a conception is, for Coleridge, a gross injustice. "Why, and on what principle of equity, were the unoffending sentenced to be born with so fearful a disproportion of their powers to their duties?" (p. 282).

Coleridge's response is, first of all, to admit as a truth recognized by all religions "the fact of a moral corruption connatural with the human race . . . of a law in the nature of man resisting the law of God" (p. 285). This fact is asserted of the individual, "not because he has committed this or that crime, or because he has shown himself to be this or that man, but simply because he is a man" (p. 286). This

---

[28] The same objection is made in FR, 395.
[29] For the same objection, see Coleridge's marginal notes on Taylor in LR, 208.

moral corruption is somehow attributable to the human will: "A moral evil is an evil that has its origin in a will. An evil common to all must have a ground common to all. But the actual existence of moral evil we are bound in conscience to admit; and that there is an evil common to all is a fact; and this evil must therefore have a common ground. Now this evil ground can not originate in the Divine Will: it must therefore be referred to the will of man. And this evil ground we call original sin. It is a mystery, that is, a fact, which we see, but can not explain" (pp. 287-288).[30] Can this corruption be attributed in any meaningful sense to the sin of Adam? No, because to do so would be to violate the nature of the will itself. "The corruption of my will may very warrantably be spoken of as a consequence of Adam's fall, even as my birth of Adam's existence; as a consequence, a link in the historic chain of instances, whereof Adam is the first. But that it is on account of Adam; or that this evil principle was, *à priori,* inserted or infused into my will by the will of another—which is indeed a contradiction in terms, my will in such case being no will—this is nowhere asserted in Scripture explicitly or by implication." Rather, "it belongs to the very essence of the doctrine, that in respect of original sin every man is the adequate representative of all men. What wonder, then, that where no inward ground of preference existed, the choice should be determined by outward relations, and that the first in time should be taken as the diagram!" In fact, Coleridge goes on, the very name of Adam is a generic one: "It is *the* Adam, so as to express the *genus* . . ." (p. 289).[31]

[30] There is a somewhat similar passage in Coleridge's notes on Taylor, in which he defines Original Sin as "sin that has its origin in itself, or in the will of the sinner, but yet in a state or condition of the will not peculiar to the individual agent, but common to the human race"; see *LR,* 206. The same insistence on the character of guilt (although not hereditary guilt) in Original Sin is found in Coleridge's notes on Taylor in *LR,* 217-218, in Notebook 43 (1830), f. [57], and in Notebook 44 (1830), ff. 12ᵛ-13.

[31] The Hebrew word Adam means "the man." Coleridge also objects to the conception of Original Sin as hereditary guilt in *NTPM,* 327, and in his marginal notes on Jeremy Taylor in *LR,* 195, 202, 205, 212-217. Despite his rejection of hereditary guilt, however, Coleridge continued to insist on the solidarity of mankind in Adam, that Adam was somehow "a representative Man virtually containing all men—that he was not only Man but Mankind." Notebook 41 (1829-1830), f. [8]. See also *LR,* 204, 489-490; and Notebook 43, ff. [38ᵛ-39ᵛ].

Further light may perhaps be shed on Coleridge's conception of the solidarity of all men in guilt by an undated note (possibly from the 1820's) in Notebook 29. "If *with* Adam we all suffer the penalty, individually and personally—does not the parity of reason require, that *with* Adam we must commit the offence?—Must not 'in' contain the sense of the 'with'—not in respect of Time or Place—but of co-presence as to that which is wholly *irrelative* to Time

What has Coleridge done, then? First, he has rejected forcefully the conception of Original Sin as hereditary guilt. Second, he has insisted upon the universality of the corruption of man's will, and in fact the "connaturality" of this corruption with human nature. Finally, he has insisted that this corruption is in some undefined way attributable to the individual will, though not insofar as it is individual but insofar as it is human.

From another point of view, what Coleridge has done is to change the location of the mystery. Traditionally, since one began with the presumption of hereditary guilt, the mystery was: what is the bond between Adam and the rest of humanity by which his sin is communicated to us? Coleridge, rejecting the notion of hereditary sin, leaves the mystery at one further remove: what is the source of the universal corruption of the human will?

Apart from this relocation of the mystery, Coleridge left the doctrine of Original Sin much as he found it—in mystery. As he saw it, man's nature is clearly diseased. This disease has its source not in his individual guilt (for it was born with him), not in the guilt of a first parent (for this would be injustice), but, somehow or other, in the human will as such. Occasionally he seems to make a disconcerting equation between Original Sin and finitude, as when he remarks in the margin of a work of Richard Field that "Field appears to have seen the truth, namely, that nature itself is a peccant (I had almost said an unnatural) state." [32] Or again, he remarked in a conversation in 1830: "A fall of some sort or other—the creation, as it were, of the non-absolute—is the fundamental postulate of the moral history of man. Without this hypothesis, man is unintelligible; with it, every phenomenon is explicable." [33] But if man's fall is identical with the "creation of the non-absolute," does not evil consist in man's very finitude, and therefore is it not useless for man to struggle against it? Coleridge nowhere reaches such a conclusion, nor must he be pushed

---

and Space—and transcendent. Therefore, I do not say that *with* Adam we *did* commit the offence—I have not said. [?] Must we not *with* Adam (i.e. as well as Adam) *have* offended?

"I am convinced that the main difficulty and perplexity respecting the admission of Original Sin results from the want of understanding and considering that the Will and the Acts of the Will are not *in* Time any more than in Space—neither *before* nor *after*—but *timeless*—even as a Thought is spaceless" (f. 79ᵛ). Is this notion akin to the modern theologian's conception of a "sin of the world"? See below, note 49.

[32] *LR*, 67.

[33] *TT*, 303.

to it. He leaves his belief, as he feels he must, in ultimate mystery. As he concludes in his 1830 conversation, "the mystery itself is too profound for human insight."[34]

It remains now to speak of the effects of Original Sin in man, especially of man's fallen will. In a very real sense, this is merely corollary to what has gone before, since Coleridge's focus of attention, in this matter as in others, has been the order of actuality. He is less interested in what has been than in what is, less interested in assigning

[34] *TT*, 303. See also *LR*, 203–204. Another aspect of the mystery of sin is the mystery of Satan, who seems to have puzzled Coleridge all his life. Although he generally does not want to accept the notion of Satan as an individual person, a fallen angel, he is faced with Scriptural references to Satan and devils. In Notebook 30 (1823–1824), ff. 34–37, Coleridge denies that the belief is derived from revelation, but in the process he sheds some light on the possible understanding of it: "Do we derive the doctrine from Revelation? Apparently *not*. There is nothing of the kind in the Old Testament. It was introduced & took root, and overspread the Jewish Church in the Intersilentium of the O. and N. Testament—and at the Birth of our Lord had already a long time become the popular faith, and passed into the popular Language.—But is then any specific Revelation of the Doctrine in the New Testament? i.e. any passage, purposely written in order to teach it? . . . Thus the doctrine of Resurrection to retributive Justice was the universal belief of the Jews, a handful of Platonizing Sadducees excepted—and our Lord repeats the words in order to confirm the Belief. Can any such passage be adduced in assertion of the existence of personal Intelligences, self-conscious Individuals, utterly yet responsibly wicked & malignant, of a diverse kind from the human, and neither men nor the disembodied Souls of Men?—I know of none. The passages, in which the Devil and Devils are spoken of anthropomorphically, are all subordinate to some other doctrine or purpose which would remain in the same strength, whether the Devils are understood literally or figuratively . . . [The writers of the Scriptures] might & probably many of the Apostles did believe as their Countrymen of the same rank with themselves believed—but they did not derive their belief from *Revelation* . . . On the other hand, I dare not deny the possibility of a finite Person *willing* evil irrevocably and beyond the powers of Repentance, & Reformation—Nay, the *Idea* is indispensable in Morality—or that this Finite Person, or Race of Persons, may have been invested with larger intellectual faculties, more enduring and subtle Bodies, than the Human Races.—But *what* or *whence*, we are not informed by Revelation, which alone could inform us—*that* there are such, is, I cannot doubt, *supposed* in several passages of the New Testament—but whether *imposed,* as a *Revealed* Truth, I dare not decide." Coleridge sheds further light in Notebook 46 (1830), ff. [10ᵛ–11], where he suggests that Satan may be an objectification of corrupt human nature: it is possible "by 'the enemy' to understand the false & alien Will, whether in the Individual as Corrupt Nature, or as from the collective Actions of all the individual Natures, as *one*, and which therefore being ab [ad?] extra for *each* individual, becomes *objectivized*, as the Satan, the Devil, the Evil Spirit." This harks back to a note of many years before, in Notebook 17, ff. 99–100 (1812): "With what contempt even in later years have I not contemplated the doctrine of a Devil!! [?Yet] now I see its' intimate connection, if not as existent Person, yet as Essence & Symbol, with Christianity—& that so far from being identical with Manicheism, it is its' surest Antidote—(i.e. rightly understood)." The key to the final parenthetical phrase may be an earlier sentence in the same passage, where Coleridge speaks of his "reflections on the Fact, that Christianity *exclusively* has asserted the *positive* being of Evil or Sin—'of Sin the exceeding Sinfulness'." Is it possible that this is much the same as his later view of Satan as an objectification of "the false & alien Will"? For other comments on the Devil, see *CL*, III, 2 (February 7, 1807); *LR*, 88–89, 104–105, 244, 284–285, 300–301, 303; *NTPM*, 225; Notebooks 18 (ff. 160ᵛ–161ᵛ), 34 (f. 20) and 46 (f. [22]).

guilt than in taking stock of the present situation of fallen man. As Shedd remarked of Coleridge, "sin, for him, as for many contemplative minds in the Christian Church—as it was for Origen in the early Church, for the Mystical Theology of the Middle Ages, for the school of Schleiermacher at the present time—was too disproportionately the corruption and disharmony of the human soul, and not sufficiently its guilt." [35] Whatever one may think of the judgment of value expressed here, one can hardly disagree with it as a reading of Coleridge.

In assessing the moral state of fallen man, Coleridge's constant preoccupation is to strike a balance between the easy optimism of the Shaftesbury sort, which fails to take account of man's real weakness of will, and a Calvinistic insistence on man's total depravity. Occasionally he seems to weight the balance a bit more heavily on one side, as when he said in one of his 1819 philosophical lectures: "I say of the whole human race that they have lost their Will. There is not one that would dare put his hand on his heart and say, 'In all things I act and feel as I know I ought to do.'" [36] But this is part of the rhetoric of the moment. Elsewhere, his statements are more tempered. Once again, the clearest declaration of his views is in the *Aids to Reflection*. "I profess a deep conviction that man was and is a fallen creature, not by accidents of bodily constitution or any other cause, which human wisdom in a course of ages might be supposed capable of removing; but as diseased in his will, in that will which is the true and only strict synonyme of the word, I, or the intelligent Self." At the same time, he differs radically from those who insist on "exaggerating the diseased weakness of the will into an absolute privation of all freedom, thereby making moral responsibility, not a mystery above comprehension, but a direct contradiction." The truth is that man's will is weakened, but it is not taken away: "I utterly disclaim the notion, that any human intelligence, with whatever power it might manifest itself, is alone adequate to the office of restoring health to the will: but at the same time I deem it impious and absurd to hold that the Creator would have given us the faculty of reason, or that the Redeemer would in so many varied forms of

[35] Introductory Essay, Shedd, I, 51.
[36] *PL*, 225.

argument and persuasion have appealed to it, if it had been either totally useless or wholly impotent." [37]

Coleridge's thinking at this point is profoundly Pauline. St. Paul wrote: "I delight in the law of God, in my inmost self, but I see in my members another law at war with the law of my mind and making me captive to the law of sin which dwells in my members" (Rom. 7:22–23). In Coleridgean terms this "law of the members" becomes the conflict of the individual will with its "higher reason," and hence with the Absolute Reason and Will. Man cannot help but be aware of "the sense of a self-contradicting principle in our nature, or a disharmony in the different impulses that constitute it." [38] It is "the Mystery of the false and alienated Will." [39] And yet, though "false and alienated," man's will is sufficiently free to be responsible for its actions. "As there is much beast and some devil in man, so is there some angel and God in him." [40]

One can hardly treat the nature of human freedom in a theological context without reference to the much vexed problem of Predestination. The problem turns, of course, around the seeming contradiction between God's free election of those who will be saved and man's free will in choosing to respond or not to respond to God's grace. Expressed from another point of view, it is the paradox of the coexistence of the freedom of man's action with God's foreknowledge of how man will act. In whatever terms it is expressed, the focal point of the problem is the protection of both God's sovereignty and man's freedom.

Coleridge did not write often of the problem, and what he had to say was in the last analysis quite simple. The realities themselves were for him beyond question: God is sovereign both in the order

---

[37] *Aids*, 195–197. Coleridge spoke often of man's radical need for Redemption; see *LR*, 47–48, 286–287, and *CL*, III, 463 (December 19, 1813). Its most positive aspect is revealed in a comment of Coleridge on his feelings at the time of the composition of his poem "Baptismal Birthday" (1833): "There are permitted moments of exultation through faith, when we cease to feel our own emptiness save as a capacity of our Redeemer's fulness." It is transcribed by Mrs. Lucy Watson in *Coleridge at Highgate*, p. 151, from a manuscript in the hand of her grandmother, Mrs. James Gillman. H. N. Coleridge records the same sentence in *TT*, 473 (August 10, 1833).

[38] *FR*, Appendix B, 529.

[39] Notebook 54 (1833), f. [13ᵛ].

[40] *TT*, 364 (August 1, 1831). For other references to the corruption of nature in fallen man, especially his weakness of will, see *LR*, 98–99, 201, 527–528, 552–553; *TT*, 418; *CL*, I, 396, III, 478–479, IV, 574–575; Notebook 44, ff. 17ᵛ–18.

of foreknowledge and of election; at the same time, even after Original Sin man is a free agent. The problem, then, was one of formulation: how to express the two realities in human terms without making them sound contradictory. The key he offered was a double one. It is found in several brief notes, but its best expression is in a note on *Pilgrim's Progress,* probably written in 1830.

First of all, he insists that the divine Absolute Will must not be considered apart from the Supreme Reason, with which it is identified, and from the finite reason and will, which participate in the light and virtue of the divine Reason and Will. This is the mistake of many Calvinist theologians, he feels, who speak of an absolute decree by God's Will of those who are to be saved, without regard to the necessary identity of God's Will with his Reason by which he knows from all eternity the merits and free acts of men, which are themselves finite participations of that Will and that Reason.

Mournful are the errors into which the zealous but unlearned preachers among the dissenting Calvinists have fallen respecting absolute election, and discriminative, yet reasonless, grace;—fearful this divorcement of the Holy Will, the one only Absolute Good, that, eternally affirming itself as the I AM, eternally generateth the Word, the Absolute Being, the Supreme Reason, the Being of all Truth, the Truth of all Being:—fearful the divorcement from the reason; fearful the doctrine which maketh God a power of darkness, instead of the God of light, the Father of the Light which lighteth every man that cometh into the world! This we know and this we are taught by the holy Apostle Paul; that without will there is no ground or base of sin; that without the law this ground or base can not become sin (hence we do not impute sin to the wolf or the tiger, as being without or below the law); but that with the law cometh light into the will; and by this light the will becometh a free, and therefore a responsible will.[41]

[41] *LR,* 264. See also *LR,* 444, 509–510 (1825); and *NTPM,* 170–171. There is a strikingly similar passage in Notebook 48 (1830), whose date lends support to my probable dating (1830) of the above-cited note. At one point it distinguishes two conceptions of Election: "Still, however, between two Divines, both professing and supporting this doctrine in its' fullest form, viz. that a pre-established Elect, the fulfilment of whose foreknown number is to be the end and consummation of the EON . . . a momentous difference may exist—the one, *more Calvinistarum* [after the fashion of the Calvinists], finding the ground of the election in the absolute (which in *their* sense means *reasonless*) Sovereignty of the incomprehensible Will, whose Self affirmation is the Eternal I AM, God the Father; the other seeking a

He continues: "This freedom, then, is the free gift of God; but does it therefore cease to be freedom?" Implicit here is Coleridge's Augustinian conception of freedom, discussed earlier in this chapter. The perfection of human freedom is "its perfect self-determined Subordination to Reason, 'whose service is perfect Freedom.'"[42] Ultimately, there can be no contradiction between man's freedom and God's free election, because man's perfect freedom is the conformity of his finite will with the Absolute Will of God.

Secondly, Coleridge rejects the conception of a priority of time in the relationship between God's foreknowledge and eternal decree of election and man's free action. "All the sophistry of the Predestinarians rests on the false notion of eternity as a sort of time antecedent to time. It is timeless, present with and in all times." In God's decree of election, man's free choices are already—that is, always—present to God. "Those who will persevere, will persevere, and God foresees."[43] A notebook entry of the same period takes the matter one step further, pointing out that the merits of Christ, in all their application to the individual Elect, are present to the Father in the eternal decree of election. "What Jesus did in time, and all the Elect each in time and numerically, that Christ did ἀχρόνως [outside of time], inclusively of all by an *elevant* Act—the former being the manifestation of the latter: Hence the necessary connection of the doctrine of Election and Foreknowledge or Predestination with the Pauline Doctrine of Redemption."[44]

Beyond this Coleridge refuses to speculate. For "if the self-examinant will abandon this position, and exchange the safe circle of religion and practical reason for the shifting sand-wastes and *mirages* of speculative theology; if instead of seeking after the marks of Election in himself, he undertakes to determine the ground and origin, the possibility and mode of Election itself in relation to God; in this case . . . we can only regret that the inquirer had not been better

---

ground in the *Word* co-eternally begotten of the Father (= the Logos, *the Being*, the Reason of all Reason) and [as] such, the *Pleroma*, or Fullness of the Father, in whom (as by a shadow of similitude the supersensual Truths or Ideas in the Human Spirit) the Sabaoth, the whole Host of Heaven had distinct existence." Notebook 48, f. [36ᵛ].

[42] Notebook 26, f. 31ᵛ.

[43] LR, 264–265. See also LR, 439 (1825), 508–509 (1825); and NTPM, 279 (1808); and Notebook F, ff. 6–7 (1825) and 36ᵛ (1826).

[44] Notebook 41 (1829–1830), f. [36ᵛ].

instructed in the nature, the bounds, the true purposes and proper objects of his intellectual faculties." [45]

It remains for us to relate Coleridge's writings on Original Sin to the theological tradition. It is admittedly difficult to place Coleridge's rather untraditional views on Original Sin in an historical perspective. Perhaps it might be helpful to distinguish several significant moments in the development of this doctrine and then to suggest Coleridge's position in reference to each of them.

The first such moment is St. Augustine's synthesis of the doctrine in the fourth century, a synthesis which has dominated theological reflection on this question in the Western Church. It is summarized in the following passage from Augustine's *Enchiridion:* "Exiled after his sin, the first man has drawn with him into death and condemnation his posterity, which through his sin he had poisoned in himself as in its root. Thus original sin is incurred by all the descendants who were to be born from him and his partner . . . through carnal concupiscence, which is itself a punishment of concupiscence. By original sin they are drawn over all kinds of errors and pains to the last punishment without end . . . Thus, sin has come into the world, and through sin death; and so sin has passed on to all men on account of him through whom all have sinned." [46]

As a recent commentator on Augustine has written, "for Augustine the sin of Adam and our connection with him are so great that he conceives original sin in children wholly in the line of a sinful attitude, of a personal guilt." [47] Augustine's position was later corrected and refined in several particulars (notably with regard to his overly stern views on the everlasting punishment of children who die before baptism), but the main lines of his position were normative for the classic doctrine of the Western Church.

The second great moment in the development of the doctrine was the Thomistic synthesis. In discussing the characteristics of human nature before the Fall, St. Thomas Aquinas distinguished between what was proper to that nature as such and what had been super-added as a gratuitous gift of God, that is, between its natural and its

---

[45] *Aids*, 213; see also 209–214, and *NTPM*, 67–68 (1823).

[46] *Enchiridion*, 26, in *Patrologia Latina*, ed. Migne, v. 40, col. 245; transl. J. Donceel in *Man and Sin: A Theological View*, by Piet Schoonenberg, S.J. (Notre Dame, Indiana, 1965), p. 153.

[47] Schoonenberg, *Man and Sin*, p. 152.

supernatural attributes.[48] This view is clearly an optimistic addition to the classic doctrine: Original Sin did lose for human nature the supernatural power by which man had complete mastery of his animal appetites, but it did not destroy the substantial integrity of man's natural powers including his will.

The third crucial stage in the history of this doctrine came with the Reformers, particularly with the view of Luther and Calvin that Original Sin destroyed man's freedom, and that this condition continued even after Baptism.

Coleridge reacted in some degree against all these positions, that is to say, against major elements of the classic doctrine as well as against the stern view of pristine Calvinism. In contradistinction to the traditional teaching in the line of Augustine, Coleridge rejected, as we have seen, the notion of hereditary guilt. Second, unlike the traditional post-Thomistic conception of supernatural privileges of man before the Fall—and therefore of an essentially integral state of nature to which man was now reduced—Coleridge believed that man's nature, especially his will, is itself corrupted. In other words, for Coleridge Original Sin was not, as in the post-Thomistic scholastic tradition, a fall from grace; it was a fall from the perfection of nature. Finally, in opposition to a strict Calvinistic determinism, Coleridge turned to a more Arminian position which, like the Council of Trent, affirms man's essential freedom and responsibility.

Coleridge's conception of Original Sin in its relation to fallen man is, to be sure, ultimately unsatisfying. If he has made a positive contribution to the theology of Original Sin, it must be in his focus on the community binding together all mankind and in his insistence that the guilt of Original Sin is due somehow, he does not know how, not merely to a first parent but to all men.[49] Negatively, his rejection of hereditary guilt in effect leaves the mystery one step farther away

---

[48] *Summa Theologica,* pars I–II, qq. 81–84.

[49] The bent of Coleridge's mind on Original Sin is similar to that of certain modern theologians who feel that the hereditary aspect of Original Sin has at least been overemphasized and that some attempt should be made to take into account the possible role of the personal guilt of individual men. The Dutch theologian Piet Schoonenberg, for example, suggests that "for centuries the classic doctrine of original sin has been at a dead point and that it urgently needs to be integrated with other elements." He believes that Original Sin is involved with what he calls a "sin of the world," and that "Scripture speaks of the sinfulness of all men not only in connection with 'Adam,' or the very texts which speak of 'Adam' mention a more sinful influence than that which derives from one first ancestor alone. To this we must add that our whole conception of the world urgently inquires whether the extraordinary importance which the classic doctrine attributes to the chronologically first man is really deserved." *Man and Sin,* p. 177.

from understanding and has besides the disadvantage of flying in the face of the whole Christian doctrinal tradition.

But one should not ask too much of what was, after all, an incompletely developed theology. Besides, the doctrine of Original Sin "is an idea, and all ideas are inconceivable"; [50] like other "ideas," it must be left ultimately in mystery. Finally, it must never be forgotten that Coleridge's theology is in the last analysis a theology of practice, of positive moral action. The speculative mystery of Original Sin will be swallowed up in the greater practical mystery of the Redemption.

[50] *LR*, 207.

❀ VI. THE REDEEMER, REDEMPTION, AND JUSTIFICATION

Like St. Paul, Coleridge always saw the Fall and the Redemption as correlates. From this point of view, the speculative foundation for Coleridge's views on the Redemption has already been laid in the preceding chapter. If it is true that it is theoretically possible for the finite will to assert its selfhood in independence of the Absolute Will, it also remains theoretically possible for the finite will, having done so, to establish once again its proper conformity with the Absolute Will. This much is clear, and it is as far as Coleridge can go in the a priori order. How this can be done in actuality is a matter of historical and theological fact. Hence this chapter will proceed in the a posteriori order.

The order of things will be Coleridge's own, since he has given us in the *Aids to Reflection* a schematic outline of the doctrine of Redemption. It may be helpful to transcribe this outline as Coleridge gives it.

SYNOPSIS OF THE CONSTITUENT POINTS IN THE DOCTRINE OF REDEMPTION, IN FOUR QUESTIONS, WITH CORRESPONDENT ANSWERS.

QUESTIONS.

Who (or What) is the
1. *Agens causator?*
2. *Actus causativus?*
3. *Effectum causatum?*
4. *Consequentia ab effecto?*

ANSWERS.

I. The Agent and personal Cause of the Redemption of mankind is— the [co-eternal] Word and only begotten Son of the Living God, incarnate, tempted, agonizing (*agonistes* ἀγωνιζόμενος), crucified, submitting to death, resurgent, communicant of his Spirit, ascendent, and obtaining for his Church the descent and communion of the Holy Spirit, the Comforter.

II. The Causative Act is—a spiritual and transcendent mystery, *that passeth all understanding.*

III. The Effect Caused is—the being born anew; as before in the flesh to the world, so now born in the spirit to Christ.

IV. The Consequences from the Effect are—sanctification from sin, and liberation from the inherent and penal consequences of sin in the world to come, with all the means and processes of sanctification by the Word and the Spirit: these consequents being the same for the sinner relatively to God and his own soul, as the satisfaction of a debt for a debtor relatively to his creditor; as the sacrificial atonement made by the priest for the transgressor of the Mosaic Law; as the reconciliation to an alienated parent for a son who had estranged himself from his father's house and presence; and as a redemptive ransom for a slave or captive.[1]

Following Coleridge's lead, we will treat first his conception of Christ as the agent of Redemption. We will speak then of the act of Redemption itself and how Coleridge believes it should be conceived and expressed. Finally, we will explain his position on the controverted question of Justification, the primary and essential effect of Redemption.

Since there is in Coleridge's writings no extended treatment of Christology, his views on the nature and role of Christ must be drawn from comments, often marginal, in other contexts. This is not to say that there is any dearth of material. Although never at length, Coleridge did write often of the central role of Christ in the Christian revelation.

We have noticed already, in treating Coleridge's idea of the Trinity, his emphasis on the Logos as the Alterity of the Father and in turn as the pattern of all creation. Now, in moving into a discussion of the historical role of Christ in the world, it is perhaps wise to refer back to this conception, since the view of Christ as the eternal Logos is linked intimately with the idea of Christ as the Redeemer of creation. As the finite will is capable of conforming itself anew to the Absolute Will only because that Will was its original pattern, so is creation capable of Redemption by the Logos precisely because the Logos was its original pattern. It is for Coleridge a matter not so much of change as of return to original integrity.

It is this belief in the central importance of the Logos that explains

[1] *Aids,* 316–317.

Coleridge's insistence that "the only-begotten Son never *became*; but all things *became* through him." [2] It is this that explains his preoccupation with the eternal generation of Christ, manifested most strikingly in his interpretation of the reference to Christ in Colossians 1:15, commonly translated as "firstborn of all creation," but which Coleridge translated as "begotten before any kind of creation" [3] or "begotten superlatively before all that was created or made." [4] The historical Christ is also the eternal Logos, eternally begotten.

To insist on this is only to insist on the central role of the divinity of Christ in Coleridge's thinking. It is clear that once his Unitarian phase was over, Coleridge very soon accepted and never again departed from his belief in the divinity of Christ. We have seen in the first chapter that Coleridge confessed the Trinity, and with it the divinity of Christ, as early as 1805-1806. By 1806 he was speaking of the divinity of Christ in terms which, although undeveloped and unsystematized, are quite consistent with the later Coleridge. [5]

In the later Coleridge, belief in the divinity of Christ is asserted in many different contexts. In the "Confessio Fidei" of 1810 Coleridge states his belief in terms of its relationship to the Redemption: "I receive with full and grateful faith the assurance of revelation, that the Word, which is from all eternity with God, and is God, assumed our human nature in order to redeem me and all mankind from this our connate corruption. My reason convinces me, that no other mode of redemption is conceivable, and, as did Socrates, would have yearned after the Redeemer, though it would not dare expect so wonderful an act of divine love, except only as an effort of my mind to conceive the utmost of the infinite greatness of that love." [6] Almost a decade later the same focus is evident, for Coleridge insists in the *Aids to Reflection* that "the sinless One who redeemed mankind from sin, must have been more than man," pointing out "the manifest absurdity and contradiction in the notion of a Mediator between God and the human race, at the same infinite distance from God as the race for whom he mediates." [7]

Very often Coleridge's expression of belief in the divinity of Christ

---

[2] *LR*, 414.
[3] *SM*, 446 and n.
[4] *LR*, 431. A similar interpretation of this text is found in *TT*, 478–479 n.
[5] See the remarkable letter to Thomas Clarkson in *CL*, II, 1193–1199 (October 13, 1806).
[6] *LR*, 16–17.
[7] *Aids*, 266.

occurs in the context of a particularly difficult text of Scripture, as when he comments on John 14:28: "I understand these words (*My Father is greater than I*) of the divinity—and of the Filial subordination, which does not in the least encroach on the equality necessary to the unity of Father, Son, and Spirit." [8]

The depth of Coleridge's concern to assure at once the equality of Christ with the Father and his subordination to the Father as "begotten" may be seen, too, in the light of his comments on the Council of Nicea and on the comparative merits of the Nicene and Athanasian creeds.[9]

But if Coleridge was concerned with upholding the divinity of Christ, he was not a whit the less concerned with asserting his humanity. It has been claimed that Coleridge had a "tendency to minimize the human nature of Christ," that he "edged away" from it "because of the enormous difficulties which the historical facts presented for his system." [10] Such a judgment seems quite unjustified, however. It is true that occasionally, but only very occasionally, Coleridge gives the impression of being uninterested in details of the life of Christ. He wrote, for example, in 1831: "But were it asked of me:

---

[8] *LR*, 430. For other such textual comments in which Coleridge asserts the divinity of Christ, see *LR*, 78–79, 160, 167–168, 276, 400–404, 445–447, 449–450, 538, and *TT*, 275–276 (May 1823), 318 (May 20, 1830). In his notes on Skelton (*LR*, 431–432), Coleridge discusses the perennial theological question of the reconciliation of Christ's divinity and his admission of ignorance of the time of the destruction of Jerusalem (Mark 13:32). For assertion of Christ's divinity in still other contexts, see *LR*, 425–426, and *CL*, III, 480–486 (April 1814), IV, 803 (January 10, 1818), and 851 (April 1818).

Although it is not often stated explicitly, it is clear from Coleridge's treatment of New Testament passages that he found the revelation of Christ's person and mission to have been only gradually realized by the Apostles. As he remarked in a late notebook entry, "nothing can be more evident than that the true conception of our Lord's Person & Office dawned on them gradually, and by a succession of hard conflicts with & conquests over the rooted & obstinate prejudice of a carnal Judaism—& not on all equally . . . but as the needs of the Church required." Notebook 47 (1830), f. [26].

[9] See above, Chap. IV.

[10] Boulger, *Coleridge as Religious Thinker*, p. 181. Only one passage is adduced in support of this judgment, and this passage is unfortunately interpreted out of context. The quoted passage reads: "Thus the sublime Idea of the Deus Patiens, the θεὸς φιλάνθρωπος ἀγονιστής [sic] symbolized in the Crucifixion is compressed into the particular fact of the second person of the Godhead, suffering bodily pain on the Cross—and the 2nd Person of the Godhead—how do they represent him to their minds!—Answer—As a superhuman Soul superinduced in a human soul, and standing to this latter in a similar bond of sympathy as this latter stands to the Organized Body." Notebook 26 (c. 1826), ff. 71ᵛ–72. Boulger takes this to be an attempt to "minimize" the human nature of Christ. The context makes it quite clear, however, that Coleridge is making a point about the nature of the Redemption, that God's mercy does not consist in "suffering Men to be punished as Monarchs are wedded, by *Proxy*" (f. 73ᵛ). What Coleridge is attacking is the merely punitive conception of the Redemption, a conception about which we shall have occasion to speak later in this chapter.

Do you then believe our Lord to have been the Son of Mary by Joseph? I reply: It is a point of religion with me to have no belief one way or the other. I am in this way like St. Paul, more than content not to know Christ himself κατὰ σάρκα [according to the flesh]. It is enough for me to know, that the Son of God *became flesh, σάρξ* ἐγένετο γενόμενος ἐκ γυναικὸς [became flesh, being born of a woman], and more than this, it appears to me, was unknown to the Apostles, or, if known, not taught by them as appertaining to a saving faith in Christ." [11] But to extrapolate from such occasional remarks (in this case a remark dictated in good measure by a doctrinal preoccupation about the Virgin Birth) and suggest that Coleridge was anything but deeply committed to the crucial importance of the human nature of Christ, is to turn one's back on too many statements to the contrary.

One need only turn to the "Confessio Fidei" of 1810 to realize how essential the humanity of Christ is to the redemptive process in Coleridge's conception. "I believe, that this assumption of humanity by the Son of God was revealed and realized to us by the Word made flesh, and manifested to us in Christ Jesus; and that his miraculous birth, his agony, his crucifixion, death, resurrection, and ascension, were all both symbols of our redemption (φαινόμενα τῶν νουμένων) and necessary parts of the awful process." [12] The same is true, a decade later, in the "Synopsis" of the doctrine of the Redemption which we have quoted from the *Aids to Reflection:* Christ is seen there as incarnate, tempted, agonizing, crucified, submitting to death.

I know of no more convincing way of emphasizing the concrete-

---

[11] Notes on Donne, *LR*, 79; see also 80–81, where Coleridge makes it clear that he does not accept the Virgin Birth as an article of faith. Coleridge speaks of the same doctrine, a bit more leniently, in Notebooks 30 (ff. 29ᵛ–30) and 33 (ff. 8–8ᵛ). In Notebook 20, in an entry written in or about 1825, the following passage manifests a still more tolerant point of view: "My outward Creed is the Apostles' as expanded in the Nicene,—save only with regard to the former, I find a difficulty in receiving as an *essential* of Faith the words 'born of the *Virgin* Mary'—seeing that there is not even an allusion to any such belief as taught or required by the Apostles in any part of the New Testament, tho' I receive it as a *point of assent* on the authority of the Church, and the certainty that it was as old as the copy of the first Gospel. But it would not be worth the discussion, but for the support it gives to the Romish Parthenolatry." Notebook 20, ff. 32–33.

Coleridge speaks against the Roman Catholic doctrine of the Immaculate Conception (the belief that Mary herself was conceived without Original Sin) in *LR*, 67–68, 532–533. He rejects what he calls Roman Catholic "worship" of the Blessed Virgin in *LR*, 520–521; *TT*, 362–363 (first note); *NTPM*, 415. See also *CL*, III, 370 (February 18, 1812); *LR*, 59–60; *TT*, 385–386.

[12] *LR*, 17.

ness of the reality in which Coleridge clothes the humanity of Christ than to cite a passage from the *Table Talk* which could have been spoken by no one but Coleridge. His view of what is involved in real and concrete human nature is uniquely his own; the passage represents Coleridge as an amateur biologist in his view of the human nature of Christ. After noting that St. John's object in his Gospel and Epistles was "to prove the divinity, and also the actual human nature and bodily suffering, of Jesus Christ; that he was God and Man," Coleridge goes on to comment on the account of Christ's death given in John 19:32–35. "St. John did not mean, I apprehend, to insinuate that the spear-thrust made the *death,* merely as such, certain or evident, but that the effusion showed the human nature. 'I saw it,' he would say, 'with my own eyes. It was real blood, composed of lymph and crassamentum, and not a mere celestial ichor, as the Phantasmists allege.' " [13] Clearly, Coleridge must be allowed to emphasize the humanity of Christ in his own way.

Although Coleridge never attempted to work out for himself a theory of the "hypostatic union," that is, of the nature of the union of the divine and human natures in the one person of Christ, it is perfectly clear that he always tried to keep the two, the divinity and humanity of Christ, in balance. He was well aware of the dangers of overemphasizing one or the other. In a notebook entry of about 1826 he referred to "the relation of Jesus to the Logos" as the "Second Great Problem," the first "Great Problem" being the problem of miracles. This relation of Jesus to the Logos "is required to be such as shall leave his Manhood entire, be capable of repetition in the person of every true Disciple ('as I am in my Father so ye are in me')—and yet preserve undiminished the proper Glory and divine honor of Jesus Christ, our Lord, our Saviour and our Mediator—one God—and *one* only Lord, and Mediator between God and Man—and further that the solution of the problem shall be reconcilable with and in-

[13] *TT,* 263 (January 6, 1823). A more detailed commentary on the same text is found in Coleridge's notes on the eighteenth-century theologian Daniel Waterland. Waterland was content to comment that the Apostle refers to the water and blood "in defence of Christ's real humanity." Coleridge adds: " 'Water and blood,' that is, *serum* and *crassamentum,* mean simply 'blood,' the blood of the animal or carnal life . . . Hence 'flesh' is often taken as, and indeed is a form of, the blood,—blood formed or organized. Thus 'blood' often includes 'flesh,' and 'flesh' includes 'blood' . . . 'Water and blood' has, therefore, two meanings in St. John, but which *in idem coincidunt:*—1. true animal human blood, and no celestial ichor or phantom:—2. the whole sentiently vital body, fixed or flowing, the pipe and the stream." *LR,* 423. There is another rejection of "Docetists" and "Phantasmasts" in Coleridge's notes on Jeremy Taylor, *LR,* 227. See also *TT,* 479 (August 17, 1833).

clude the facts of the Gospel." This need for balance is not asserted merely in the abstract, but in terms of what Coleridge sees as the theological aberrations of his own day. "Great need there is of such Solution—and urgent motives for the proposal of the Problem and for the attempt to solve it—seeing that according to the present almost universal Habit of Thought among the orthodox Churches, *Jesus,* the Exemplar of Humanity, the First-fruits of the Resurrection, the Captain of our Salvation, is well nigh lost—overpowered in the splendors of the only begotten and co-eternal *Word* that was incarnate in Jesus." [14]

In this context, it is perhaps well to point out that Nestorianism (the belief in two persons in Jesus Christ, one divine and one human) held no attraction for Coleridge. He spoke of it only occasionally and then only to reject it, at the same time clearing Nestorius himself of the charge of Nestorianism. In a late notebook entry he wrote:

Persuaded that the doctrine of two persons in Christ was *deduced* by Nestorius's Opponents, and fastened on him as a supposed *consequence* of his refusal to give to Mary the title, Mother of God, tho' he willingly hailed her as "the Mother of Him who was God"—and convinced that the two-personity [sic] is no legitimate consequence of the position, and that it was injuriously attributed to Nestorius, I do not hesitate to avow myself a *Nestorian*—Nay, an Ultra-Nestorian—inasmuch as with the fullest and profoundest faith in, and belief of, the great fundamental Article of the Church, that Christ was & is one Person with *the Word,* the only-begotten Son; and that the Father with the only-begotten Son, and the Spirit proceeding, is the one only God . . . I yet—without positively rejecting—attach no religious belief, no belief *of faith,* to the Christopaedia, prefixed to the first and to the third Gospel. [15]

It is possible that Coleridge's most profound insights into the Incarnation and its relationship to the Redemption are conceived in terms of his notion of symbol, by which he can express his vision of Christ as a "sacramental" mediator between time and eternity. He writes in a note on one of Donne's sermons: "As the sacrament of the

---

[14] Notebook 39 (c. 1826), ff. 20ᵛ–21.
[15] Notebook 50 (1831–1832), ff. [27–27ᵛ]. See also *LR,* 59–60. Coleridge rejects the authenticity of the *Christopaedia* of Matthew and Luke in *LR,* 79 and 421–422; and in Notebook 30 (1823–1824), f. 29, he touches upon the same problem. On the Nestorian controversy, see J. N. D. Kelly, *Early Christian Doctrines* (New York, 1958), pp. 323–330.

Eucharist is the epiphany for as many as receive it in faith, so the crucifixion, resurrection, and ascension of Christ himself in the flesh, were the epiphanies, the sacramental acts and *phaenomena* of the *Deus patiens,* the visible words of the invisible Word that was in the beginning, symbols in time and historic fact of the redemptive functions, passions, and procedures of the Lamb crucified from the foundation of the world;—the incarnation, cross, and passion,—in short, the whole life of Christ in the flesh, dwelling a man among men, being essential and substantive parts of the process, the total of which they represented." [16] For Coleridge, this Jesus Christ who is the "co-eternal Deity" is just as surely "the Son of Mary, in whom the Word . . . *tabernacled.*" [17] The two natures may be distinguished, either as nature or as function, but they are not separate; the one is a sacramental sign of the other.[18]

One might expect this sign-value to be bodied forth most effectively in Coleridge's view of the Risen Christ, who is traditionally taken as the pledge of man's own ultimate resurrection. Although Coleridge never elaborated a theology of the Resurrection of Christ, he did see the Risen Christ as the efficacious sign of man's future life. This will be better discussed later, however, in the light of Coleridge's views on the future life. For the moment, it will suffice to point out that the Resurrection seems never to have constituted a problem for Coleridge. He accepted it as an integral part of his acceptance of the Gospels. Nor does he seem to have been concerned about details of the manifestation of the Risen Christ in the world; what was important

---

[16] *LR,* 83–84.

[17] Notebook 35 (c. 1827), f. 18ᵛ.

[18] In explaining certain scriptural passages, Coleridge uses a distinction between "Christ as God" and "Christ as Man." For example, in Notebook 37 (1828), f. 19, he says: "The Son of God became the Son of Man, but tho' whatever we say of the latter, we may rightly affirm of the former; the converse would carry us into strange errors . . . Who will dare assert that the Gospel represents *Jesus* as omniscient, in his personal Consciousness as Jesus?" James Boulger (*Coleridge as Religious Thinker,* p. 182) refers to this distinction as a "dichotomy" and seems to treat it as a kind of evasion, but it is clear in Coleridge that it is a question of distinction without dichotomy. For example, in Notebook 41 (1829–1830), f. [35], he begins his note on Philippians 2:6–11 by saying: "This very difficult passage I can at present see no other way of understanding but by a distinction, tho' without division, of the Jesus from the Logos." Although it would have been clearer had Coleridge used here the more traditional theological distinctions between person and nature in Christ and between his divine and human natures, what he is saying implicitly is sufficiently clear: although the Logos, with all the attributes of God, *is* from all eternity, the humanity of Christ *is not* from all eternity, but is born with him in time.

The distinction is also used elsewhere in the notebooks: in Notebook 48 (1830), f. [25], for example, and, somewhat more implicitly, in *LR,* 75, 269–270, and 431.

was the fact, and his belief in the fact is sufficiently attested by his constant adherence to the Apostles' and Nicene Creeds.[19]

During the last few years of his life, Coleridge seems to have reflected often on a Christological doctrine which, until then, had held no special place in his thinking: the doctrine of the Mystical Body of Christ. Beginning in 1827, there are at least five distinct notebook entries on the Mystical Body. In Notebook 36, in a comment on the typology of the Psalms, he speaks of David as "a complex type—now of the Church as the mystic Body of Christ in all her different states, and now of Christ himself as the Head and Indwelling Principium Vitae of the Mystic Body."[20] In Notebook 41, discussing St. Paul's conception of Christ as the second Adam (Romans 5), Coleridge follows out the parallel in greater detail. As Adam "must be contemplated as a representative Man virtually containing all men—that he was not only Man but Mankind—how much more then must Christ

[19] Coleridge does, however, make several interesting comments on the nature of the Second Coming of Christ (Matt. 24–25, Mark 13, Luke 21, I Thess. 4–5). In his notes on Luther's *Table Talk*, for instance, he writes: "Are Christians bound to believe whatever an Apostle believed,—and in the same way and sense? I think St. Paul himself lived to doubt the solidity of his own literal interpretation of our Lord's words.

"The whole passage in which our Lord describes his coming is so evidently, and so intentionally expressed in the diction and images of the Prophets, that nothing but the carnal literality common to the Jews at that time and most strongly marked in the disciples, who were among the least educated of their countrymen, could have prevented the symbolic import and character of the words from being seen . . .

"The unhappy effect which St. Paul's (may I not say) incautious language respecting Christ's return produced on the Thessalonians, led him to reflect on the subject, and he instantly in the second epistle to them qualified the doctrine, and never afterwards resumed it; but on the contrary, in the first Epistle to the Corinthians, c. 15, substitutes the doctrine of immortality in a celestial state and a spiritual body." *LR*, 277. For much the same view, see also *LR*, 513–514. The Second Coming is also touched upon in *LR*, 175–176, 210–212, 520, and in *TT*, 496 (December 21, 1833), as well as in several entries in the later notebooks.

One exception to Coleridge's general lack of concern with details about the Risen Christ is a comment on Jeremy Taylor. Taylor had remarked that after the Resurrection "Christ's body, his natural body, is changed into a spiritual body, and it is not now a natural body, but a spiritual, and therefore can not be now in the Sacrament after a natural manner, because it is so nowhere, and therefore not there; *It is sown a natural body, it is raised a spiritual body.*" Coleridge commented: "But mercy on me! was this said of the resurgent body of Jesus? a spiritual body, of which Jesus said it was not a spirit. If tangible by Thomas's fingers, why not by his teeth, that is, manducable?" *LR*, 228.

Coleridge also spoke several times of the "descent of Christ into Hell." He believed the Apostles' Creed to have been originally a baptismal creed, much shorter than its present form, which was "gradually augmented as heresies started up. The latest of these seems to have consisted in the doubt respecting the entire death of Jesus on the Cross, as distinguished from suspended animation. Hence in the fifth or sixth century the clause—'and he descended into Hades,' was inserted;—that is, the indissoluble principle of the man Jesus, was separated from, and left, the dissoluble, and subsisted apart in *Scheol* [sic], or the abode of separated souls;—but really meaning no more than *vere mortuus est* [he truly died]." *LR*, 421. See also *LR*, 107 and 278.

[20] Notebook 36 (1827), ff. 51–50ᵛ.

be considered not only as a spiritual divine Man but as the essential Divine Humanity . . . The psychical Humanity was all in Adam, the spiritual Humanity all in Christ." [21] In Notebook 53, Coleridge speaks of "the Son of God, the only-begotten *Word,* the eternal *Reason* & Supreme Being (= Jehovah, ὁ ὤν) by his own condescension & in the mystery of love identified with the suffering humanity, and as one with the Body (the Church) of which he is at once the Head and the Fullness." [22]

This is neither a very clear nor a very developed view of the doctrine of the Mystical Body (according to which all Christians are united as members of the Church, the Body of Christ, and so are one with Christ) but it is an intriguing one. With these passages in mind,

[21] Notebook 41 (1829–1830), f. 8.
[22] Notebook 53 (1833), f. [4ᵛ]. The other pertinent notebook entries are Notebook 48 (1830), ff. [25–26], where Coleridge does not use the term Mystical Body, although the conception is much the same; and Notebook 50 (1831–1832), f. [19]. From this same period, see also *CCS* (1830), 101 n., and 102–103. I have found two earlier references to the Mystical Body, in *CL,* II, 1197 (October 13, 1806) and IV, 582 (August 2, 1815). There is also a suggestive, if somewhat puzzling, undated note in Coleridge's copy of Kant's *Die Religion innerhalb der Grenzen der blossen Vernunft* (1793), which is quoted by Muirhead, *Coleridge as Philosopher,* pp. 249–250. After admitting that the regeneration of human nature is ultimately a mystery, Coleridge finds suggestive analogies in "the undoubted influence of example, of education, in short of all the administrants and auxiliaries of the Will. The will may be acted on not only by ourselves (through the cultivation of habits), but by the will of others, nay even by nature, by the breeze, the sunshine, by the tender life and freshness of the sensation of convalescence, by shocks of sickness." He then refers to George Herbert's poem "The Sonne," and goes on to suggest, "Why not then an influence of influences from the Sun of God, with the Spirit of God acting directly on the *homo noumenon,* as well as through the *homo phaenomenon?* This would make a just distinction between grace and redemption and providential aids: the direct action on the *noumenon* would be the grace—the call—the influence on the *noumenon* through the *homo phaenomenon* by the prearrangement of outward or bodily circumstances would be, as they are commonly called in pious language, providences. Finally, on such a view might not Christ be the World as revealed to human knowledge—a kind of common sensorium, the idea of the whole that modifies all our thoughts? And might not numerical difference be an exclusive property of phenomena so that he who puts on the likeness of Christ becomes Christ?" Muirhead interprets this *noumenon/phaenomenon* distinction as "a distinction between the real and the apparent man, which was designed to admit of miraculous incursions from another world" (p. 251). If Coleridge is here simply taking over Kant's distinction, then Muirhead's reading is perhaps sensible. If, however—as seems to me more likely, knowing Coleridge's propensities —Coleridge is using Kant's distinction for his own devices, I should think it more reasonable and more consistent with Coleridge's thinking to read this as a distinction between "spiritual" and "sensible." This would correspond better with the crucial distinction between reason and understanding, both of which are for Coleridge faculties of the "real," the one of spiritual reality, the other of sensible reality. It is consistent, too, with Coleridge's view of Christ as the Logos, the Supreme Reason to whose likeness the reason of man must strive to conform. The terms might also be translated in Coleridge's context, I should think, as "free" and "determined," as they have been taken to mean in Kant himself; see D. W. Gotshalk, "The Central Doctrine of the Kantian Ethics," in *The Heritage of Kant,* ed. G. T. Whitney and D. F. Bowers (New York, 1939), pp. 191–192. In any event, the passage remains a puzzling one.

perhaps other earlier reflections may take on larger meaning. Years earlier, for example, Coleridge had written in *The Friend* of the "divine humanity" as the "final cause of all creation." After reflecting on the providential ordering of the irrational creation, Coleridge continued: "If then we behold this economy everywhere in the irrational creation, shall we not hold it probable that by some analogous intervention a similar temperament will have been effected for the rational and moral? Are we not entitled to expect some appropriate agency in behalf of the presiding and alone progressive creature? To presume some especial provision for the permanent interest of the creature destined to move and grow towards that divine humanity which we have learnt to contemplate as the final cause of all creation, and the centre in which all its lines converge?" [23]

Had Coleridge developed these hints, would he have applied them to his views on the evolution of the world, that "nature in her ascent leaves nothing behind, but at each step subordinates and glorifies," [24] and to his "theory of life," which concludes that "this must be the one great end of Nature, her ultimate production of the highest and most comprehensive individuality"? [25] Would he have developed in this context his suggestion that the Incarnation of the Logos was necessary, even apart from the Redemption, as the natural culmination of the evolution of the created universe, that "man must have had a Christ, even if Adam had continued in Paradise"? [26] This is something one can only guess at, but the speculation is an intriguing one.

---

[23] *FR*, 466–467. See also *UL*, II, 358 (July 1825). There is a remarkable resemblance here to the thought of the modern Jesuit scientist and theologian of evolution, Pierre Teilhard de Chardin, who sees Christ (the "Omega point") as the final cause and culmination of the evolutionary ascent toward unity. See especially *The Phenomenon of Man*, transl. Bernard Wall (New York, 1961), which, like Coleridge, is profoundly influenced by Pauline theology.

[24] *LR*, 326. Other notes on evolution are found in *PL*, 239; *Aids*, 180–181; *NTPM*, 248–249; and *TT*, 270. Coleridge accepted the notion of an ever-ascending manifestation of Nature in different forms, differing in kind, but not the idea of the evolution of man from a lower species. It is a dynamic evolution of ever developing progress: plant forms ascend to animal forms, simple animal forms to more complex. It is only when he comes to man that he stops short. There is, he says in his essay on the "Theory of Life," a "wide chasm between man and the noblest animals of the brute creation, which no perceivable or conceivable difference of organization is sufficient to overbridge." See *Hints towards the Formation of a more Comprehensive Theory of Life*, in *Aids*, Appendix C, 381–382. The *Theory of Life* was posthumously published, as a separate tract, in 1848. There is an excellent treatment of Coleridge on evolution in Muirhead, *Coleridge as Philosopher*, pp. 130–136. See also Craig W. Miller, "Coleridge's Concept of Nature," *Journal of the History of Ideas*, XXV (1964), 77–96, esp. 84–86 and 93–96.

[25] *Theory of Life*, in *Aids*, Appendix C, 391.

[26] *LR*, 209. See also *LR*, 196–197.

One can only regret that Coleridge did not turn his attention earlier, or more methodically, to an idea which was clearly so congenial to him.

One other aspect of Coleridge's Christology merits consideration, if only because it seems to be singularly his own. It involves a view of the Incarnation not merely as a discrete moment in history but also as part of a long and developing redemptive process. Although Coleridge's reflections on the Incarnation were obviously focused on the New Testament, in the last years of his life he turned more and more to what he saw as the beginnings of its revelation in the Old Testament. For Coleridge, the Old Testament manifestations of God as Jehovah and his manifestations through the prophets and law givers were already manifestations of the Logos, a gradual revelation "proceeding from dim dawn to full noontide."[27] These revelations were already "so many distinct Epiphanies of one and the same Person, El Jah [= Jahweh?], Elijah (or Elias), the Son of Man, and finally in the final fulfilment Son of God."[28] As Coleridge wrote in a commentary on Genesis 31:3 (God's covenant with Jacob): "I know few points in Scripture, which it more concerns a Christian to bear in mind than that Christ as the Logos Θεάνθρωπος was the Jehovah of the Old Testament." Coleridge goes on to assert that "the Divinity, the Filial Godhead, was humanized before he was incarnate—i.e. manifested himself *focally* (ut in foco) in an individual Man."[29] His view is clarified somewhat in a notebook entry the following year: "I would again & again enforce the necessity of bearing in Mind, that the Logos had willed to be the covenanted King of the Hebrew Nation and tho' not yet *incarnate* (οὐκ ἐγένετο σάρξ), yet in a legitimate sense we may assert—ἐγένετο ἐν ὁμοιώματι ἀνθρώπου [he was in the likeness of man]."[30] Several pages later he refers to "the beau-

---

[27] *NTPM*, 136.

[28] Notebook 49 (1830), f. [23ᵛ].

[29] Notebook 42 (1829), ff. [61–62].

[30] Notebook 44 (1830), ff. [62–62ᵛ]. The passage continues: "and if I am not mistaken, some of the Greek Fathers considered the Lord's assumption of Humanity as anterior to his incarnation." It is difficult to know to which Fathers Coleridge is referring—and they would not, I think, express it as an "assumption of Humanity"—but there are references to manifestations of the action of the Logos in the Old Testament (through Moses and the prophets) in St. Theophilus of Antioch's *Ad Autolycum* (c. 181–182) and St. Hippolytus's *Philosophumena* (post 222). See *Enchiridion Patristicum*, ed. M. J. Rouet de Journel, 21st ed. (Barcelona, 1959), n. 179, 182, 398. Something akin to this is also found in Justin Martyr (c. 100-c. 165). See Aloys Grillmeier, S.J., *Christ in Christian Tradition: From the Apostolic Age to Chalcedon (451)*, transl. J. S. Bowden (London, 1965), pp. 105–111.

tiful Harmony between this State and the Λόγος ἀνθρωπόμορφος—the manifested yet invisible King." [31]

Elsewhere in Notebook 44, Moses is also seen as a manifestation of the Logos: "The Jehova Word, the Christ under the Veil of Moses, is here by the mystery of condescending Love to man . . . the exemplar of a Covenanted (i.e. constitutional) King—even as in his incarnation he in sundry ways became, yea, acted and suffered in order to be, the exemplar of the universal, spiritual Man." Moses was "he [to] whom had been delegated the temporary function, the prophetic fore-running Shadow, of the Son's essential and of his freely chosen, Mediatorship . . . the Jehovah condescended to be and to manifest himself as the Head of a particular Nation." [32]

There need be nothing unorthodox in all this. Coleridge's idea of the Jehova-Word manifests his profound sense of the unity of the two Testaments, the old Covenant developing toward the fullness of revelation in the new, and of the central role of the Logos in all God's revelation of himself to man. Coleridge makes no claim that the doctrine of the Trinity had already been revealed in the Old Testament but simply that the word God there spoke to man was the eternal Word, the Logos. At the same time, he is at pains to make it clear that the Word had not yet become flesh but only revealed himself through the instrumentality of other men, the prophets and the kings. Coleridge's conception has the great merit of emphasizing, in the person of the Logos, the singleness of purpose in God's redemptive design for mankind.

Turning to the redemptive act itself, we find that the central statement is to be found once again in the *Aids to Reflection*.[33] It is, in fact, Coleridge's only extended discussion of the Redemption, although he often touched upon it elsewhere.

A problem arises immediately in the very conception of this act itself. The Redemption may be considered in two ways, either "in relation to the antecedent, that is, the Redeemer's act, as the efficient

---

[31] Notebook 44, f. [64].

[32] Notebook 44, ff. [18ᵛ–19ᵛ]. Other notebook entries on the idea of the "Jehova-Word" are in Notebooks 42 (1829), ff. [66ᵛsq.]; 45 (1830), f. 11ᵛ; and 55 (1834), f. [18]. See also *NTPM*, 136–137, 277–278, and *TT*, 478 (August 17, 1833).

[33] *Aids*, 295–320. There is what Shedd calls a "rough original" of part of this discussion in Coleridge's notes on Field, *LR*, 56–58. The argument corresponds closely to *Aids*, 307–317, and the note is dated May 4, 1819.

cause and condition of redemption," or "in relation to the consequent, that is, the effects in and for the Redeemed." The problem is that "the mysterious act, the operative cause, is transcendent. *Factum est:* and beyond the information contained in the enunciation of the fact, it can be characterized only by the consequences" (p. 308). Hence, even though it is possible for Coleridge to distinguish in his "Synopsis" between the act and its effects, in practice one comes to know the act only in terms of its effects.

This was necessarily, therefore, the approach of the Apostle Paul, as Coleridge points out, and it is Paul's lead that he is following. "It is the consequences of the act of Redemption, which the zealous Apostle would bring home to the minds and affections both of Jews and Gentiles." But since most of Paul's "opponents and gainsayers" were Jews, and since Paul himself was a Jew, it is natural that "his reasoning would receive its outward forms and language, that it would take its predominant colors, from his own past, and his opponents' present, habits of thinking; and that his figures, images, analogies and references would be taken preferably from objects, opinions, events, and ritual observances ever uppermost in the imaginations of his own countrymen" (pp. 308–309).

Coleridge turns, then, to the four basic metaphors used in the Pauline theology to express "the blessed consequences of Christ's redemption of mankind." They are: "1. Sin offerings, sacrificial expiation. 2. Reconciliation, atonement . . . 3. Ransom from slavery, redemption, the buying back again, or being bought back. 4. Satisfaction of a creditor's claims by a payment of the debt" (pp. 309–310). As to St. Paul's intention in using them, "the very number and variety of the words or *periphrases* used by him to express one and the same thing, furnish the strongest presumptive proof that all alike were used metaphorically" (p. 310). All are used metaphorically, Coleridge believes, but each one does give an insight into the results of Christ's action on behalf of mankind. A man rejoices when a ceremonial offering to the priest removes a "civil stain" from his name and he is restored to his privileges among his brethren; here is "an atonement which takes away a deeper and worse stain, an eating canker-spot in the very heart of your personal being" and gives "the privilege to become sons of God." A man is grateful to one who reconciles him to a dear friend from whom he had been alienated; here is "the intercession, which had brought you back . . . to your father's arms." A man is grateful to one who has ransomed him from slavery; here is "redemption from a far direr slavery, the slavery of sin unto death." A man is deeply moved when a friend pays for him a heavy and pressing debt which he himself is unable to pay; here is a debt paid for us that is "a debt of death to the evil nature." Each of the metaphors is used to describe "from similitude of effect" the "superlative boon" (pp. 311–312). They remain, however, only metaphors.

It is precisely here that Coleridge departs from theological tradition. The history of the doctrine of the Redemption has been distinguished into three stages: the first (sometimes called the "classic" theory) saw the Redemption in terms of a struggle, as a victory of Christ over the forces of evil in the world; the second (or "Anselmian" view) treated the Redemption as a debt of satisfaction paid by Christ to God's justice; the third (or "subjective" view) saw the Redemption in terms of man's action rather than Christ's, as a matter of conversion and amendment.[34] Here (at least in the first two views, which treat the Redemption as an objective reality) there is no metaphor, but reality. The terms "struggle," "justice," and "satisfaction" are used analogously, to be sure—there is a difference between God's justice and man's—but they are viewed as truly representative of the reality. Coleridge, on the other hand, rejects the use of such figures as anything but metaphorical. They are not *"nomina propria,* by which the very nature of Redemption and its occasion are expressed," but only "figures of speech for the purpose of illustrating the nature and extent of the consequences and effects of the Redemptive Act, and to excite in the receivers a due sense of the magnitude and manifold operation of the boon, and of the love and gratitude due to the Redeemer" (p. 313).

Coleridge's main target for attack is the abuse of the figure of satisfaction for a debt of justice, which he takes as symptomatic of a general overliteral interpretation of the Pauline theology of Redemption. He takes, by way of example, the common theological conception "that sin is, or involves, an infinite debt . . . owing by us to the vindictive justice of God the Father, which can only be liquidated by

---

[34] For this threefold division, see Gustaf Aulén's classic work *Christus Victor: An Historical Study of the Three Main Types of the Idea of the Atonement,* transl. A. G. Hebert (London, 1931).

the everlasting misery of Adam and all his posterity, or by a sum of suffering equal to this" (p. 313).[35] But what, he asks, is the meaning of justice in such a conception of Redemption? "If you attach any meaning to the term justice, as applied to God, it must be the same to which you refer when you affirm or deny it of any other personal agent—save only, that in its attribution to God, you speak of it as unmixed and perfect. For if not, what do you mean? And why do you call it by the same name? I may, therefore, with all right and reason, put the case as between man and man" (p. 314). Coleridge uses then a case involving justice between human beings to show that the conception of vicarious satisfaction of a debt of justice is totally inadequate to express the relationship between God and man, that is, if one takes the conception to be expressive of the essential character of the redemptive act itself; such a conception leaves entirely out of account, for example, the elements of divine love and of the personal response of the individual sinner. And this is precisely Coleridge's complaint, "that this metaphorical naming of the transcendent causative act through the *medium* of its proper effects from actions and causes of familiar occurrence connected with the former by similarity of result, has been mistaken for an intended designation of the essential character of the causative act itself; and that thus divines have interpreted *de omni* what was spoken *de singulo,* and magnified a partial equation into a total identity" (p. 317).[36]

Are these metaphors of our Redemption useless then? No, not in

---

[35] Some form of this conception has been, for example, the most common theory of Redemption in Roman Catholic theology, following the tradition of St. Anselm's *Cur Deus Homo?* (c. 1097).

[36] There is a similar comment in a letter of the same period; see *UL,* II, 335 (January 12, 1825). Coleridge's most biting attacks are usually reserved for the idea of "vicarious satisfaction" of a debt of suffering owed to God, which he calls a "gross perversion of the sublime idea of the Redemption by the cross." *LR,* 74–75. See also *CL,* III, 128 (December 3, 1808); *BL,* I, 136–137; *LR,* 437–438; Notebook 49 (1830), f. [28].

Professor Shedd argues, it seems to me very cogently, that Coleridge's aversion to the idea of vicarious satisfaction explains his failure to stress sufficiently the aspect of guilt in his views on the Redemption: "The scheme which Coleridge presents in the *Aids to Reflection* is defective in not insisting with emphasis upon the truth, that as the *essential* nature of sin . . . is *guilt,* so an *essential* element in any remedial plan must be atonement or expiation. The correlate to guilt is atonement, and to attempt to satisfy those specific wants of the sinful soul, which spring out of remorse of conscience, which is the *felt* and *living* relation of sin to law and justice, by a mere provision for spiritual sanctification, however needed and necessary this may be, in its own place, must be like the attempt to satisfy thirst with food. Coleridge was repelled from the doctrine of vicarious atonement, by some of the mechanical schemes and forms under which it has been exhibited, but if, as the best theology of the church has generally done, he had looked at it from the view-point of the *absolute nature of justice,* and had brought it under the category of want and correlate—one of the most vital of all, and one with which Coleridge's own mind was thoroughly familiar—it seems to us that he would

the light of Coleridge's practical Christianity. It is by means of these metaphors that the Christian, following the lead of St. Paul, can associate his Redemption by Christ with the pattern of his own life, "with whatever was eminently dear and precious to erring and afflicted mortals, and (where no expression could be commensurate, no single title be other than imperfect) seek from similitude of effect to describe the superlative boon, by successively transferring to it, as by a superior claim, the name of each several act and ordinance, habitually connected in the minds of all his hearers with feelings of joy, confidence, and gratitude" (p. 311).[37]

Coleridge finds St. John, on the other hand, speaking without metaphor: "John, recording the Redeemer's own words, enunciates the fact itself, to the full extent in which it is enunciable for the human mind, simply and without any metaphor, by identifying it in kind with a fact of hourly occurrence—expressing it, I say, by a familiar fact the same in kind with that intended, though of a far lower dignity." It is the analogy, a proper analogy, of life. "In the redeemed it is a re-generation, a birth, a spiritual seed impregnated and evolved, the germinal principle of a higher and enduring life, of a spiritual life." And as there is a spiritual life, there is spiritual

---

have seen, that although the terms *ransom* and *payment of a debt,* when applied to the agency of the Redeemer, are indeed metaphorical, the term *sacrificial expiation,* is not." Had he looked at it from this point of view, Coleridge would have seen "that there is a rational necessity for the expiation of guilt—a necessity founded secondarily, in the rational nature and moral wants of man, and therefore primarily, in the nature and attributes of that infinitely Holy Being, who made man in His own image and after His own likeness." Shedd, I, Introductory Essay, 51–52. Italics in the original.

[37] Later, Coleridge caught a hint of a more positive approach to the metaphor problem. In a late notebook he wrote: "In the *Aids to Reflection* I was standing on the same ground with those, whose opinions I strove to rectify—& consequently, took the terms, Sacrifice, Vicarious Sacrifice, Debt, Satisfaction, Atonement, &c. with the whole *caput mortuum* of the conceptions, which those, I was addressing, had formed, from the facts and usages of the World. To apply these, therefore, to the Deity, to the relations of the Father to the co-eternal Son, and of both to Man, without debasing the Idea of the Divine, I was constrained to interpret them *per metaphoram.* Far otherwise will it be, if beginning from the ideas I move descensively, tracing the Light into the Darkness in the diminutions, refractions, & [?turbid] stains. Then these very terms would become *Symbols,* having the *reality* of their relations in the Divine Acts, of which they are the . . . appropriate representatives—and in this [?course] I should be among the first & most strenuous assertors of their *literal* truth, of their being the *proper* expressions of the Ideas signified." Clearly, what he had in mind was to conceive the symbol in terms of the prime analogate, on the level of the Absolute, and apply it in turn to its human analogues. "The difference between me & the modern pseudo-Calvinists is—that I use the *Idea* to ennoble the human [?analogues]—they the relation to degrade & inturbidate the Idea." Notebook 53 (1833), ff. [6–6ᵛ]. As he wrote later in the same notebook, "much, I foresee, will depend on the right understanding of the Symbolic, or real; and vice versà, of a reality that is nevertheless a Symbol" (f. [10ᵛ]). It is difficult to see how Coleridge could expect to achieve the pure ideas without beginning with their human analogues, and unfortunately he does not develop these hints more at length.

death, the death of the soul that comes from sin. "Thus the regeneration to spiritual life is at the same time a redemption from the
spiritual death" (pp. 310–311). By this we know that the redemptive
act is, in a real though analogous sense, a life-giving act mediated by
the Eternal Word made flesh. And, we may add, though Coleridge
does not take the step in this immediate context, it is by means of
this new life mediated by Christ that man's will is restored to integrity: "By this provision of transcendent Goodness God has permitted and enabled us to divide our personal Will from our corrupt
and evil Nature." [38] But "more than this, the mode, the possibility,
we are not competent to know" (p. 311).

Mysterious though this redemptive act may be, there remain
several important characteristics of it, implicit in what has already
been said, which can be further defined.

First of all, it is clear that Coleridge views this "life-giving" act as
intrinsically affecting man in his spiritual faculties; it is not merely
an action which affects man from without, whether as example or as
efficient cause. Christ acts in both these latter ways, of course, and
Christians will find themselves "looking to him as their pattern both
in doing and in suffering, and drawing power from him for going
through both" (p. 297). But the profounder causality of Christ's redemptive act involves union, a common life shared by the Redeemer
and the redeemed. He writes (seemingly taking for his purpose the
words of Leighton): "There is that union betwixt them and their
Redeemer, that they shall rise by the communication and virtue of
his rising: not simply by his power—for so the wicked likewise to
their grief shall be raised: but *they by his life as their life*" (p. 298).
As Coleridge had written to Dr. Green several years earlier, "no
power can be redemptive which does not at the same time act in the
ground of the life as one with the ground, that is, must act in my
will and not merely *on* my will." Further, he goes on, the Redeemer
who can so act must necessarily be God, for "whatever is less than
God, may act *on,* but cannot act in, the will of another. Christ must
become man, but he cannot become *us,* except as far as we become
him, and this we cannot do but by *assimilation;* and assimilation is a
vital real act, not a notional or merely intellective one." [39] In the same

[38] Notebook 46 (1830), f. [12ᵛ].
[39] *LSTC,* II, 710 (May 25, 1820).

vein, Coleridge wrote in the last year of his life that Christ "caused himself to become Man, that he might *be* (not *teach*) *the Resurrection* and the *Life!*" [40]

Second, it is clear that Coleridge has here again brought into balance the objective (or historical) and subjective poles of religion. *"God manifested in the flesh* is eternity in the form of time. But eternity in relation to time is as the absolute to the conditional, or the real to the apparent, and Redemption must partake of both;—always perfected, for it is a *Fiat* of the Eternal;—continuous, for it is a process in relation to man; the former the alone objectively, and therefore universally, true" (p. 303 n.). He insists particularly on the conception of the Redemption as objectively an *opus perfectum,* presenting as the teaching of all the orthodox Reformed Churches, Lutheran and Calvinist alike, as well as the "most learned divines of the Roman Catholic Church," that "Redemption is an *opus perfectum,* a finished work, the claim to which is conferred in Baptism: that a Christian can not speak or think as if his redemption by the blood, and his justification by the righteousness of Christ alone, were future or contingent events, but must both say and think, I have been redeemed, I am justified" (p. 303 n.). Accordingly, his heaviest fire is reserved for "the contrary doctrine, according to which the baptized are yet each individually to be called, converted, and chosen, with all the corollaries from this assumption, the watching for signs and sensible assurances, the frames, and the states, and the feelings, and the sudden conversions, the contagious fever-boils of the (most unfitly, so called) Evangelicals, and Arminian Methodists of the day" (p. 304 n.).[41] In short, it is important to lose sight of neither one nor the other: Christ's completed redemptive act and man's free response of acceptance. Commenting later on the *Aids to Reflection,* he wrote: "I have already in the 'Aids' & elsewhere observed that this is the most difficult & delicate point of Theology—so to handle the justifying and completing efficacy of the Redemption as not to weaken the foundations of Morality, and so to support Morality as not to evacuate the Redemptive Act & Boon of its Worth & Value." [42] This will be a focus of attention, too, in considering Coleridge's belief

---

[40] Notebook 55 (1834), f. [15]. See also *LR,* 365, 489–490, and Notebook F, ff. 5ᵛ–6 (?1825).

[41] See also *CL,* IV, 698 (?1816).

[42] Notebook 26 (c. 1826), f. 104.

concerning Justification: the respective roles of God and man in the work of man's sanctification.

One further characteristic of the redemptive act remains to be noted. Although Coleridge does not explicitly say so in his discussion of the Redemption in the *Aids to Reflection,* he seems to view the Redemption implicitly in terms of his usual continuity (or is it indistinction?) between the natural and the supernatural. In a long footnote (pp. 300–301), Coleridge rejects the view of "some Arminian divines" that what Adam lost for himself and his posterity were supernatural graces; in this view the Redemption would be, by implication, the restoration of these supernatural gifts. In rejecting this view, Coleridge seems to regard the Redemption simply as the restoration of the natural order itself and not an elevation to an order above nature. This is consistent with his views expressed elsewhere about the relationship of nature and revelation, particularly a remarkable marginal note in Henry More's *Theological Works:*

> Yet if Christianity is to be the religion of the world, if Christ be that Logos or Word that *was in the beginning,* by whom all things *became*; if it was the same Christ who said, *Let there be light;* who in and by the creation commenced that great redemptive process, the history of life which begins in its detachment from nature, and is to end in its union with God;—if this be true, so true must it be that the book of nature and the book of revelation, with the whole history of man as the intermediate link, must be the integral and coherent parts of one great work: and the conclusion is, that a scheme of the Christian faith which does not arise out of, and shoot its beams downward into, the scheme of nature, but stands aloof as an insulated afterthought, must be false or distorted in all its particulars. In confirmation of this position, I may challenge any opponent to adduce a single instance in which the now exploded falsities of physical science, through all its revolutions from the second to the seventeenth century of the Christian aera, did not produce some corresponding warps in the theological systems and dogmas of the several periods.[43]

From this point of view, as Coleridge wrote in several of his late notebooks, Creation is "the commencement of the Redemption."[44] This is consistent, too, with Coleridge's idea (discussed earlier in this

---

[43] *LR,* 113. See also *LR,* 89.
[44] Notebook 41 (1829–1830), f. 75^v.

chapter) of Christ as the final cause of the whole universe, material as well as spiritual. "We may say—The World was made for the Gospel or that Christianity is the final Cause of the World. If so, the Idea of the Redemption of the World must needs form the best central Reservoir for all our knowledges, physical or personal. Every fact must find it's place, as a component point in some one or other of the converging Radii." [45]

We turn now to the effects of the redemptive act. In his "Synopsis" of the Redemption, Coleridge spoke of the "effect caused" as "being born anew" and of the "consequences from the effect" as sanctification from sin and liberation from its penal consequences with "all the means and processes of sanctification by the Word and the Spirit." Actually, this division is atypical and more than a little misleading. In this area, Coleridge was more prone to unify and synthesize than to distinguish. He was ready to concede that "we, according to the necessity of our imperfect understandings, must divide and distinguish. But surely justification and sanctification are one act of God, and only different perspectives of redemption by and through and for Christ. They are one and the same plant, justification the root, sanctification the flower; and (may I not venture to add?) transubstantiation into Christ the celestial fruit." [46]

"By and through and for Christ" is the key. Coleridge's "theology" of Justification—if such it can be called—is profoundly Christocen-

---

[45] *UL,* II, 358 (July 1825). Several other passing comments of Coleridge on aspects of the Redemption are worthy of note. In an early note (1810), Coleridge suggests that the suffering of Christ was not necessary, that the result would have been the same had Christ only "worked his miracles . . . and taught the same doctrines" without shedding his blood; the result Coleridge points to here seems to be, however, simply that of giving authority to his teaching. *LR,* 481. Later, the result of Christ's redemptive act was for Coleridge, as we have seen, an intrinsic and effective change in the redeemed humanity itself; for this, Coleridge accepted the fittingness, if not clearly the necessity, of the blood of Christ as the fitting sign of the completeness of his self-giving. See, for example, *Aids,* 311–312. Coleridge had misgivings later about this aspect of his thinking on the Redemption. "Is my Idea of Redemption compatible with the doctrine of atonement by the *sufferings* of Jesus Christ? Does my system give a distinct causativeness, a distinct efficiency, to 'the stripes by which *we* are healed'? If not, I am prepared to deem it imperfect & by omission at least false.—Much, I foresee, will depend on the right understanding of the Symbolic, or real; and vice versà, of a reality, that is nevertheless a Symbol." Notebook 53 (1833), f. [10].

In an undated note on Richard Baxter's *Catholick Theologie* Coleridge made a rare reference to the role of the Church in Redemption, speaking of "the first admission within the pale of the alone saving Church" as "the condition & inceptive of Redemption." See *Coleridge on the Seventeenth Century,* ed. Roberta F. Brinkley (Durham, North Carolina, 1955), p. 360.

[46] Notes on Luther's *Table Talk, LR,* 288.

tric. It is the work of Christ, and of the Spirit, within the individual that interests Coleridge, and distinctions often fall away in the face of this truth.

Earlier in this chapter, we spoke of Coleridge's view of the humanity of Christ as a "sacramental sign" of the Godhead. In seeing the incarnate Son of God as the great "sacrament," it should be made clear that Coleridge viewed him not merely as an exemplar, a model for imitation, but as an efficacious sign which is capable of bringing about in men what it signifies for them. What Christ is, through Redemption man must become; what Christ did, man must be enabled to do. As Christ suffered, so will redeemed man suffer; as Christ was glorified, so will redeemed man be glorified. "The sum of my Belief is, that nothing happened to Jesus, which in and thro' him must not happen to every elect Believer." [47] And all this is to take place through the indwelling of Christ in the Christian. The essential effect of the Redemption is "transubstantiation into Christ."

Coleridge nowhere treats at length of Justification and Grace. We must glean his views, even his understanding of the terms, from a variety of contexts. One thing is clear throughout, however: his emphasis is constantly on the action of God indwelling and working within man. This is evident even as early as 1810 in his marginal comments on an anonymous work on evangelical preaching, signed "a Barrister." The Barrister wrote of John 3:3–8 (during Christ's interview with Nicodemus): "The true meaning of being *born again,* in the sense in which our Saviour uses the phrase, implies nothing more or less, in plain terms, than this:—to repent; to lead for the future a religious life instead of a life of disobedience; to believe the Holy Scriptures, and to pray for grace and assistance to persevere in our obedience to the end. All this any man of common sense might explain in a few words." Coleridge is indignant. "Pray, then . . . what does the man of common sense mean by grace?" The only aspect of grace which the man of common sense could hope to explain would be "the circumstances *ab extra,*" but to reduce grace to this "would be mere mockery and in direct contradiction to a score of texts." [48]

In the *Aids to Reflection,* although Coleridge clearly distinguishes

[47] Notebook 39 (c. 1826), f. 21–21^{v}.
[48] *LR,* 474–475.

between "actual" grace and "habitual" grace, his emphasis is on the indwelling of God in the soul and therefore on habitual grace.[49] "There is a great and worthy sense in which we may believe the Apostle's assurance, that not only doth *the Spirit help our infirmities;* that is, act on the will by a predisposing influence from without, as it were, though in a spiritual manner, and without suspending or destroying its freedom . . . but that in regenerate souls it may act in the will; that uniting and becoming one with our will or spirit it may *make intercession for us.*"[50] Elsewhere, Coleridge speaks of "the indwelling Christ in the Soul."[51] Again, he speaks of Christ's own declaration to the Apostles "that he had dwelt a brief while *with* or *among* them, in order to dwell *in* them permanently."[52]

But perhaps the clearest and most dramatic insight into Coleridge's view that Justification, man's "being made righteous," is essentially union with the indwelling Christ, is a notebook entry dated March 15, 1828:

Suggested to my mind during prayer. It is most true, and a truth of unspeakable Consolation, that we cannot be saved by our own righteousness but only by the already perfected Righteousness of the Son of Man. Yet it is no less true, that the Son of God . . . did according to the Will of the Father endow Man with the Capability of being raised to the knowledge and Desire of the Creator as his ultimate End—and likewise in as many as are chosen in actual *Capacity* of the Righteousness of Christ, a potenziation of the Will by the Leading of the Father—for whom the Father leadeth to the Son, in *him* God is both to will and to do—and this actual Capacity, if to be mentally distinguished from, is however necessarily inductive to, a nascent or germinal state, in the language of the Apostles a Seed, a Graft-bud . . . not indeed as the Believer's own Righteousness, but the Righteousness of Christ in him. Sed quicquid in Deo est, est Deus. [But whatever is in God, is God.] The Righteousness which is in Christ *is* Christ: and therefore with strictest propriety, however the phrase may have been soiled by Familists and Quakers, it may be spoken of under

[49] Habitual or sanctifying grace is commonly taken to be the gift of God habitually dwelling in the soul, by which the regenerate man is made a sharer in the divine life. Actual grace is a divine assistance given to the soul, by which one is enabled to perform some particular good act. Prevenient grace, clearly implied in the passage quoted below, is that actual grace by which God enables the as yet unregenerate to perform good acts and draws them toward justification.

[50] *Aids*, 152–153. The biblical allusion is to Romans 8:26.

[51] Notebook 48 (1830), f. [15ᵛ].

[52] *LR*, 424.

the analogy of Birth, as a newly born, an infant Christ. In *practical* Divinity we are bound to insist on this, as the indispensable *condition,* and the means or medium of that spiritual immanence in the glorified Body of our Redeemer, as constituting for each of the Elect and for the whole Number the spiritual continuum between them and their Redeemer, by which, as Archbishop Leighton beautifully observes [cf. *Aids,* 298] "They shall rise by the communication and virtue of his Rising: not simply by his *power*—for so the wicked likewise to their grief shall be raised—but *they by his life as their life"* . . . the Mediator between the Creature and the Creator is likewise himself the Medium between the Creature and Himself. He is "the Way, the Life and the Resurrection." [53]

What can be said, then, of Coleridge's view of Justification and Grace? First of all, the terms Justification, Grace, and Sanctification are essentially interchangeable; the use of one term merely highlights one or another aspect of man's regeneration. Justification emphasizes man's new state of "righteousness" before God. The term Grace stresses the character of divine gift, freely given. Sanctification places the emphasis on man's new state of holiness, or union with God. Second, whatever term is used, there is clearly an intrinsic change in the regenerated man. Third, the process of regeneration involves a dynamic union with God, who now acts in the soul. Finally, this union is mediated through Christ and the Holy Spirit, although now one, now the other is stressed.

In this context, it might be noted just what is Coleridge's understanding of the classic Reformation doctrine of "imputed righteousness." Until fairly recently, it was commonly supposed that Luther meant by the doctrine that Justification worked no intrinsic change in man, and that the righteousness of Christ was merely imputed by a kind of legal fiction to the regenerate, who remained a sinner; the regenerate was therefore *simul justus et peccator.* This was distinguished from the Catholic position that the righteousness of Christ was not only imputed but actually "imparted" to the sinner, working an inner change in him from a state of sin to a state of grace. Coleridge speaks of the doctrine only rarely, but when he does, it is to defend quite a different understanding of the classic Lutheran position. In *Aids to Reflection,* for example, he is convinced that "the doctrine of IMPUTED righteousness, rightly and Scripturally inter-

[53] Notebook 37, ff. 56–57.

preted, is so far from being either irrational or immoral, that reason itself prescribes the idea in order to give a meaning and an ultimate object to morality." [54] And in a late notebook entry he says: "Inherent Rights suppose inherent righteousness. He alone is a Christian, who has learnt with his whole soul to acknowledge, that he has no righteousness of his own, but that, a sinner, a fallen creature, he is saved by and in the righteousness of Christ. This Righteousness is, & only can be, an *imputed* Righteousness." [55] In the light of modern studies of Luther, it is by no means clear that the great Reformer rejected the intrinsic justification of the regenerate, and Coleridge's reading of the classic Reformation doctrine may well be correct.[56] In any case, what Coleridge wants to defend above all is the primary and essential role of Christ in the process of Justification: man is not justified by his own righteousness but by the righteousness of Christ, a belief certainly common to both Catholic and Reformer. Beyond this he believed—and here again he may have been at one not only with Catholic but also with Reformation teaching—that this Justification involves a real intrinsic change in the regenerate sinner.

The inevitable problem that must arise in any theology of grace is its relationship to man's free will. Whether it be actual grace (the supernatural assistance given for a particular act) or habitual grace (the indwelling and relatively permanent supernatural life), the influencive action of God on or in man's spiritual faculties must somehow be related to man's own inner-directed action, whether to override it or to work harmoniously with it. Historically, this has proven to be the central problem in the controversies over grace. Although Tertullian was already aware of the problem, it was St. Augustine who first endeavored to come to grips with it. Augustine's attempt to save free will in man involved a distinction between prevenient grace (that is, grace given before justification) and subsequent grace. Prevenient grace was completely gratuitous on God's part; subsequent grace involved cooperation between God's action and man's. Augustine also distinguished merely sufficient grace (that is, subsequent grace which in the event proved not to have man's free

---

[54] *Aids*, 180.
[55] Notebook 50 (1831–1832), f. [47]. See also *TT*, 457 (June 8, 1833).
[56] See Hans Küng, *Justification: The Doctrine of Karl Barth and a Catholic Reflection*, transl. T. Collins, E. Tolk, D. Granskou (New York, 1964), pp. 217 ff. For the Council of Trent's condemnation of the "extrinsicist" understanding of Justification, see Session VI, Decree on Justification, Canon 11, in Denzinger-Schönmetzer, n. 1561.

cooperation) from efficacious grace (with which man freely coop-
erated). These distinctions became the staples of theological speculation and controversy over grace throughout the Middle Ages and the
Renaissance. The pendulum swung back and forth, from school to
school and from theologian to theologian, between emphasis on
man's freedom on the one hand and God's omnipotence on the other.
A climax was reached in the Reformation, when both Luther (at least
the earlier Luther) and Calvin taught absolute predestination, the
complete determination of man's salvation by God's grace.[57]

Although Coleridge adverted occasionally to these controversies
as historical problems, and although he occasionally distinguished
between prevenient and "auxiliary" grace, he seems not to have interested himself in these speculations as such.[58] He was concerned
simply with maintaining certain basic truths. On the one hand, anything that derogated from God's omnipotence and man's total dependence on God in the order of justification and salvation would
have been anathema to him. Christ taught that men "must perish—
utterly perish—if they relied on themselves, or if they sought for a
realization of that perfection, which yet remained even the only
ground of a safe morality, in aught but a reliance on a superior
power." [59] On the other hand, in Coleridge's practical Christianity
anything that threatened man's imperative need for vigorous moral
action was equally suspect. For "what the plant is by an act not its
own and unconsciously—that must thou make thyself to become—
must by prayer and by a watchful and unresisting spirit, join at least
with the preventive and assisting grace to make thyself, in that light
of conscience which inflameth not, and with that knowledge which
puffeth not up!" [60]

[57] One of the best modern treatments of the history of the theology of grace is in Henri
Rondet's *Gratia Christi: Essai d'Histoire du Dogme et de Théologie Dogmatique* (Paris,
1948).

[58] Coleridge comments in 1826, for example, on a passage from Luther's *Table Talk*, in
which Luther speaks of the inefficacy of man's will: "Luther confounds free-will with efficient power, which neither does nor can exist save where the finite will is one with the
absolute Will. That Luther was practically on the right side in this famous controversy, and
that he was driving at the truth, I see abundant reason to believe. But it is no less evident that
he saw it in a mist." *LR,* 280. For examples of Coleridge's use of prevenient and auxiliary
grace, see *FR,* 395, and *LR,* 105.

[59] *PL,* 222. For similar assertions of man's dependence on divine grace in the order of
salvation, see *LR,* 155, 262, 480, 494–495; *PL,* 216, 221–226; *NTPM,* 162–164; *CL,* IV, 709
(February 28, 1817); Notebook 21½, f. 46ᵛ.

[60] *SM,* Appendix B, 462.

Beyond this, as in so many other areas, he was content to accept the mystery. Obviously, the mystery implied a tension between the two truths, but this tension, this polarity, was precisely the mystery. One of his best statements of his view is in a note dated May 4, 1829. It is worth quoting in full:

More and more strenuously to impress on myself and render intelligible to others the great principle—that all truths of religion are *practical,* and by their *practicability,* not their intellectual conceivability to be tried or judged of. Thus: I not only believe, that by Faith alone can I be justified, and that if I live at all, except this life-in-death under the curse of a most holy but for me impracticable Law, it is not I, but Christ that liveth in me (Gal. ch. [ii], 11–20) and that this faith is not *mine* but of Grace—the faith of the Son of God, Who communicates it to me, and whose righteousness is the alone righteousness by which I can be saved—and yet there must be an act of receiving on my part—but this very act is the effect of Grace. What shall I say then? Am I no longer responsible? God forbid! My Conscience would scream a *Lie* in my face if I but tried to think it. No! but that I am applying the petty Logic of Cause & Effect, where they are utterly inapplicable. But does there exist any practical difficulty? Can I not with my whole heart abjure my own righteousness and feel that I must be transferred & transplanted to another *Ground* of my Individuality, a higher *Nature,* that is indeed above *Nature*—and can I not feel & know that however ardently I may desire this, I have no power to bring it about? Nay, that this very desire I could not have had, had I not been a Christian? In the practice there are no difficulties—and all Works of Religion must be tried by this rule—are the Duties they dictate incompatible with each other? If not, laugh or turn away with pity from all logical Objections.[61]

The act by which man is justified is a free act of a free man, and yet it is somehow "graced" in its very freedom. And salvation, the fulfillment of man's justification, is also the perfection of man's freedom. "Redemption is in the Absolute Act of Freedom thro' Grace & in faith by which we overcome this Self-being." [62] And there, for Coleridge, is the heart of the mystery.

[61] Notebook 40, ff. 25–25ᵛ. This note was also transcribed by Mrs. Watson, who edited the text somewhat, expurgating Coleridge's reference to the "for me impracticable Law." See *Coleridge at Highgate,* p. 141. For other evidences of Coleridge's acceptance of the mystery of the cooperation of grace and free will in man, see *Aids,* 307; *LR,* 165, 198–199, 280–281, 474; and Notebook 20, ff. 33ᵛ–34.
[62] Notebook 39 (c. 1826), f. 37.

There is one aspect of the theology of Justification which demands particular attention: the controverted problem of Justification by Faith. It arises in Coleridge in two distinct contexts, the one that of the classic Reformation controversy of Faith and Good Works, the other the question of Infant Baptism. The second belongs more properly to a discussion of the sacraments and will be treated in the following chapter.

The problem of Faith versus Works is really a corollary of what we have seen already on the relationship of grace and free will. Here again, what is at issue is the relationship of what God does and what man does in the process of salvation. Here again, too, Coleridge was primarily interested neither in the speculative attempts to reconcile the action of God and the action of man, nor in the historical controversies, but simply in maintaining the two basic truths. Historical background is necessary, therefore, more by way of perspective than for its own sake.

Although a tension already appears in the early Church on the question, represented in the seemingly contradictory statements of Paul (Rom. 3:28) and James (James 2:24) about the role of Faith and Works, in post-Reformation times it is basically a Protestant-Catholic dispute. Luther's emphasis on the importance of faith, joined with the sixteenth-century disenchantment with indulgences, relics, pilgrimages, and the like—all of which had come to be grossly abused and enormously overemphasized—resulted in the Reformers' teaching that it is *sola fides* that justifies, that justification is by faith alone. Man cannot merit by his works; he can only hope for the completely gratuitous gift of God. The Council of Trent countered with a formal declaration that man can properly merit by his good works; he cannot merit the initial grace of justification, to be sure, but he can earn the increase of grace and the reward of eternal life after death.[63] Obviously, the Catholic was then left with the problem of preserving somehow the gratuity of God's grace. One attempted solution was the Schoolmen's distinction between condign merit in the strict sense (what is due in strict justice) and condign merit in a less strict acceptation (due not in justice but because of God's love and his

---

[63] Council of Trent, Session VI, Decree on Justification; see Denzinger-Schönmetzer, n. 1545–1549, 1576, 1582.

faithfulness to his promises).[64] The Protestant, on the other hand, was faced with the problem of preserving man's motivation for good acts. The solution generally offered was that good works are the external signs of grace.

The Church of England, in codifying the Articles of Religion in their final form in 1571, took a conciliatory stance on the question of good works, attempting to mollify both the rigorous Calvinists and the more liberal High Church theologians.[65] The advent of the liberal Arminian theology into England during the seventeenth century heightened controversy over the interpretation of the Articles, and the Calvinist-Arminian differences became a focal point in English theology for the next three centuries. What is important to note here is that the Arminian theology gave wide scope to man's free will and to the value and efficacy of good works. When there was compromise, therefore—as there was even in the sixteenth century—it involved giving a broader field for the works of the individual.[66] James Boulger summarizes very well the significance of such a compromise: "The loose or moderate form of Calvinism, which had been adopted as a compromise in the sixteenth century, followed the spirit of Luther himself by insisting upon justification as a personal and continuous victory for the individual, while rejecting the Calvinistic deductions of election, predestination, and, at worst, antinomianism.

[64] Condign merit is itself distinguished from congruous merit, which is due only in the sense that it is fitting.

[65] Article XI holds, like the Council of Trent, that initial justification is completely gratuitous on the part of God, and therefore "that we are justified by faith only is a most wholesome doctrine." Article XII ("Of Good Works") says nothing of merit, but speaks of Good Works as outward signs of Faith; they are "pleasing and acceptable to God in Christ, and do spring out necessarily of a true and lively faith, insomuch that by them a lively faith may be as evidently known as a tree discerned by the fruit." These articles were clearly open to either Calvinist or Arminian interpretations.

[66] Coleridge summarizes the main lines of development himself in Notebook 26 (c. 1826), f. 70: "The first Assault of Protestantism was on the Romish Doctrine of ritual merits; & the gifts to religious purposes (i.e. priestly uses); and to alms, given in the spirit of compensation & as equivalent for duties omitted or transgressed—in short, against the scheme of *good works*, in the churchly acceptation of the Word. In opposition to this most pernicious Doctrine, the Reformers preached *Faith* as the only principle or subjective Source of Salvation. —The second [assault was] against the *Romish* Doctrine of Faith (i.e. implicit confidence) in the Pope & Bishops, instead of Faith in Christ & Belief of the Scriptures—in opposition to this, they preached Faith working obedience by Love. Then came the division between Protestants—and Arminianism obtained the outing over Calvinism in all the higher orders of Christians, and the consequence has been a finer form of the old doctrine of meritorious [?works] —the Protestants forgetting the living Faith in a lifeless Morality, the Romanists overlooking true morality in a lifeless Faith."

Scholastic theologians in the Established Church were often forced into a dualism of speculative Calvinism and practical Arminianism in their attempts to defend the Church's Article." [67]

In a sense, as Boulger suggests, it is this modified Calvinism (to which Coleridge gave the name "pure Lutheranism") that best represents Coleridge's point of view.[68] There is one important difference, however, in that Coleridge rather effectively avoided the resulting dualism by simply refusing to dwell on the speculative side. He was interested in the implications for practical Christian life, and this involved bearing always in mind two truths: man works, and God works in him. It is a matter of "the reconciling of distinctity with unity,—ours, yet God's; God's, yet ours." [69]

As a good Protestant, Coleridge felt constrained—at least in an earlier period of his theological reflection—to attack occasionally the "Romish" doctrine of Works for "asserting the merits of creatures so as, though not avowedly, to deny, yet, effectively to make vain the sole redemption by, and mediation of, Christ." [70] In his more tolerant moments, however, it becomes clear that what he is inveighing against is not the doctrine but the practice, that is, the excesses and abuses of traditional Roman Catholic prayers, devotions, and practices: veneration of relics of the saints, priestly absolution, indulgences, and the like—all of which, if unwisely used, could and did lead to superstition, or at least to overemphasis on the value of external works. Coleridge wrote in the margin of one of Hooker's works: "I am persuaded, that the practice of the Romish church tendeth to make vain the doctrine of salvation by faith in Christ alone; but judging by her most eminent divines, I can find nothing dissonant from the truth in her express decisions on this article." Even further, he continues, "I neither do nor can think, that any pious member of the Church of Rome did ever in his heart attribute any merit to any work as being his work." [71] He finds nothing incompatible with his own

---

[67] *Coleridge as Religious Thinker*, p. 42. Boulger's lengthy treatment of the historical background of the controversies in England over Justification by Faith, and its relationship to Coleridge's thought, has been particularly helpful; see *Coleridge as Religious Thinker*, pp. 37–64.

[68] *Coleridge as Religious Thinker*, p. 50.

[69] *LR*, 92.

[70] Notes on Chillingworth (1809), *NTPM*, 73–74. See also *LR*, 470, and *CL*, IV, 845 (March 3, 1818).

[71] *LR*, 49–50. Shedd here quotes Canons 24 and 32 of Session VI of the Council of Trent (see Denzinger-Schönmetzer, n. 1574, 1582) in contradiction of this assertion. He seems to

beliefs in the essential Catholic teaching on Good Works: even though man cannot perform an act effective for salvation without God's help, God has promised that man will be rewarded for his good works done in cooperation with God's grace; man works while God works in him.

Ironically enough—in view of his opposition to Romanism in so many areas—this is what Coleridge quite consistently teaches. Occasionally he does speak of the traditional Protestant "sign value" of good works, as when he writes in *The Friend:* "But man knows not the heart of man; scarcely does any one know his own. There must therefore be outward and visible signs, by which men may be able to judge of the inward state; and thereby justify the ways of God to their own spirits, in the reward or punishment of themselves and their fellow-men. Now good works are these signs, and as such become necessary." [72] But this is by way of exception. Elsewhere and often, he insists on the need for good works as a requisite principle of Christian morality itself. "No article of faith can be truly and duly preached without necessarily and simultaneously infusing a deep sense of the indispensableness of a holy life." [73] Discussing the efficacy of prayer, he says: "Whatever efficacy we may, and by the constitution of our Being *must,* attribute to our *Actions,* considered as appointed means to rightly desired ends, the same with equal rationality we assign to our petitionary prayers." [74] For faith is not "a substitute for what we *can* do, but for what we cannot, and yet but for Christ *must* do or perish." It is "the principle which alone can make the little, which in our corrupt nature we can do, acceptable to a holy God . . . the Principle, which will increase our power of obedience, and enable us thro' Grace to do what without it we should be unable ever to attempt." [75]

---

have misread Canon 32, however. The canons do assert, it is true, that man can merit an increase of grace and eternal life, but the insistence of Canon 32 that the good works of the justified man are done by him "per Dei gratiam et Iesu Christi meritum (cuius vivum membrum est)" makes it clear that such meritorious actions are themselves "graced" and are therefore the work of God. This is even more evident in the chapter of Session VI on which these canons are based (Denzinger-Schönmetzer, n. 1545–1549), where the Council clearly teaches that these actions which God wills to be meritorious for man are themselves "gifts of God."

[72] *FR,* 288. See also *FR,* 286–289, and *LR,* 483.
[73] *TT,* 418 (January 7, 1833).
[74] *UL,* II, 395 (1827). See also *CL,* IV, 676 (September 22, 1816).
[75] Notebook 41 (1829–1830), f. [55^v].

What is crucial for Coleridge in all this is that credit for both the the faith and the good work belongs to God, since the act which tends toward God is itself graced and the very power to work toward salvation is a grace of God. "If the faith worketh the works, what is true of the former must be equally affirmed of the latter;—*causa causae causa causati* [the cause of the cause is also the cause of the thing caused] . . . The faith and the righteousness of a Christian are both alike his, and not his—the faith of Christ in him, the righteousness in and for him. *I am crucified with Christ: nevertheless I live; yet, not I, but Christ liveth in me: and the life which I now live in the flesh I live by the faith of the Son of God, who loved me, and gave himself for me.* [Gal. 2:20]" It is "ours, yet God's; God's, yet ours."[76]

But since Coleridge accepted the mystery of the union of the Christian with Christ through grace, the problem of Faith versus Good Works had already ceased to be a "problem"; it is rather part of the larger "mystery." If the agent is one, however mysteriously so, the action will be one. In the mystery of Christ are reconciled "distinctity with unity"; faith and good works; "ours, yet God's; God's, yet ours." The living faith that has brought union with Christ will of itself flow over into good works, of whom the agent is both God and man:

Now contrast with this [the Old Law] the process of the Gospel. There the affections are formed in the first instance, not by any reference to works or deeds, but by an unmerited rescue from death, liberation from slavish task-work; by faith, gratitude, love, and affectionate contemplation of the exceeding goodness and loveliness of the Saviour, Redeemer, Benefactor: from the affections flow the deeds, or rather the affections overflow in the deeds, and the rewards are but a continuance and continued increase of the free grace in the state of the soul and in the growth and gradual perfecting of that state, which are themselves gifts of the same free grace, and one with the rewards; for in the kingdom of Christ which is the realm of love and inter-community, the joy and grace of each regenerated spirit becomes double, and thereby augments the joys and the graces of the others, and the joys and graces of all unite in each;—Christ, the head, and by his spirit the bond, or unitive *copula* of all, being the spiritual sun whose entire image is reflected in every individual of the myriads of dew-

[76] Notes on Donne, *LR*, 92. Italics in the original. See also *Aids*, 189–191, and *LR*, 465–466.

drops. While under the Law, the all was but an aggregate of subjects, each striving after a reward for himself,—not as included in and resulting from the state,—but as the stipulated wages of the task-work, as a loaf of bread may be the pay or bounty promised for the hewing of wood or the breaking of stones! [77]

So, for Coleridge, the wheel has come full circle. The agent of Redemption is Christ, God and man, but now seen as Christ present in the Christian; for the grace by which man is justified is the participated life of God, indwelling in man. Because the divine and human natures have been united in the Person of Christ, mankind is enabled to share in the divine life as the first fruits of its Redemption.

[77] LR, 284. See also LR, 263.

❋ VII. CHURCH, SACRAMENTS, AND PRAYER

Bringing the Church and the Sacraments together into a single chapter has perhaps more basis in tradition than in Coleridge. After all, as we have noted already, Coleridge did fail to develop the idea of the Mystical Body of Christ, which would have allowed him to view the sacraments primarily as works of the Church, that is, as symbolic actions by which the divine life of the Mystical Body is communicated to the faithful. Nevertheless, the juxtaposition of the Church and the Sacraments, together with Prayer, is a natural one: they are all instruments of man's sanctification. About these instruments, especially the Church, Coleridge has much to say that is valuable.

The central statement of Coleridge's idea of the Church is in his essay *On the Constitution of the Church and State* (1830), the last work published during his lifetime.[1] It is built upon a dual distinction. Coleridge distinguishes first between the National Church and the Christian Church, while the latter is further distinguished into the visible Church of Christ and the invisible or spiritual Church. "As many and fearful mischiefs have ensued from the confusion of the Christian with the National Church, so have many and grievous practical errors, and much un-Christian intolerance, arisen from confounding the outward and visible Church of Christ, with the spiritual and invisible Church, known only to the Father of all Spirits."[2]

Using "the language of Queen Elizabeth," Coleridge explains his

[1] This pamphlet was written in criticism of certain elements of the Catholic Emancipation Bill of 1829, with which Coleridge agreed in principle but with some of whose provisions he was dissatisfied. For the background of its composition, see James Dykes Campbell's *Samuel Taylor Coleridge: A Narrative of the Events of His Life* (London, 1894), pp. 271–272.

[2] *CCS*, 107. Coleridge's distinction between the National Church and the Christian Church is a late development. The earliest references I have found are in his notes on Skelton, dated 1825 (*LR*, 438–439) and on Hooker's *Laws of Ecclesiastical Polity*, at least one of which is dated 1826 (*LR*, 30, 32, 34). See also *LR*, 349–350 (1829), 255 (c. 1830), 136 (1833); and *TT*, 382–383 (February 22, 1832). A notebook entry of 1824 (Notebook 30, ff. 59–58ᵛ) and a passage in the *Aids* (291) speak of the Church in such a way as to indicate that Coleridge had not yet formulated the distinction with any clarity. In the notes on Skelton cited above, Coleridge says that he had expressed the distinction in his "Essay on Establishment and Dissent"; this essay, if it ever existed, has not been discovered.

idea of the National Church in terms of the ancient three estates of the realm. The first estate were the landowners, made up of Barons and Franklins, who insured permanence. The second estate, the artisans, manufacturers, and merchants, provided for "progressiveness and personal freedom." The third estate, including the clergy and the other educated and teaching classes, worked for the continuity of the nation's cultural values, including the spiritual.[3] It is this third group which, in Coleridge's view, constitutes the National Church or "Clerisy." C. R. Sanders calls it a veritable "broad church."[4] Coleridge himself has still another name for it. If the Christian Church is the *ecclesia,* the communion of those who are "called out of the world, that is, in reference to the especial ends and purposes of that communion," then the National Church or Clerisy might properly be called an *enclesia,* or "an order of men chosen in and of the realm, and constituting an estate of that realm" (p. 53). The Clerisy of the nation comprises not only the religious leaders and theologians but also "the learned of all denominations, the sages and professors of the law and jurisprudence, of medicine and physiology, of music, of military and civil architecture, of the physical sciences . . . in short, all the so-called liberal arts and sciences, the possession and application of which constitute the civilization of a country" (p. 53). Within this order the theologian takes precedence, "because the science of theology was the root and the trunk of the knowledges that civilized man, because it gave unity and the circulating sap of life to all other sciences, by virtue of which alone they could be contemplated as forming, collectively, the living tree of knowledge" (p. 54).

The aim of the National Church, therefore, is to preserve and build up "the treasures of past civilization," but especially to "diffuse through the whole community and to every native entitled to its laws and rights that quantity and quality of knowledge which was indispensable both for the understanding of those rights, and for the performance of the duties correspondent." Just as the object of the first two estates was to insure permanence and progression, "law with liberty," so the object of this third estate was "to secure and

[3] For this division, see *CCS,* 51.
[4] *Coleridge and the Broad Church Movement,* p. 86.

improve that civilization, without which the nation could be neither permanent nor progressive" (p. 52).[5] Clearly, such an object does not of itself require one church or another. The Clerisy of its very nature is nonsectarian.

Up to this point, Coleridge has been speaking of an idea of the National Church, not "the history of the Church established in this nation" (pp. 60–61). Ultimately, he must face the question of the relationship of Christianity to the National Church. "In relation to the national Church, Christianity, or the Church of Christ, is a blessed accident, a providential boon, a grace of God." A typical Coleridgean footnote asks that the "religious reader" be not offended by the word "accident." He means by it "only that Christianity is an aid and instrument, which no State or realm could have produced out of its own elements, which no State had a right to expect. It was, most awfully, a GOD-SEND!" (pp. 59–60)

The Christian Church must be carefully distinguished not only from the National Church but also from other churches which pretend to be the true Christian Church. With this in mind, Coleridge outlined a set of four "distinctions, or peculiar and essential marks, by which the Church with Christ as its head is distinguished from the National Church, and separated from every possible counterfeit, that has, or shall have, usurped its name" (p. 105). Bearing in mind Coleridge's strong antipapal sentiments, as well as the fact that the *Constitution on the Church and State* was written in the heat of controversy over the Catholic Emancipation Bill of 1829, it is not surprising to find Coleridge's four marks of the true Church directed at least in part against the Roman Catholic Church.[6] Even more pointedly anti-Roman are the two "absolute disqualifications" for any office as trustee or functionary of the true Christian Church, with which Coleridge prefaces his list of the marks of the Church: "Allegiance to a foreign power, or an acknowledgment of any other visible head of the Church but our sovereign lord the King; and

[5] One of the fullest discussions to date of Coleridge's idea of the National Church, as well as of the broader question of the Church-State relationship, is in David P. Calleo's *Coleridge and the Idea of the Modern State* (New Haven, 1966). See especially pp. 96–99, 114–119, 130–131.

[6] In his prefatory remarks to the *Constitution of the Church and State* (29–30) and in his concluding section (117–129), Coleridge is at some pains to insist that he is strongly in favor of Catholic Emancipation, and only objects to the failure of the 1829 Bill to provide adequate safeguards against the encroachment of Rome-based power.

compulsory celibacy in connection with, and dependence on, a foreign and extra-national head" (p. 97).

The first essential mark of the ideal Christian Church is that it is not a kingdom of this world, nor is it "an estate of any such realm, kingdom, or state; but it is the appointed opposite to them all collectively—the sustaining, correcting, befriending opposite of the World; the compensating counterforce to the inherent and inevitable evils and defects of the State" (p. 98). In return for these services, "she asks only protection and to be let alone." But even these she asks "only on the ground that there is nothing in her constitution or in her discipline inconsistent with the interests of the State, nothing resistent or impedimental to the State in the exercise of its rightful powers, in the fulfilment of its appropriate duties, or in the effectuation of its legitimate objects" (p. 98). The Christian Church "asks nothing for her members as Christians, which they are not already entitled to demand as citizens and subjects " (p. 99). The question of a union of Church and State has no place here, since "the Christian Church, as such, has no Nationalty intrusted to its charge" (p. 99). There can be no "Establishment" of the Church of Christ but only of the National Church. C. R. Sanders makes the point well: "The national church . . . since it was an 'estate' of a worldly kingdom, was not to be identified with the Christian church, the ideal institution. It drew strength from the Christian church, but it was not the Christian church." [7]

The second mark of the Christian Church is its visibility. The Church Coleridge is speaking of in all this is not the invisible Church, the "kingdom of God which is within." It is "the Church visible and militant under Christ," an "institution consisting of visible and public communities" (p. 99).

The third mark is the "absence of any visible head or sovereign, and by the non-existence, nay the utter preclusion, of any local or personal centre of unity, of any single source of universal power" (p. 100). What Coleridge has in mind here is obviously the papacy, but it applies as well to the King, who is head of the National Church but not of the Church of Christ.[8] This is not to be construed, how-

---

[7] *Coleridge and the Broad Church Movement*, p. 85.

[8] Coleridge's rejection of the "pretensions" of the Papacy was unremitting. See, for example, *LR*, 64, 177–179; *NTPM*, 71; *CCS*, 100, 101–103 (note), 105–107; *TT*, 448 (May 6, 1833) and 514 (May 31, 1834). See especially the section of *CCS* (108–116) entitled "On the Third

ever, as a rejection of authority in the Church, for Coleridge goes on to maintain strongly, as he did through all the years of his allegiance to the Church of England, the function and authority of the episcopacy. His ideal is, of course, the primitive Church, where "every altar had its own bishop, every flock its own pastor, who derived his authority immediately from Christ, the universal Shepherd, and acknowledged no other superior than the same Christ, speaking by his spirit in the unanimous decision of any number of bishops or elders, according to his promise, *Where two or three are gathered together in my name, there am I in the midst of them*" (p. 101).[9] Even now, despite aberrations like the papacy, usurpation of temporal power by the bishops, and the like, the Bishops of the Church of Christ possess "a spiritual power, which neither King can give, nor King and Parliament take away. As Christian Bishops, they are spiritual pastors, by power of the spirits ruling the flocks committed to their charge" (p. 104).[10] Coleridge wrote in the *Aids to Reflection:* "My fixed principle is: that a Christianity without a Church exercising spiritual authority is vanity and delusion."[11] This implied for him

Possible Church, or the Church of Antichrist," where the "third possible church" is identified with the Roman Church and Antichrist with the Pope. The Roman Catholic doctrine of Infallibility comes particularly under fire in *LR*, 32–33, 176–177, and 333–334. Coleridge seems to vacillate on the role of Councils in the Church. Although we have noted before his general acceptance of the earlier Councils, he speaks elsewhere of the "abuse of Councils" progressively from Nicea to Trent (*LR*, 39) and questions the validity of Councils in matters of doctrine—although he is willing to admit they may be useful in matters of order and discipline. See *LR*, 180–181.

[9] The Scripture reference here is Matthew 18:20.

[10] For other brief comments on the episcopacy, generally affirming its role in the Church—although with varying degrees of acceptance of a privileged episcopal charisma—see *LR*, 31, 142, 146, 270, 323, 330–331; *NTPM*, 143–144; and *NED*, I, 125.

Linked with the question of authority in the Church is the matter of toleration, a virtue for which Coleridge esteemed the Church of England most highly. See his "Apologetic Preface to 'Fire, Famine, and Slaughter,' " written about 1815, in which he speaks of the Church-Establishment as "the greatest, if not the sole safe bulwark of toleration"; see *The Complete Poetical Works of Samuel Taylor Coleridge*, ed. Ernest Hartley Coleridge, 2 vols. (Oxford, 1912), II, Appendix III, 1107–1108. Coleridge's attitude toward toleration itself is generally benevolent. In *Aids* (238 n.), he distinguishes between the belief and the believer, and insists on the need for toleration with respect to the person: "Tolerate no belief that you judge false and of injurious tendency: and arraign no believer. The man is more and other than his belief: and God only knows, how small or how large a part of him the belief in question may be, for good or evil. Resist every false doctrine: and call no man heretic." See also *FR*, 93; *LR*, 87, 131–132, 166, 173. Elsewhere he speaks out against the right of the civil authorities to punish errors in belief; see *NED*, I, 123, and II, 12–14, 23. Once or twice, however, he argues the right of the civil arm to punish heretics, although he admits on one occasion that the right should not be exercised because in practice it has not been successful; see Coleridge's contributions to Southey's "Omniana" (1812) in *NTPM*, 319–321, and *TT*, 498–499 (January 3, 1834).

[11] *Aids*, 295 n.

no rejection of the right of private judgment—although he cautions the unlearned against too easily trusting their own judgment in matters of scriptural interpretation—but rather an insistence on the need for the spiritual activity of both the individual and the Church.[12] The Church's reflection on the spiritual ideas of religion is an endless and developing progress, not so much of intellectual comprehension as of moral growth. In this light, there must be authority on the part of the Church and a reverent docility on the part of the individual. And yet, from another point of view, the individual *is* the Church and so partakes of authority in some degree. The Church is a democracy: there should be "focal points in it, but no superior." [13] As D. G. James expresses Coleridge's idea, "authority must partake of docility, and docility of authority. There cannot fail to be a tension between these two poles of the religious life; but the tension is none the less necessary and healthy." [14]

The last essential mark of the Christian Church is its universality. The Church is "neither Anglican, Gallican, nor Roman, neither Latin nor Greek." The "Catholic and Apostolic Church of England" should more properly be called "the Church of Christ in England" (p. 104). Wherever the characteristics of the true Church are found, there is the one Universal Church present, for "through the presence of its only Head and Sovereign, entire in each and one in all, the Church Universal is spiritually perfect in every true Church, and of course in any number of such Churches, of which from circumstance of place, or the community of country or of language, we have occasion to speak collectively" (p. 105).

A further word remains to be said about the question of Church and State. Although Coleridge rejected the relevance of the phrase in speaking of the Christian Church, he is quite aware of the importance of the question vis-à-vis the National Church. "The Christian Church is not to be considered as a counterpole to any particular State," since its only true contraposition is "the World"; "the phrase, Church and State, has a sense and a propriety in reference to the National Church alone" (p. 99). We have seen already that the relationship of Church and State in the context of the ideal Christian Church

---

[12] *Aids,* 294–295 and n.
[13] *TT,* 316 (May 18, 1830).
[14] *The Romantic Comedy,* p. 236.

is no problem for Coleridge. They are related as two completely distinct entities which cooperate insofar as it is necessary, but "without interference or commixture" (p. 98). Enter the idea of the National Church, and the Church-State problem is immediately relevant, for it is here that Establishment takes place. This is so precisely because, in the Establishment of a National Church, a nation chooses the clergy of a particular church for posts of direction and authority in its Clerisy. The problem arises, therefore, because the spiritual leaders of the Christian Church become also functionaries of the National Church, that is to say, bishops are also prelates.

Concretely, problems of money, land, authority, legal jurisdiction, and the like, are the inevitable result of an "Ignorance respecting the true nature & purpose of a National Church and it's Prelacy: and of it's essential distinction from the Christian Church and it's Episcopacy." This is not to say that it may not be desirable to have the two functions performed by the same individual. "What are distinct, yea different, need not therefore be separated. Two distinct trusts and functions may be vested in and exercised by the same Person: nay, the perfection of the lower of the two Trusts may depend on this union." [15] It is to say, however, that it must always be made clear which function is being exercised. If this is not done, there is constant danger of decisions regarding spiritual matters being made, for example, on the basis of finances or of legal precedent. And historically, Coleridge asserts, this has proven to be the case. As he laments in his notes on Donne's sermons, "O, that our clergy did but know and see that their tithes and glebes belong to them as officers and functionaries of the nationalty,—as clerks, and not exclusively as theologians, and not at all as ministers of the Gospel;—but that they are likewise ministers of the Church of Christ, and that their claims and the powers of that Church are no more alienated or affected by their being at the same time the established clergy, than they are by the common coincidence of being justices of the peace, or heirs to an estate, or stockholders." Coleridge goes on to criticize Donne and his contemporaries for "announcing and enforcing" the claims of the Christian Church on a purely legal basis, often forgetting in the

---

[15] Notes on Richard Baxter's *Catholick Theologie*, in *Coleridge and the Seventeenth Century*, ed. Brinkley, pp. 360–361.

process the more important spiritual values which are not negotiable at law. "This is one evil consequence, though most unnecessarily so, of the union of the Church of Christ with the national Church, and of the claims of the Christian pastor and preacher with the legal and constitutional rights and revenues of the officers of the national clerisy. Our clergymen in thinking of their legal rights, forget those rights of theirs which depend on no human law at all." [16] Thus, although we have already seen that Coleridge does not consider the Church-State problem relevant to the ideal Christian Church, conretely we find him having to face the problem in the dual role of the English churchman. Coleridge's ideal solution is for the spiritual leader of the Christian Church who is also a functionary of the National Church to exercise each of his functions with an awareness both of its distinction and independence from the other and of its need to respect the other's independent rights and obligations—and all this "without interference or commixture." [17]

Up to now, we have spoken only of the visible Church of Christ. One would like to follow this by a detailed explanation of Coleridge's idea of the invisible or spiritual Church. Unfortunately, he has left us only hints and guesses, most of which we have seen already in discussing Coleridge's fragmentary treatment of the doctrine of the Mystical Body of Christ. This much may be said, however, by way of recapitulation. The invisible Church is the spiritual equivalent of the visible Christian Church. The totality of its members, however, are known to God alone, who can alone discern true and false among the Christian churches and who can alone know who of their adherents are truly adherents in their hearts. Its head, like that of its visible counterpart, is Christ alone, and it is by means of the headship of Christ that the Church is one, despite its seeming division, locally and temporally, into particular Christian sects. Christ is the head who gives life to the members of his Mystical Body, the Church.[18]

Throughout his discussion of the nature of the National Church

---

[16] *LR*, 89–90. For other comments of Coleridge on abuses due to confusion of functions, see *LR*, 142–143, 146–147, 332–333; and *NED*, II, 20–21.

[17] *CCS*, 98. See also *FR*, 91–92; *LR*, 363; and *TT*, 343–344 (September 19, 1830), 381 (December 28, 1831).

[18] In addition to the passages cited in the discussion of the Mystical Body (Chapter VI), see *LR*, 180, 182–183, 237, and *CCS*, 102–105, 107.

and the Christian Church, Coleridge is untroubled about his own allegiance to the Church of England. He was thoroughly convinced of the need for an Established Church. Only two months before his death, he spoke feelingly of its importance: "The National Church requires, and is required by, the Christian Church, for the perfection of each: for, if there were no national church, the mere spiritual church would either become, like the papacy, a dreadful tyranny over mind and body, or else would fall abroad into a multitude of enthusiastic sects, as in England in the seventeenth century. It is my deep conviction that, in a country of any religion at all, liberty of conscience can only be permanently preserved by means, and under the shadow of, a national church—a political establishment connected with, but distinct from, the spiritual church." [19] Despite its failings as a National Church and despite the fact that it did not always live up to the ideal of the Christian Church, Coleridge considered the Church of England the best embodiment in the world of the idea of the Church. On September 23, 1833, Coleridge wrote in one of his notebooks that his reason for being "by free preference a Member of the Reformed Church of England" is that it presents "in its' Articles, Liturgy, and intended Constitution and Organization, the purest form of a Christian Church in union with the National Church or Clerisy of a Christianized Country." [20]

In his treatment of the Sacraments, it might be said with some justification that Coleridge is generally orthodox but unenlightening. Except for his rather polemical discussion of Baptism in the *Aids to Reflection,* Coleridge never wrote at length on the Sacraments, but from his frequent brief comments elsewhere it is clear that he was

[19] *TT,* 514 (May 31, 1834).
[20] Notebook 51, ff. [23–23ᵛ]. See also *CL,* IV, 849 (April 1818) and *LR,* 28 (1831). In a conversation on March 9, 1833, he insisted: "There should be no *party* politics in the pulpit, to be sure; but every church in England ought to resound with national politics,—I mean the sacred character of the national church." *TT,* 428. Despite his pride in the Church of England, it is tempered by the human realities. In Notebook 26 (c. 1826), ff. 78–78ᵛ, he wrote of the Established Church that "her Ministers should be attached to her conscientiously on those grounds of fair & decided preference, which an Institution established by human authority, and a scheme of Doctrine, Worship, and Government framed by the imperfect tho' eminent wisdom and piety of men who not only laid no claim to any special & super-human immunity from error for themselves, but demanded of all Fiduciaries of the Church the refusal of such immunity to any particular Church, National or Provincial, their own included, [should call for]."

faithful to the Thirty-Nine Articles.[21] This allegiance still allowed him considerable leeway, however, since the Articles were not intended to be narrowly precise statements of doctrine. They were codified in a time of controversy and in a spirit of compromise. It has been said that "much variety of interpretation has been put upon many of them without improperly straining the text, and probably this license was deliberately intended by their framers." [22]

The object of Article XXV, the general article on the Sacraments, is threefold: to condemn the incomplete view propounded by the Zwinglians and Anabaptists (that the Sacraments are merely "badges or tokens of Christian men's profession") and to insist on the true efficacy of the Sacraments; [23] to distinguish between the two "Sacraments of the Gospel" (Baptism and the Eucharist) and the five "commonly called Sacraments" (Confirmation, Penance, Orders, Matrimony, Extreme Unction); and to insist on the necessity of a worthy disposition in the recipient.[24]

---

[21] It might be noted at the outset that Coleridge was faithful, too, to the form of administration of the Sacraments in the Book of Common Prayer. Bishop Gilbert Burnet (1643–1715) had written in his *History of the Reformation in England* that "the Book of Common Prayer and Administration of the Holy Sacraments set forth by the authority of Parliament, is agreeable to the Scriptures, and that it is Catholic, Apostolic." When he was reading this passage, probably in 1823, Coleridge wrote in the margin: "Amen; as far as the knowledge of its fallible origin is not contradicted by this assent." *NTPM*, 71.

[22] "The Thirty-Nine Articles," *The Oxford Dictionary of the Christian Church*, ed. F. L. Cross (London, 1963), p. 1349.

[23] On Zwingli and the Anabaptists, see G. W. Bromiley, *Baptism and the Anglican Reformers* (London, 1953), p. 173.

[24] See E. C. S. Gibson, *The Thirty-Nine Articles*, II, 588. The text of Article XXV reads, in part, as follows: "Sacraments ordained of Christ be not only badges or tokens of Christian men's profession, but rather they be certain sure witnesses, and effectual signs of grace and God's goodwill towards us, by the which He doth work invisibly in us, and doth not only quicken, but also strengthen and confirm our faith in Him.

"There are two Sacraments ordained of Christ our Lord in the Gospel, that is to say, Baptism, and the Supper of the Lord.

"Those five, commonly called Sacraments, that is to say, Confirmation, Penance, Orders, Matrimony, and Extreme Unction, are not to be counted for Sacraments of the Gospel, being such as have grown partly of the corrupt following of the Apostles, partly are states of life allowed in the Scriptures; but yet have not the like nature of Sacraments with Baptism and the Lord's Supper, for that they have not any visible sign or ceremony ordained of God.

". . . in such only as worthily receive the same, have they a wholesome effect or operation."

It should perhaps be noted that the Article has no intention of rejecting the five "commonly called Sacraments." With the exception of Extreme Unction, which had fallen into disuse, they were "had in reverend estimation" by the Church of England; the point is simply that they are not to be placed on the same level with the two "Sacraments of the Gospel." See Gibson, II, 602–605. Even the Council of Trent insisted that the Sacraments are not all of equal value and importance. See Session VII, Canon 3, in Denzinger-Schönmetzer, n. 1603.

The most that can be said of Coleridge's conception of the efficacy of the Sacraments is that it is vaguely loyal to the Reformation. The Reformers had reacted strongly against Scholastic sacramental theology, which emphasized the role of the material sign as a vehicle of divine grace, and which in turn sometimes led to an overemphasis on what is often called the *ex opere operato* effect of the sacrament, that is, without regard for the dispositions of the recipient.[25] Calvin, for example, avoided this danger of a "magical" element in the sacraments by avoiding entirely the idea of infused grace as a result of sacramental action; he preferred to speak of "the benefits rather than the effects, and of the assurance of the deletion of sins rather than the deletion itself."[26] Luther insisted, especially in his discussion of Baptism, that the proper work of the sacrament is as a work of faith, hence that an act of faith by the recipient is essential for the efficacy of the sacrament, and that the power of the sacrament is in the words rather than in the material elements.[27] By the time of the final codification of the Thirty-Nine Articles in 1571, the common understanding of the efficacy of the Sacraments in the English Church was a Reformed rather than a Scholastic interpretation. G. W. Bromiley suggests that the viewpoint of the Anglican Reformers may be summed up in a statement of the sixteenth-century divine, John Whitgift: "It is a certain and true doctrine to all such as profess the gospel, that the outward signs of the sacrament do not contain in them grace, neither yet that the grace of God is of necessity tied unto them, but only that they be seals of God's promises, notes of Christianity, testimonies and effectual signs of the grace of God."[28]

[25] The phrase *ex opere operato* is used in distinction from *ex opere operantis*, which latter may refer to the dispositions either of the recipient or of the minister of the sacrament. See Karl Rahner and Herbert Vorgrimler, *Theological Dictionary*, ed. Cornelius Ernst, transl. Richard Strachan (New York, 1965), pp. 325–326. This firm stand against the *ex opere operato* effect of the sacraments is borne out in an interesting but incomplete discussion of sacraments in Notebook F, ff. 37^v–38 (1826). Coleridge defines a sacrament there as "a Symbol or Mystery consisting of a sensible sign and a *spiritual* substantiative act—the predicate spiritual distinguishing this act from a physical, and even from a *moral* act, unless in the latter case the act of the soul shall be correlative to an act of the Divine Spirit, and the medium thro' which the gracious influence of the Divine Spirit is conveyed to the Believer." He makes it quite clear that the "medium" of grace in the sacrament is not the sensible sign, but a spiritual act of or in the soul of the believer.

[26] Bromiley, *Baptism and the Anglican Reformers*, p. 173. Bromiley's entire treatment of the historical development of sacramental theology, particularly with reference to Baptism, is excellent. See especially pp. 168–206.

[27] Bromiley, p. 187.

[28] Quoted by Bromiley, p. 193.

It is clear that Coleridge was faithful to this understanding of the efficacy of the sacraments; it is equally clear that he did little to define it further. He seemed not to have been interested in how the sacraments were "effectual signs of grace," except to deny the efficacy of the material sign itself and to insist on the importance of faith and of worthy dispositions in the recipient. In his 1819 lecture on the Schoolmen he traced the genesis of what he considered sacramental superstition:

here was the spiritual degraded into an image, and secondly, the image was unnaturally made to possess spiritual powers . . . Man cannot deprive himself of his moral feelings altogether. He cannot deprive himself of that instinct which still teaches him that there is something which is better than his senses or the mere organs of his body can present to him; but he has it in his power to confound what he cannot destroy, and to give to the spirit the attributes of the body, and to give to the body the attributes of the spirit, to make an image real, to make a wafer possess omnipresence, and to make the spiritual corporeal, the heterogeneous homogeneous. This is the character of superstition in all ages: it is the confounding of the spiritual with the bodily.[29]

In 1828, evidently after rereading what he had written of Baptism in the *Aids to Reflection,* Coleridge wrote in one of his notebooks of his desire to prove "the substantial accordance of my Scheme with that of our Church." He then went on to reassert, somewhat more clearly, the position he had taken in *Aids:* "I still say that an act of the Spirit *in time,* as that it might be asserted, the moment of the uttering the words, I baptize Thee in the name of, &c., *Now* the

---

[29] *PL,* 267–268. Coleridge spoke out often against "superstitious abuses" of the sacraments, like the early practice of "deferring of the Baptismal rite to a late period of life, and even to the deathbed, in the belief that the mystic water would . . . send him pure and spotless into the other world." *Aids,* 339. For another example of his attack on belief in the spiritual power of the material sign, see *LR,* 251–252.

In the philosophical lecture preceding the one quoted above, Coleridge spoke more tolerantly of Christian ceremonies, praising them as a practical expression of speculative truth. "The Christian religion as an historical fact differed from all the institutions of the ancients in this point, that great truths were connected with all its ceremonies . . . Christianity first of all destroyed the pernicious distinction between truth and reality, between the practical and that which was merely speculative . . . And even in an excess of ceremonies, still there was a more or less visible connexion between each ceremony and an opinion represented thereby." *PL,* 260–261. Somewhat the same idea seems to be suggested in *Aids,* 128, and *LR,* 83–84. This may be contrasted with his "pious condescension" to such vestiges of popery as holy water, relics, and the like, in *LR,* 45.

Spirit *begins* to act—is false in Philosophy and contrary to Scripture."[30] What was of crucial importance to Coleridge, as to the Reformers, was faith; for it is faith which justifies, not external works, whether these be "meritorious actions" (as in the preceding chapter) or material sacramental signs. As he wrote in the *Aids to Reflection:*

> . . . it is neither the outward ceremony of Baptism, under any form or circumstances, nor any other ceremony, but such a faith in Christ as tends to produce a conformity to his holy doctrines and example in heart and life, and which faith is itself a declared mean and condition of our partaking of his spiritual body, and of being *clothed upon* with his righteousness,—that properly makes us Christians, and can alone be enjoined as an article of faith necessary to salvation, so that the denial thereof may be denounced as a damnable heresy. In the strictest sense of essential, this alone is the essential in Christianity, that the same spirit should be growing in us which was in the fulness of all perfection in Christ Jesus. Whatever else is named essential, is such because, and only as far as, it is instrumental to this, or evidently implied herein.[31]

It seems fairly clear that Coleridge has left the way open to some kind of efficacy for the sacramental sign, and yet an efficacy not of its own but derived from the faith of which it is an external sign. Is it in effect a kind of sacramental occasionalism, in which God grants grace on the occasion of the sacramental sign but has in no way bound himself to do so? We can only guess, since Coleridge has clarified the matter no further.

Coleridge accepted, of course, the distinction between the two "Sacraments of the Gospel" and the others, and naturally enough the two Great Sacraments drew his attention most often.[32] With regard to Baptism, almost the entire focus of his attention was taken up

---

[30] Notebook 37, f. 80. The same passage later indicates Coleridge's belief that the external sign gives certainty only of the recipient's acceptance by the Church, not of the inner action of the Spirit: "Except the time when the Church receives the subject into her own body, and co-organizes the person therewith, no time can be specified for the Spirit's descent and incoming. For the operations of the Spirit are as little referable to Time as to Space." In one's conduct toward and judgment of the person baptized, however, he must presume the "regenerate presence of the Holy Spirit" promised to the members of the Mystical Body. The whole of this notebook passage is transcribed by Shedd in *Aids,* 347–349.

[31] *Aids,* 338. The original draft of this passage is in Notebook 24, ff. 51–51^v.

[32] Coleridge speaks of the distinction in *LR,* 236 (where he suggests the term "Mysteries" for the former, "Sacraments" for the latter), and in *LR,* 356 (where he refers to the latter group as *"quasi sacramenta"*).

with his polemic against Infant Baptism. This is not to say that he was not a respecter of the traditional Anglican ceremony. He loved it dearly, was deeply moved by it, and several times acted as godfather for the children of his friends. He is quoted as saying in conversation in 1832: "I think the baptismal service almost perfect. What seems erroneous assumption in it to me, is harmless. None of the services of the church affect me so much as this. I never could attend a christening without tears bursting forth at the sight of the helpless innocent in a pious clergyman's arms." [33]

But Coleridge did not always consider the "erroneous assumption" to be quite "harmless." From other sources, one may guess that the first assumption Coleridge has in mind is that there is a need for the baptism of infants. He makes it clear very often that he does not believe there is such a need, that the practice of Infant Baptism was not the practice of the early Church, and that it was only introduced in the fifth century when St. Augustine, "in the fever of his Anti-Pelagian dispute had introduced the Calvinistic interpretation of Original Sin, and the dire state of infants dying unbaptized." [34] What is involved is the conception of "Original Sin in the sense of actual guilt," and the practice of Infant Baptism on the basis of such a conception "supposes and most certainly encourages a belief concerning a God, the most blasphemous and intolerable." [35] Children are guiltless, and therefore are not liable to punishment. "Did not the Lord himself say of *unbaptised* children 'of such are the kingdom of heaven'?" [36] For, in fact, "the infant is *de se* of the kingdom of heaven. Christ blessed them, not in order to make them so, but because they already were so." [37]

At first glance, one is tempted to ask how this innocence of infants is reconcilable with Coleridge's belief in a doctrine of Original Sin. But a moment's recollection of the nature of Coleridge's idea of Original Sin makes it clear that in his mind there was probably no contradiction at all. For Coleridge, Original Sin is essentially the

---

[33] *TT*, 410 (August 9, 1832). See also *LR*, 186; the "Letter to His Godchild" (July 13, 1834), written for Adam Steinmetz Kennard twelve days before Coleridge's own death, in *LR*, 565–567; and the poem "My Baptismal Birth-Day" (*Poems*, I, 490), together with the reflection on his own state of mind when composing it, preserved by Mrs. Watson in *Coleridge at Highgate*, p. 151.

[34] *Aids*, 337 n. On Coleridge's denial of the practice of Infant Baptism in the early Church, see also *LR*, 34, and *NED*, II, 9–10.

[35] *LR*, 192.

[36] *NED*, II, 12.

[37] *LR*, 187. See also *LR*, 188.

corruption of the human will, innate and ultimately mysterious. Where there is no operable will, as in an infant, it would be meaningless to talk of such a corruption. Original Sin only becomes real when the will becomes real, that is, when the child reaches the age of reason. To my knowledge, Coleridge never made this illation in his writings, but it is reasonable to suppose that the two beliefs were interdependent in his thinking. At any rate they are remarkably consistent with one another.

Closely linked with Coleridge's denial of the need for the Baptism of infants is another assumption implicit in the practice: that a sacrament can be efficacious in any except those who "worthily receive the same" (Article XXV). Since an infant does not yet have the use of reason and will, "an ordinance of admission to Christian membership, pre-requiring on the part of the competitor knowledge, repentance, and faith, is a definition that will not agree with Infant Baptism." And yet, Coleridge goes on, one cannot deny "the positive, oft-repeated injunctions of Christ and Scripture, demanding previous faith and repentance in the subject to be baptised." [38]

Despite Coleridge's theoretical objections to Infant Baptism, he had no difficulty about accepting the practice of his Church and the recommendation of Infant Baptism in Article XXVII as "most agreeable with the institution of Christ." He had only to consider the Baptism of the infant as a sign pointing toward the future, an acceptance of the child by the Church in some sense, to be ratified by the child's later act of faith. As he wrote in 1815, Infant Baptism must be regarded as "a sacrament of *conditional promise* and as a *means of grace*, but not as a sacrament of *effect,* and an immediate *conveyance* of grace." [39] In 1828, he accepted an invitation to be godfather with the comment: "I shall be much gratified by standing beside the

[38] *NED,* II, 48. See also *NED,* II, 30, and *LR,* 187–188, 190–192. In *LR,* 273, Coleridge rejects Luther's belief that faith is actually given to the infant in preparation for Baptism, "although with our natural sense and reason we neither see nor understand it." A single notebook entry of 1828 admits the possibility of the influence of God on the infant's soul, but Coleridge does not pretend to know any more of it beyond what is suggested by the obvious presence of nascent reason: "I do not deny (God forbid!) the possibility or the reality of the influence of the Spirit on the Soul of the Infant. The first smile bespeaks a Reason (the *Light* from the Life of the Word)." Notebook 37, f. 79.

[39] *CL,* IV, 581 (August 2, 1815). See also pp. 581–582 of the same letter, where Coleridge indulges in some rather specious arguments to the effect that one of the prayers in the baptismal ceremony of the Book of Common Prayer "evidently implies that the actual operation of the Spirit is future and conditional." One need only read through the whole text of the ceremony to find this assertion contradicted.

baptismal font as one of the sponsors of the little pilgrim at his inauguration into the rights and duties of Immortality, and he shall not want my prayers, nor aught else that shall be within my power, to assist him in *becoming* that of which the Great Sponsor who brought light and immortality into the world has declared him an emblem." [40]

In his occasional comments on the sacrament of the Eucharist, Coleridge remained faithful to Article XXVIII, on the Lord's Supper.[41] Coleridge followed the Article, first of all, in his consistent assertion of the real presence of the Body and Blood of Christ in the sacrament. For the mature Coleridge, this was never in doubt.[42] What did occasionally attract his attention was the matter of *how* Christ is present in the Eucharist. Although he never approached a satisfactory solution to the problem, his most serious suggestion involves a distinction between the noumenal and the phenomenal Christ, which seems to correspond, though somewhat vaguely, to a distinction between spiritual and sensible. His clearest explanation of it is in the form of a comment on a passage of Jeremy Taylor. Taylor had raised the question "whether, when we say we believe Christ's body to be really in the Sacrament, we mean 'that body, that flesh, that was born of the Virgin Mary, that was crucified, dead, and buried?' I answer, that I know none else that he had or hath: there is but one body of Christ natural and glorified." Coleridge retorts: "This may be true, or at least intelligible, of Christ's humanity or personal identity as νόητόν τι [an intelligible entity], but applied to the phenomenal flesh and blood, it is nonsense. For if every atom of the human frame be changed by succession in eleven or twelve years,

---

[40] *LSTC*, II, 750 (August 14, 1828).

[41] Article XXVIII says, in part: "The Supper of the Lord is not only a sign of the love that Christians ought to have among themselves one to another; but rather it is a sacrament of our redemption by Christ's death: insomuch that to such as rightly, worthily, and with faith, receive the same, the bread which we break is a partaking of the body of Christ; and likewise the cup of blessing is a partaking of the blood of Christ.

"Transubstantiation (or the change of the substance of bread and wine) in the Supper of the Lord, cannot be proved by Holy Writ; but is repugnant to the plain words of Scripture, overthroweth the nature of a sacrament, and hath given occasion to many superstitions.

"The body of Christ is given, taken, and eaten, in the Supper, only after an heavenly and spiritual manner. And the mean whereby the body of Christ is received and eaten in the Supper is faith."

[42] See, for example, Coleridge's notes on several of Jeremy Taylor's works on the Eucharist, in *LR*, 218–230, passim; also *SM*, Appendix B, 469; *Aids*, 305–306 and note; *TT*, 316–317 (May 20, 1830).

the body born of the Virgin could not be the body crucified, much less the body crucified be the body glorified, spiritual and incorruptible." His idea is clearly that of a nonsensible intelligible humanity which perdures beneath the inevitable changes of growth and corruption and so gives continuity to the individual being. It is in this sense that he asserts that "Christ, both in the institution of the Eucharist and in the sixth chapter of John, spoke of his humanity as a *noumenon,* not of the specific flesh and blood which were its *phaenomena* at the last supper and on the cross." [43]

In the last analysis, however, Coleridge himself seems to be impatient at these attempts to explain the mystery of the presence of the Body of Christ in the Eucharist. He concludes his own attempt, just quoted from his notes on Taylor, with a suggestion for a straightforward expression of belief on which the Lutheran, the English, and the Roman Churches could agree. He suggests that the formula worked out by the Colloquy of Poissy in 1561, "used with implicit faith, shall suffice." It reads: *"Credimus in usu coenae Dominicae vere, reipsa, substantialiter, seu in substantia, verum corpus et sanguinem Christi spirituali et ineffabili modo esse, exhiberi, sumi a fidelibus communicantibus."* [44] A briefer expression of this same acceptance of the mystery is found in a notebook entry of the 1820's, in which Coleridge characterizes Luther's final position on the Eucharist as "the true Christian doctrine of the Sacrament—Christus est *spiritualiter* in Sacramento. Quo modo, non nobis est perscrutari. Nam credimus: Modum nescimus." [45]

[43] *LR,* 222. In this context, Coleridge refers to a passage of Clement of Alexandria quoted by Taylor. Coleridge says that he himself, unlike Taylor, interprets Clement's words literally, and that they "perfectly express my opinion." I quote the passage as it is transcribed by Shedd: "Dupliciter vero sanguis Christi et caro intelligitur, spiritualis illa atque divina, de qua ipse dixit, Caro mea vere est cibus, &c., vel caro et sanguis, quae crucifixa est, et qui militis effusus est lancea." Translation (my own): "The blood and flesh of Christ is understood in a double sense: that spiritual and divine [flesh and blood] of which he said, 'My flesh is truly food, etc.'; or the flesh which was crucified, and the blood which poured forth at the thrust of the soldier's lance." For this same distinction, see also *Aids,* 306 n.; *LR,* 64–65, 219, 220; *TT,* 453 (May 15, 1833); *NTPM,* 72 (1823). See also *LR,* 245. For other hints and guesses as to the mode of Christ's presence in the Eucharist, see Coleridge's notes on Jeremy Taylor, *LR,* 218–230.

[44] *LR,* 223. Translation (my own): "We believe that in the practice of the Lord's Supper, the true Body and Blood of Christ truly, really, substantially (that is, in substance), in a spiritual and inexpressible manner, is present, is manifested, and is received by the faithful who communicate."

[45] Notebook 22½, f. 39ᵛ. Translation (my own): "Christ is *spiritually* present in the Sacrament. How this is so, it is not for us to search out. For we believe: the means we know not."

Coleridge follows Article XXVIII, too, in his consistent rejection of the Roman Catholic doctrine of Transubstantiation, according to which the substance of bread and wine is changed into the substance of the body and blood of Christ, "which thereby become present while the empirical realities as phenomena ["species" or "accidents"] of bread and wine remain." [46] The Article condemns the doctrine of Transubstantiation on four grounds: it cannot be proven from Scripture; it is, in fact, repugnant to Scripture; it destroys the nature of a sacrament (because if the bread no longer remains after consecration, the "outward visible sign" of the sacrament has been destroyed); and it has been the occasion of superstitious practices.[47] Coleridge is much less positive in his rejection. "I find no necessary absurdity in Transubstantiation," he wrote in his notes on Taylor. "The substrate or *causa invisibilis* may be the *noumenon* or actuality, *das Ding in sich,* of Christ's humanity, as well as the *Ding in sich* of which the sensation, bread, is the appearance." The problem is that "there is not a word of sense possible to prove that it is really so." [48] The only objection Coleridge offers in common with the Article is its lack of basis in Scripture: "I honestly confess that I should confine my grounds of opposition to the article [of Transubstantiation] thus stated to its unnecessariness, to the want of sufficient proofs from Scripture that I am bound to believe or trouble my head with it." [49] Ultimately, Coleridge seems to reject Transubstantiation because it serves no useful function. He does not see that it offers any real understanding, any insight into what is finally a mystery. "I say again and again, that I myself greatly

[46] Rahner-Vorgrimler, *Theological Dictionary*, p. 466. The doctrine of Transubstantiation was defined by the Council of Trent in Session XIII, Canon 2; see Denzinger-Schönmetzer, n. 1652. It has often been presumed (e.g. Gibson, *The Thirty-Nine Articles*, II, 656) that Trent was here defining the Eucharist in terms of the Scholastic theory of substance and accidents. Modern theologians and historians of theology find it clear, however, that no such definition of the mode of Christ's presence was intended: " 'Substance' means that which, taken in its ultimate being and significance, makes the offering bread (and nothing more) or the Body of Christ; 'species' means that which in the world of ordinary human experience is accessible to us." Rahner-Vorgrimler, p. 466.

[47] See Gibson, *The Thirty-Nine Articles*, II, 656–658.

[48] *LR*, 245. The passage goes on to object further that Christ himself declared that "his words were to be understood spiritually, that is, figuratively." See also *LR*, 227, 382. In a somewhat similar passage in the *Aids*, Coleridge objects that he can find in himself no faculty "by which there can be presented to me a matter distinguishable from accidents, and a substance that is different from both. It is true, I have a faculty of articulation; but I do not see that it can be improved by my using it for the formation of words without meaning, or at best, for the utterance of thoughts, that mean only the act of so thinking, or of trying so to think." *Aids*, 224–225.

[49] *LR*, 219–220.

prefer the general doctrine of our own Church respecting the Eucharist,—*rem credimus, modum nescimus* [we know the fact, how it is so we know not]." [50]

The third major element of Eucharistic belief emphasized in Article XXVIII is the essential role of faith in the sacrament of the Eucharist. Coleridge articulated this role only rarely in the context of this sacrament, but probably he saw little need to emphasize it. One rare expression of it merits attention, however, since his argument is the same he used against Infant Baptism: without will there is no faith, without faith there is no sacrament. "Surely the wafer and the tea-spoonful of wine might be swallowed by an infant, as well as water be sprinkled upon him. But if the former is not the Eucharist because without faith and repentance, so can not the latter, it would seem, be Baptism. For they are declared equal adjuncts of both Sacraments." [51]

So little did Coleridge depart from the Article of his Church on the Lord's Supper that a summary by E. C. S. Gibson of the Anglican teaching on the Eucharist may well stand as almost an epitome of Coleridge's own belief on the question:

. . . while the doctrine of the real Presence is distinctly taught, and the theory of Transubstantiation is condemned, there is an entire absence of any counter theory of the manner of the Presence. And in this lies the real strength of the position taken up by the Church of England. She devoutly accepts her Lord's words. She does not attempt to explain them away or to resolve them into a mere figure. But, on the other hand, she is content to hold them as a mystery. Her Lord has not explained them. He has nowhere revealed "how" His Body and Blood are present; and therefore she declines to speculate on the *manner,* and rejects as no part of the Church's faith all theories on the subject presented to her, whether that of Transubstantiation, or the Lutheran tenet of Consubstantiation.[52]

---

[50] *LR,* 227. See also *LR,* 382. But contrast this with his undated note on Donne in *LR,* 84–85, in which he speaks of the phrase *"rem credimus, modum nescimus"* as a "poor evasion." Probably for much the same reason of uselessness, Coleridge also rejects the theory of "Impanation" and Luther's theory of "Consubstantiation," both of which involve the Real Presence of Christ together with the substance of bread and wine. See *LR,* 84, 227, 382.

[51] *LR,* 190. See also *LR,* 83–84.

[52] Gibson, *The Thirty-Nine Articles,* II, 662–663. We should add here a touching notebook entry of 1827: "Christmas day. Received the Sacrament—for the first time since my first year at Jesus College. Christ is gracious even to the Laborer that cometh to his vineyard at the eleventh hour—33 years absent from my Master's Table. Yet I humbly hope, that spiritually I have fed on the Flesh & Blood, the Strength and the Life of the Son of God

Coleridge has little to say of the other sacraments, the five "commonly called Sacraments." Generally speaking, he seems to adopt the somewhat ambiguous stance of Article XXV: they do not qualify as "Sacraments of the Gospel" since they "have not any visible sign or ceremony ordained of God," and yet they are revered and (except for Extreme Unction) reverently employed in the Church. For the Anglican Church, Confirmation is a rite of Apostolic origin, as is clear from Acts 8:17 and 19:6, but was not clearly instituted by Christ himself in the Gospel. Penance was instituted by Christ (John 20:23), but it does not have a visible sign ordained by God. Orders, too, was instituted by Christ (John 20:21–23), but the outward sign of the imposition of hands is not found in the Gospel. Matrimony is an "honourable estate" and is symbolic of the union between Christ and his Church, but it does not have its origin in the Gospel and has no visible sign instituted by God. Extreme Unction, long fallen into disuse in the Church of England, may perhaps be traced to James 5:14–15, but was not ordained by Christ.[53]

To his acceptance of the belief and practice of his Church concerning Confirmation, Coleridge adds one interesting argument in its favor. He feels that Protestant divines would be well advised to turn away from attempts to relate the explicit teaching of the Fathers on Confirmation to the "remote, arbitrary, and fine-drawn inferences from the few passages of the New Testament which can be forced into an implied sanction of a rite nowhere mentioned." Instead, they should consider the value of the rite in itself as a ratification of the promises of Baptism. "How much more rational and convincing . . . would it have been to have shown, that when from various causes the practice of Infant Baptism became general in the Church, Confirmation or the acknowledgment *in propria persona* of the obligations

---

in his divine Humanity during the latter years. The administration of Communion Service of our church is solemn & affecting—& very far to be preferred both to the Romish, which may excite awe & wonder in such as believe the real transmutation of the Bread & Wine, but [?assuredly] no individual comfort or support—and to the form among our Dissenters, who practice what to the shame of our Church the great majority of our own Clergymen teach—& cold and flat the ceremonial is, as how can it be otherwise, when the Eucharist is considered as a mere and very forced visual metaphor for the mere purpose of reminding the Partakers of a single event, the sensible crucifixion of Jesus, and without any connection with that masterful Mystery revealed in John VI, of which the Eucharist is at once symbol & instance." Notebook 36, ff. 32^v–33.

[53] On the Anglican teaching concerning these sacraments, see Gibson, *The Thirty-Nine Articles*, II, 602–610.

that had been incurred by proxy was introduced; and needed no other justification than its own evident necessity." [54]

When Coleridge speaks of the sacrament of Penance, it is generally to inveigh against the attribution to a human instrument of the power to forgive sins, against the belief that "the mere will of a priest could have any effect on the everlasting weal or woe of a Christian." [55] All that is required for God's forgiveness is faith and repentance. If these are present a priest may declare remission of sins, but this is only "declarative" and not "operant." [56]

In spite of his own unfortunate marriage, Coleridge had a lofty view of the sacrament of Matrimony. "It might be a mean [sic] of preventing many unhappy marriages," he wrote in the *Aids to Reflection*, "if the youth of both sexes had it early impressed on their minds, that marriage contracted between Christians is a true and perfect symbol or mystery; that is, the actualizing faith being supposed to exist in the receivers, it is an outward sign co-essential with that which it signifies, or a living part of that, the whole of which it represents." Marriage is, he continued (referring to Ephesians 5:22–23), "symbolical of the union of the soul with Christ the Mediator," and it is "perfectly a sacramental ordinance." It was not kept among the sacraments by the Reformers, first, because the sign of marriage is not proper to the Christian Church alone and because its origin is not in the Gospel itself, and second, because it is not a means of grace for all members. "It is not a sacrament of the Church, but only of certain individual members of the Church." It remains, however, truly sacramental and a "great mystery." [57]

[54] Notes on Jeremy Taylor, *LR*, 247. On Confirmation, see also *LR*, 146, 250–251; *NED*, II, 31, 35. Coleridge refers to his own Confirmation in *LR*, 250.

[55] *LR*, 315.

[56] *LR*, 200–201. See also *NTPM*, 74 (1809), and *LR*, 279. Also see *LR*, 212, where Coleridge suggests that the command of John 20:23 ("Whose sins you shall forgive, they are forgiven them . . .") necessarily involves the gift of "reading the hearts of men," and that it "amounts to no more than the rejection or admission of men according to their moral fitness or unfitness, the truth or unsoundness of their faith and repentance." He suggests further that "the promise, like the miraculous insight which it implies, was given to the Apostles and first disciples exclusively, and that it referred almost wholly to the admission of professed converts to the Church of Christ." It might be recalled that private auricular confession was not the practice of the Church of England in Coleridge's day.

[57] *Aids*, 138 n. See also *TT*, 349 (September 27, 1830). There is some vacillation in Coleridge's mind, however, on the sacramentality of marriage. In 1826, the year following the publication of the *Aids*, he specifically retracted (in Notebook F, f. 37ᵛ) the note in *Aids* which we have just cited. He reasoned that to be perfectly a sacramental ordinance, "the substantiative act must be *spiritual* . . . and not merely a *moral* Act." In 1827, however, he

Of Holy Orders Coleridge wrote nothing, except for several marginal references in favor of the imposition of hands in the ceremony of Ordination. This imposition is "more and other than a mere delegation of office, a mere legitimating acceptance and acknowledgment." The imposition, with the words "Receive the Holy Spirit," involves "some infusion of power or light, something given and inwardly received, which would not have existed in and for the recipient without this immission by the means or act of the imposition of the hands." [58] Of Extreme Unction Coleridge wrote nothing at all.

It is difficult not to be disappointed in Coleridge's treatment of the Church and the Sacraments. His discussion of the Church has much that is rich and exciting, it is true—his insights, for example, into the nature of a National Church—but his failure to develop the idea of the Church as the Mystical Body of Christ is a disappointment, and his fragmentary treatment of the Sacraments yields, we have seen, only sporadic insights. One might have hoped for him to place the Sacraments, and the Church as the "great Sacrament," in the context of his expansive idea of the nature of symbols as products of the imagination, "that reconciling and mediatory power, which incorporating the reason in images of the sense, and organizing (as it were) the flux of the senses by the permanence and self-circling energies of the reason, gives birth to a system of symbols, harmonious in themselves, and consubstantial with the truths of which they are the conductors." [59] As it is, one can only be grateful for the moments of insight—and wonder what might have been.

There remains one other "means of sanctification" of which Cole-

---

seems to have returned to his original position, citing St. Paul, who "so profoundly calls Marriage a great Mystery, or Sacramental Symbol"; see Notebook 35, f. 41.

In *LR*, 179, Coleridge hierarchizes the ends of Christian marriage: the "proper and essential ends" are "the moral, social, and spiritual helps and comforts"; the procreation of children is a "contingent consequence." On the latter, see also his notes on the Book of Common Prayer, *LR*, 24.

An interesting note in Notebook 29 (ff. 46–46ᵛ) suggests an Old Testament foundation for marriage as a religious institution. He sees the account of the creation of woman in Genesis not as a description of a physical action of God, but as a "poetic Myth (μῦθος)" which represents "the institution of Marriage as a *positive* ordinance of Religion."

[58] *LR*, 145; and see 359.

[59] *SM*, 436. Very occasionally Coleridge reaches tantalizingly for his idea of symbol in the context of the Sacraments, only to leave the link undeveloped. See, for example, the passage on marriage quoted above from *Aids* (128); and *LR*, 224 and 293–294.

ridge wrote: prayer.[60] In an early poem, writing of God, Coleridge had said:

> Of whose omniscient and all-spreading Love
> Aught to *implore* were impotence of mind.[61]

Shortly afterwards, he recanted the sentiment of these lines, "it being written in Scripture, '*Ask,* and it shall be given you,' and my human reason being moreover convinced of the propriety of offering *petitions* as well as thanksgivings to Deity." [62] He was never to swerve from this attitude, and the passage of years only deepened his conviction.

As he came to realize more and more the innate weakness of man's finite will, Coleridge came more and more to see prayer as an essential means of achieving the necessary union of the finite will with the Absolute Will. Prayer became for him "the effort to connect the misery of the self with the blessedness of God." [63] And yet this act is supernatural, performed under the influence of grace, and so is an act both of God and of man. God's "Gifts, Aids, and Defences will be bestowed on man in such manner that they shall be the product and consequents of his own Act and Will; but from another no less indispensable Postulate we are compelled to declare them the results of the Divine Act and Will; . . . the gifts, aids and interventions of the Divine Power . . . are consequent on an Act and Will of the Recipient, which yet is at the same time the Act and Will of the

[60] The concern here is primarily with "prayer of petition." The importance of prayer of praise and thanksgiving is generally presumed in Coleridge. See, for example, his beautiful "Nightly Prayer" (1831) in *LR*, 19–21.

[61] "To a Friend," *Complete Poetical Works*, I, 79. The poem was written for Charles Lamb in 1794.

[62] The "recantation" appeared in the 1797 and 1803 editions of Coleridge's poems; I quote it from E. H. Coleridge's note in the *Complete Poetical Works*, I, 79. It should be noted that prayer, for Coleridge, is to be directed to God alone, not to saints or other intercessors. In his copy of Richard Field's treatise *Of the Church* he notes that, since we do not know whether or not the saints pray to God for us, we "ought to act as if we knew they did not . . . for whatever ye do, do it in faith"; *LR*, 63. See also *LR*, 60, 517; *NTPM*, 276–277; and Notebook F, ff. 47ᵛ–48, 59 (c. 1826). In another marginal comment on Field, however, there is a suggestion that his opposition may really be to the particular practices of Roman Catholic "worship" of the saints: "The communion and intercession of Saints is an idea, and must be kept such. But the Romish church has changed it away into the detail of particular and individual conceptions, and imaginations, into names and fancies"; *LR*, 66.

[63] Huntington MS. on the Divine Ideas, as quoted by Muirhead, *Coleridge as Philosopher*, p. 220. Muirhead's folio reference is incorrect, but I have been unable to ascertain the correct one.

Divine Spirit . . . Now these conditions can be found realized only in Faith and Prayer." This, then, is the "Idea of Prayer": a "state of Being, in which the productive energy is the produce, where the agent is at the same moment and the self-same Act the patient, & wrestling conquers for himself what is yet bestowed on him of free grace." [64] This "produce" is, of course, union of the finite will with the Absolute Will.

Prayer as Coleridge conceived it was no easy matter. It will be noticed that he referred to it as "wrestling." As he said to his nephew Henry Nelson Coleridge two years before his death, "*to pray, to pray* as God would have us; this is what at times makes me turn cold to my soul." He continued: "Believe me, to pray with all your heart and strength, with the reason and the will, to believe vividly that God will listen to your voice through Christ, and verily do the thing he pleaseth thereupon—that is the last, the greatest achievement of the Christian's warfare on earth. *Teach* us to pray, O Lord!" With that, Henry Coleridge reports, he burst into tears and begged his nephew to pray for him. [65] Such wrestling is warfare indeed, for it involves wrestling for the submission of one's own will. "Prayer is faith passing into act; a union of the will and the intellect realizing in an intellectual act. It is the whole man that prays. Less than this is wishing, or lip-work; a charm or a mummery." [66]

Within the context of such prayer, man may properly pray not only for his spiritual good but even for temporal needs. "Provided only that our *spiritual* interests be, generally, the predominant, and *always* the ultimate Object, neither our bodily, nor our temporal, needs and concernments are excluded from the requests that may be offered in Faith." [67] The presumption is that man, who sees only fit-fully the pattern of his life, is ready to accept the Will of God, who

---

[64] Notebook 34 (1827), ff. 10–12ʳ. In the same notebook, f. 8, Coleridge wrote: "No Liberty but by co-incidence with the Divine Will—& hence the doctrines of the Spirit—No faith but by the Father's leading—no effectual Prayer but by the *Spirit.*" For this same insistence on the need of God's grace for true prayer, see *LR*, 292. A fine passage in *CCS*, 132–134, insists on the need for the exercise of one's human faculties in a reasonable way, that is, that prayer does not take away one's responsibility for thought and decision. Coleridge inveighs against the belief that men should "wilfully blind themselves to the light, which [God] had himself given them, as the contra-distinguishing character of their humanity, without which they could not pray to him at all."

[65] *TT*, 327 n. For a similar expression, see *CL*, III, 478 (April 26, 1814).

[66] Notes on the Book of Common Prayer, *LR*, 21 (probably c. 1827).

[67] *UL*, II, 395 (1827).

sees man's life whole; that is to say, man's "ultimate object" must be his spiritual good. With this proviso, there will be no conflict between man's will and the Divine Providence. Man can know his ultimate goal of union with God, but in the choice of means toward that goal he has less certainty. He chooses as best he can, but when he works and prays for them, he must leave his reason open to the clearer light of the Absolute Reason. In this sense, whether one's particular petition has been granted or whether Divine Providence has moved him into a better way unknown to him, his prayer has been answered. "Of *the End* we can safely judge, for Revelation & Reason have determined it. Whenever therefore we contemplate a linked series of facts in the light of a known *end* as means to that end, by this [?render] a *synopsis* of those facts, we reason safely—but when on the contrary we anticipate the end by inference from any particular fact, or desire a particular event as *the* means to an ultimate *end,* we forget our imperfections & fallibility, prescribe to God, & worship in appetite & passion, not in Spirit & a conformed Will." [68]

Coleridge's position has not been better summarized than by J. H. Muirhead: "If the Whole is spiritual, and therefore in the end providential, it is not by having things altered from without that we have to seek the goal of union with Its spirit, but by accepting them, whether in the natural or the moral world, just as they are and turning them to the ends of the spirit. Even as man's material progress is wrought not by magic but by the ministry of physical nature, so his moral and religious progress is wrought by the ministry of psychical nature. If prayer, as Coleridge held it to be, is the effort to live in the spirit of the Whole, it attains its highest level not in the assertion of our will, as in petition, but in the acceptance of God's will as including ends beyond the particular and the present, in the words 'not as I will, but as Thou wilt.' " [69]

If a common note has been struck in this treatment of the "means of sanctification" in Coleridge, surely it is that of the cooperation of God and man in the work of man's sanctification. The Church is divine and human: there is the National Church and the Church of Christ; there is a visible Church and a Church unseen and unnum-

[68] Notebook 47 (1830), ff. [10ᵛ–11].
[69] Muirhead, *Coleridge as Philosopher*, pp. 232–233.

bered; there is visible human authority but under the invisible head-ship of Christ. The Sacraments are efficacious signs of God's grace, but they require the cooperation of man's worthy disposition of faith. Prayer is man's effort, aided by grace, to achieve union of his finite will with the Absolute Will. The sign of the Incarnation is every-where in Coleridge. God has become man, and man in turn must strive, with God's help, to become one with the God-Man.

❀ VIII. THE LAST THINGS

Traditionally, the last things are Death, Judgment, Heaven and Hell. Coleridge was little interested in the first two of these; he was more taken up with the nature of life after death than with death itself. He spoke of death only in passing, usually moving on quickly to speak of the eternal life which death portends. Coleridge criticized his admired Jeremy Taylor because he "greatly degrades the mind of man by causelessly representing death as an evil in itself." He concedes that death may be looked upon as a "crisis, or phenomenal change, incident to a progressive being," but even in such a conception it "ought as little to be thought so, as the casting of the caterpillar's skin to make room for the wings of the butterfly. It is the unveiling of the Psyche." [1] Physical death is only a passage to further life.

Coleridge touched on several arguments for man's immortality. In his most extended discussion of man's future life, in the *Aids to Reflection,* he began with the classic argument from the inequity of the present order of things, the evident "disproportion between moral worth and worldly prosperity" which must somehow be redressed in a future life.[2] This reflection has the unquestionable value, Coleridge says, of "exciting well-disposed and spiritually awakened natures . . . to mature the presentiment of immortality into full consciousness, into a principle of action and a well-spring of strength and consolation." Of itself, however, it is not enough. "It must be referred to far deeper grounds, common to man as man." [3] This "deeper ground" is the instinctiveness and universality of man's belief in his own immortality. Just as, for example, the bull-calf butts

1 *LR,* 203. See also *LR,* 282, 548–549, 551–552. Coleridge speaks of the Last Judgment in *LR,* 244, but only of the general judgment at the end of the world, not of a particular judgment.

2 *Aids,* 327. On this argument, see also *TT,* 517 (June 23, 1834). The entire discussion of man's future life is in *Aids,* 326–333. In a long note in *Aids,* 300–301, Coleridge discusses, without settling it one way or the other, the question of whether man's immortality is a supernatural gift or a property of his very nature.

3 *Aids,* 328–329.

before he has grown horns ("with smooth and unarmed brow"), so "throughout animated nature, of each characteristic organ and faculty there exists a pre-assurance, an instinctive and practical anticipation; and no pre-assurance common to a whole species does in any instance prove delusive." [4] Such an instinctive and universal drive of man as his desire for immortality must have a corresponding fulfillment, and this is the deepest natural source of man's belief in life after death. A notebook entry from the same period seems to be saying the same thing in other terms when it says of immortality: "What is it but the impossibility of believing the contrary? The inevitable Rebound of the *I am*—itself the fearful Rebound of Life. The moment that the Soul affirms, I am, it asserts, I cannot cease to be—For the *I am* owns no antecedent, it is an act of absolute Spontaneity & of absolute necessity." [5]

But Coleridge's discussion in the *Aids to Reflection* does not stop with this. Up to this point, he has been speaking in the "assumed character of a mere naturalist, to whom no light of revelation had been vouchsafed." [6] But a revelation has been vouchsafed, and Coleridge moves quickly into the realm of faith. Immortality is, after all, an idea; it is, therefore, ultimately an object of the higher reason which is faith. Coleridge agreed with the dictum of Leighton that "only He that gives [the happiness to come], gives faith likewise to apprehend it, and lay hold upon it." [7]

J. H. Muirhead has noted very perceptively that Coleridge's appeal to scriptural authority here is not, as one might expect, to the *locus classicus* on immortality, I Corinthians 15, which focuses on the resurrection of the body and the ultimate victory over physical death. Coleridge looks rather to the Epistles to the Romans and the Hebrews, where the question turns about Christ's victory over spiritual death and man's salvation from "the curse of the law." [8] Clearly, Coleridge is less concerned with temporal death than with sin, the death of the soul. For "we all know, that it was not from temporal death, or the penalties and afflictions of the present life, that believers

---

[4] *Aids*, 329. See also *Aids*, 187–188; *LS*, 216; *PL*, 212; and *LR*, 267.
[5] Notebook 39 (c. 1826), f. 36ʳ. In a much earlier note (1811), Coleridge also spoke of conscience as a ground for belief in a future life; see *LR*, 551–552.
[6] *Aids*, 329.
[7] *LR*, 367.
[8] See Muirhead, *Coleridge as Philosopher*, p. 235.

had been redeemed." [9] Even beyond this, he sees that the question in St. Paul is not one that requires a simple affirmative or negative answer: "Whether there was a judgment to come, and souls to suffer the dread sentence?" The proper question is rather: "What are the means of escape; where may grace be found and redemption?" Coleridge's answer, therefore, like St. Paul's, goes far beyond the mere affirmation of a future life: "Not therefore, that there is a life to come, and a future state; but what each individual soul may hope for itself therein: and on what grounds: and that this state has been rendered an object of aspiration and fervent desire, and a source of thanksgiving and exceeding great joy; and by whom, and through whom, and for whom, and by what means, and under what conditions—these are the peculiar and distinguishing fundamentals of the Christian Faith. These are the revealed lights and obtained privileges of the Christian Dispensation. Not alone the knowledge of the boon, but the precious inestimable boon itself, is the *grace and truth that came by Jesus Christ.* I believe Moses, I believe Paul; but I believe in Christ." [10]

Here, then, is the ultimate pledge of man's future life: Jesus Christ, who himself conquered death so that all men might be saved from death. The Risen Christ is the pledge, an efficacious sign, of man's future life. "If then it be health and comfort to the faithful that Christ descended into the grave, with especial confidence may we meditate on his return from thence, *quickened by the Spirit:* this being to those who are in him the certain pledge, yea, the effectual cause of that blessed resurrection for which they themselves hope. There is that union betwixt them and their Redeemer, that they shall rise by the communication and virtue of his rising: not simply by his power—for so the wicked likewise to their grief shall be raised: but *they by his life as their life.*" [11]

There is much that is mystery, of course, about the life to come, but Coleridge was clear about certain of its essential qualities. First of all, it will consist essentially in union with God. It is for this reason

---

[9] *Aids,* 332.

[10] *Aids,* 332–333.

[11] *Aids,* 298. See *CL,* IV, 851 (April 1818), where somewhat the same idea is touched upon. Coleridge believed, too, that the Old Testament already adumbrated, however dimly, the fuller New Testament revelation of a future life; see *LR,* 96–97; *CL,* IV, 559 (March 24, 1815); and *TT,* 275 (c. May 1823).

that he could write in the *Aids to Reflection,* echoing Archbishop Leighton—and ultimately St. Augustine's famous *"Inquietum est cor meum, Domine"*—that man's heart, even when it wanders far from God, "retains that natural relation to God, as its centre, that it hath no true rest elsewhere, nor can by any means find it. It is made for Him, and is therefore still restless till it meet with Him." [12] Or, as he wrote in a notebook, probably in the early 1820's: "The very end and final Bliss of the glorified Spirit is represented in Scripture as a plain aspect, an intuitive Beholding of Truth in its eternal and immutable Source." [13] And, as the Truth of God is expressed in the eternal Word, this ultimate union with God is mediated through Christ: "What must not the blessing be to be thus identified first with the Filial Word, and then with the Father in and through Him?" [14]

As one would expect from Coleridge, this union with God involves the whole man, under the guidance of his will. Man's primary task in life is, as we have seen, to prepare his finite will to exercise its proper sovereignty by conforming itself, in faith, to the Absolute Will—"in rendering the will productive, in giving the will a causative power and fitting it for a higher state." [15] This "higher state" is the ultimate act of human freedom, achieved in heaven by complete conformity of the human will with the Divine Will. Until then, man must work to make himself "capable of that freedom of moral being, without which heaven would be no heaven . . ." [16]

This future life remains as deeply personal and individual as the life which preceded it. It necessarily involves "the survival of individual consciousness," for Coleridge rejects vigorously the Spinozan view that "the survival of consciousness is the highest prize and consequence of the highest virtue, and that of all below this mark the

---

[12] *Aids,* 187.

[13] Notebook 25, f. 134ᵛ. See also *LSTC,* II, 747 (January 14, 1828), 762–763 (August 13, 1832).

[14] *LR,* 374. See also *LR,* 197–198.

[15] *PL,* 387.

[16] *NTPM,* 350. In an interesting marginal note in one of Skelton's works, Coleridge insists that it is not by any single action that a man will be judged fit or unfit for Heaven, but by the general tenor of his life. "Here we find ourselves constrained by our best feelings to praise or condemn, to reward or punish, according as a great predominance of acts of obedience or disobedience, and a continued love of the better, or the lusting after the worst, manifests . . . the radical will and proper character of the individual. So parents judge of their children; so schoolmasters of their scholars; so friends of friends, and even so will God judge his creatures, if we are to trust in our common sense, or believe the repeated declarations in the Old Testament." *LR,* 442–443.

lot after death is self-oblivion and the cessation of individual being." [17]
It involves, too, the resurrection of the body. Here again, as in his
discussion of the presence of Christ's body in the Eucharist, Coleridge
distinguishes between the phenomenal body and the noumenal body.
"Resurrection is always and exclusively resurrection in the body;—
not indeed a rising of the *corpus* φανταστικόν, that is, the few ounces
of carbon, nitrogen, oxygen, hydrogen, and phosphate of lime, the
copula of which that gave the form no longer exists . . . but the
corpus ὑποστατικὸν, ἢ νούμενον." [18] The same distinction is implied,
though in different terms, in a lengthy note in a volume of Leighton:
"It is of highest concernment that we should distinguish the personeity or spirit, as the source and principle of personality, from the
person itself as the particular product at any one period, and as that
which can not be evolved or sustained but by the co-agency of the
system and circumstances in which the individuals are placed." For
"on this hangs the doctrine of the resurrection of the body, as an
essential part of the doctrine of immortality." What is at question
here is the "incorruptible body" which St. Paul speaks of in I Corinthians 15:35-54, and which Coleridge cites in this context. "When the
spirit by sanctification is fitted for an incorruptible body, then shall it
be raised into a world of incorruption, and a celestial body shall bur-
geon forth thereto, the germ of which had been implanted by the
redeeming and creative Word in this world." [19]

All these elements of the future life touched upon by Coleridge
find expression in a notebook entry of 1827, a commentary on John
14:2 ("In my Father's house are many mansions"), which may serve
by way of summary:

Often have I lamented, & in the First Lay-Sermon & in the "Aids to

[17] *LR*, 318. There is a similar view expressed in Notebook L (1809–1818), f. 24ᵛ, where
Coleridge speaks of the "false & dangerous use of the word Eternity as applied to the future
state of man instead of immortality, or a temporal state without that particular division of
it's parts called Death." A consequence of this word is "improper absoluteness of *opposition*
to the present state, as if it were not as much & natural a part of our Being as the next, &c. &c.
—or as if the next must not be a pilgrimage to [?some] future progression &c." This added
hint of a possible "future progression" remains puzzling. For other suggestions of Coleridge's
general point of view, the continuity of the future life with the present life, with varying
degrees of conviction, see *NTPM*, 349–354; *LS*, 152 n.; and *LSTC*, II, 746 (May 3, 1827).

[18] *LR*, 516. The same distinction is used, it seems, in Notebook L (1809–1818), f. 28, except that the terms used are "body terrestrial" and "body celestial." The one "we leave
behind when it is worn out," while the other is "imperishable."

[19] *LR*, 371. On the resurrection of the body, see also *LS*, 190 n., and *LR*, 124, 127.

Reflection" expressed, my regret that the true meaning of "Spiritual" is so generally ignored—what it does *not* mean, no less than what it *does*. The History of Life from the [?] to the Spirits of the Just made perfect is comprized in one sentence—Life begins in detachment from Nature and ends in union with God. The adorable Author of our Being is likewise its' ultimate End. But even this last triumphal Crown, the summit and ne plus ultra of our immortality, even the Union with God is no mystic annihilation of individuality, no fanciful breaking of the Bottle and blending the contained water with the ocean in which it had been floating, the dreams of oriental Indolence! but on the contrary [?an] *intension,* a perfecting of our Personality . . . But where Persons are, and Community, and ever intercirculating Love, there must *Bodies* be—spiritual, or as St. Paul says, Celestial Bodies indeed, but yet Bodies—& if Bodies, then Places, Mansions. Spiritual Space indeed and heavenly Mansions, but yet Space, (i.e. perceivable Relations of distinct Forms to each other), but yet Mansions.[20]

Beyond this—about the deeper nature of this life, about the meaning of this "celestial body"—Coleridge, like St. Paul, can say no more than has been revealed. The ultimate mystery remains.

If life after death is possible to man, deprivation of that future life is also possible. As long as one strives to conform his will to the Absolute Will, he is, as all men are, "a distempered Being in order to the possibility of a recovery." If one freely rejects the relevance of the Absolute Will to his own, however, he forfeits his possibility of "recovery," of union with God. "God has not promised Heaven finally to all men, and I see nothing which authorizes me to promise it in his name . . . surely there is nothing to shock the moral sense in telling a sinner impenitent after repeated warnings, God *has not promised* that you will have the power or opportunity of repenting after death—the contrary seems the obvious sense of his revealed declarations." [21]

Coleridge's conception of the nature of this deprivation is generally clear. He would like to think that Hell is a *"poena damni negativa, haud privativa,"* that is, simply a cessation of life, not a loss that involves a positive pain. It would be, he feels, "a far stronger motive than the present; for no man will believe eternal misery of himself, but millions would admit, that if they did not amend their lives they

20 Notebook 36, ff. 63ᵛ–64ᵛ.
21 Notebook 38 (1829), ff. 26ᵛ–27.

would be undeserving of living forever." But he cannot accept the view: "So many texts against it!" [22] Whether he likes it or not, Coleridge believes that Hell involves positive pain.

This pain is not merely corrective; it is somehow bound up with the nature of guilt itself. The guilt of sin is essentially the deliberate divorce of one's will from the will of God; it is this that constitutes the essential pain of Hell. Hell is remedial, to be sure, in that it serves as a warning to sinners. For the individual after death, however, it is more than this; it is one's self-created state of eternal alienation from God. As early as 1807 Coleridge wrote in a volume of Andrew Fuller: "That all punishments work for the good of the whole, and that the good of the whole is included in God's design, I admit: but that this is the sole cause, and the sole justification of divine punishment, I can not, I dare not concede;—because I should thus deny the essential evil of guilt, and its inherent incompatibility with the presence of a Being of infinite holiness. Now, exclusion from God implies the sum and utmost of punishment; and this would follow from the very essence of guilt and holiness." [23] Coleridge never found reason to change this belief. In 1814 he wrote: "I believe, that punishment is essentially *vindictive,* i.e. expressive of abhorrence of Sin for it's own exceeding sinfulness." [24] In the following year he wrote to Joseph Cottle that "the *receding* from [God] is to *proceed* towards Nothingness and Privation," and yet that the *"nothingness* or *Death,* to which we move as we recede from God & the Word, *cannot* be nothing; but that tremendous Medium between Nothing and true Being, which Scripture & inmost Reason present as most, most horrible!" [25] And in the *Aids to Reflection,* Hell is seen as sin carried out to its eternal conclusion: "Where nothing of vice remains but its guilt and its misery—vice must be misery itself; all and utter misery." [26]

[22] *LR,* 207–208. See also *LR,* 215.

[23] *LR,* 447–448.

[24] *CL,* III, 466 (April 5, 1814).

[25] *CL,* IV, 545 (March 7, 1815).

[26] *Aids,* 144. Coleridge's letter of April 2, 1806 or 1807 (*CL,* III, 6), to his brother George, suggests that "Self-knowledge may be among the spiritual punishments of the abandoned," as well as among the joys of the blessed in Heaven. A notebook entry of 1830, however, stands somewhat in opposition to these passages, suggesting for the first time (and only time, to my knowledge) the possibility that individual consciousness may not perdure in those damned to Hell. The idea clearly stems from Coleridge's belief that the light of man's reason is a participation in the Divine Reason. "That a distinct individual self-consciousness, that a Light & such a Light as he only, the redemptive *Word,* who lighteth every man that cometh into

What of the scriptural pains of the senses in Hell? Coleridge interprets them metaphorically, as means to express the anguish of the soul cut off from God. Just as the promises of "felicity to the righteous in the future world, though the precise nature of that felicity may not be defined, are illustrated by every image that can swell the imagination," so "the misery of the *lost,* in its unutterable intensity, though the language that describes it is all necessarily figurative, is there exhibited as resulting chiefly, if not wholly, from the withdrawment of the *light of God's countenance,* and a banishment from his *presence!*—best comprehended in this world by reflecting on the desolations which would instantly follow the loss of the sun's vivifying and universally diffused *warmth.*" [27] An even more dramatic statement appears in a note of a conversation which took place sixteen years later. "Why need we talk of a fiery hell? If the will, which is the law of our nature, were withdrawn from our memory, fancy, understanding, and reason, no other hell could equal, for a spiritual being, what we should then feel, from the anarchy of our powers. It would be conscious madness—a horrid thought!" [28]

Coleridge seems generally to have believed that Hell is eternal. In the passages already alluded to, as in others, he speaks of "eternal death," "eternal misery," and the like. And in a letter of 1814, already cited, he explains: "From all experience as well as a priori from the constitution of the human Soul I gather that without a miraculous Intervention of Omnipotence the Punishment must continue as long as the Soul—which I believe imperishable.—God has promised no such miracle—he has covenanted no such mercy—I have no right therefore to believe or rely on it—It *may* be so; but wo to me! if I presume on it." [29]

---

the World, can communicate—that this heaven-sprung Light, this grace & boon to the State of Time, shall abide in the utter Darkness, in the state below Time—for such an assertion I can find as little sanction in Scripture as in Reason." Notebook 48, ff. [39–40].

[27] *CL,* III, 482 (late April 1814).

[28] *TT,* 349 (September 28, 1830). See also Notebook F, ff. 46ᵛ–47 (1826).

[29] *CL,* III, 466 (April 5, 1814). See also *Aids,* 301 n., and Notebook F, ff. 46–47ᵛ (1826). In the latter passage, Coleridge argues that since the soul is immortal Hell must be eternal, but that it is not certain whether any individual soul is actually predestined to Hell.

There is one notable contradiction of Coleridge's general position that Hell is eternal. In a letter to his friend Joseph Cottle (uncertainly dated early April 1814), Coleridge suggests reasons why Hell may perhaps not be eternal, based mainly on the general belief of men about the attributes of God, particularly their belief that God's punishments cannot be vindictive, but "either for amendment, or warning for others." But "eternal punishment precludes the idea of amendment; and its infliction, after the day of judgment, . . . renders the notion of warning to others inapplicable." *CL,* III, 468.

The doctrine of Purgatory was, of course, anathema to Coleridge, and mention of it always appears in the form of a polemic against popery.[30] This "doctrine of a middle state, and hence Purgatory with all its abominations," comes from "introducing the *idolon* of time as an *ens reale* into spiritual doctrines, thus understanding literally what St. Paul had expressed by figure and adaptation." [31] Occasionally, however, Coleridge speaks more leniently of Purgatory, seeing the chief danger not in the doctrine itself so much as in the "superstitious practices," Masses for the dead and so forth, which it has occasioned.[32] As he wrote in one of his notebooks in 1829, commenting on II Corinthians 5:10, the passage might, "more strictly following the Greek, be rendered so as to furnish a more plausible authority of the doctrine of Purgatory than the Romanists are in the habit of bringing from Scripture." As for the doctrine: "A most pernicious one, I grant; but is not its pernicious quality acquired chiefly by its connection with the papal hierarchy? Not what it is in itself, but . . . what it is capable of being shaped into in order to be instrumental to the power and gain of the Priesthood, constitutes the mischief and danger of the doctrine." [33]

In all this, it might appear that Coleridge was wary of a reward/punishment approach to the "last things." And so he was, in fact.

[30] See, for example, *NTPM*, 74, 352; *LR*, 230; and *Aids*, 306–307.

[31] *LR*, 73.

[32] It is interesting that an early (1808) marginal note of Coleridge in Sir Thomas Browne's *Religio Medici* allows prayer for the dead: "Our church with her characteristic Christian prudence does not enjoin prayer for the dead, but neither does she prohibit it." *NTPM*, 275. Much later, in the *Constitution of the Church and State* (1830), Coleridge speaks strongly against the notion of the "Communion of Saints, or the sympathy between all the members of the universal Church, which death itself doth not interrupt." He seems, however, to have in mind the evident abuses rather than the belief itself, for he goes on to see it exemplified in "St. Anthony and the cure of sore eyes, St. Boniface and success in brewing, and other such follies," seeing them as "the means and instruments of priestly power and revenue." *CCS*, 102 n.

[33] Notebook 41, ff. [26ᵛ–27]. Coleridge goes on to refer to this note as "a slight contribution to a very necessary work, viz. a re-examination of the important point controverted between Protestants & R. Catholics." See also *CL*, III, 468 (early April 1814?); *LR*, 210; and Notebook F, f. 43ᵛ (1826).

A note of 1810–1811 contains a fascinating reflection on the possible value of the interval between death and resurrection. "Who shall say that the Interval between Death and the Resurrection may not be as necessary for the growth of the Spirit, and to render it capable of the great Transition, as Sleep—or the deeper Entrancement of the Chrysalis. May not such processes be then carried on, which would be incompatible with consciousness—intolerable Torment perhaps?—May not the very best of men resemble those summer fruits, which will not ripen till after they are plucked from the Tree—Such great changes as may perhaps be necessary in this new organizing of the glorified body, would perhaps madden the soul with torture, if the sensations were converged in a focus of Consciousness, collected into one point —& so became objects of consciousness." Notebok 18, ff. 143ᵛ–144.

He was strongly opposed, for example, to the merely prudential morality of Paley, which was then the current teaching in the universities.[34] He did allow, however, that the idea of eternal reward and punishment does have its proper place in Christianity, because the true Christian idea of them is not crassly prudential. These hopes and fears are not "mere Selfishness," for "what I hope for myself, I hope for all men—I cannot hope Heaven for myself as myself, but for all good men in the number of which *I* may be included. No act of Thought or Feeling necessarily *social* can be absolutely *selfish*." [35] Beyond this, "the faith presupposed . . . gives to the motive a purity and an elevation which of itself, and where the recompense is looked for in temporal and carnal pleasures or profits, it would not have." [36] Even the fear of Hell, while not a high motive, can be a "preparatory awakening of the soul." [37]

But in the last analysis, the emphasis should probably be laid on love. Although Coleridge does not often use the word itself in this context, the idea of love seems to stand behind much of what he says about the "last things." Heaven is for him, after all, union with God, the ultimate conformity of the finite will with the Absolute Will. Heaven is love, Hell is the rejection of love. "It is a perilous state in which a christian stands, if he has gotten no further than to avoid evil from the fear of hell! . . . The fear of the Lord is the beginning of wisdom, but perfect love shutteth out fear." When the meaning of the love of God has once been realized, even the conception of Hell is seen in terms of love: a realization of what it would be not to be united with the object of that love. "To him who but for a moment felt the influence of God's presence, the thought of eternal exclusion from the sense of that presence, would be the worst hell, his imagination could conceive." [38]

For Coleridge, as for St. John and for Dante, the last thing of all is love.

---

[34] See *CL*, III, 146 (December 14, 1808), and *LS*, 194–195, first note.
[35] *CL*, III, 154 (December 30, 1808).
[36] *NED*, I, 124.
[37] *CL*, III, 468 (early April 1814?). See also *NTPM*, 278 (1808), and *LR*, 504.
[38] *CL*, III, 468 (early April 1814?).

✻ EPILOGUE

Coleridge would have been very much at home with modern religious thought. The points of tangency of his thinking with recent theological currents, some of which we have noted already, are many and varied. We can do here little more than suggest some of these points of tangency, but perhaps this will be enough to underscore his potential relevance for modern man.

One of the most notable of Coleridge's modernities, it seems to me, is his attempt to break down the old radical discontinuity between the natural and the supernatural. For too long the two had gone their separate ways. Coleridge felt, as many modern theologians feel, that one can come to grips with the supernatural only in terms of the natural. Karl Rahner's conception of the "supernatural existential," which involves a radical foundation in nature for supernatural gifts—which yet remain gratuitous on the part of God—is only one of many approaches to this problem.

Coleridge is profoundly modern, too, in his approach to the idea of faith. His strong emphasis on the role of the will, and therefore on the interpersonal aspects of man's relationship to God, anticipates the work of a number of modern theologians and philosophers of religion: Martin Buber's conception of the "I–Thou" relationship; Maurice Blondel's *L'Action,* with its insistence on the role of man's will in reaching God and the necessity for the "option"; and more generically, the introduction into the theology of faith of the concepts and terminology of modern personalist philosophy.

In the same context, we have noted that Coleridge's treatment of the evidences for faith is akin to the "new apologetics," which sees that a very vital role of apologetics is within the act of faith itself, that is, that the so-called evidences may themselves be dependent upon a previous or concomitant act of faith which gives them structure and meaning. In particular, the privileged evidences we call miracles are conceived primarily as divine signs rather than in terms of their relationship to a sometimes hypothetical order of nature, and in any case miracles can be perceived as such only by one who has already committed himself in faith.

Like several modern theologians who have written of the problem of conceiving Original Sin in terms meaningful to the modern Christian, Coleridge spoke of Original Sin not simply in terms of individual guilt but in terms of the guilt of all men. His sense of human solidarity in this guilt, as well as of redemption through mankind's solidarity in Christ, responds well to the situation of modern man, who finds himself faced with the new phenomenon of a community of nations. We have noted especially the resemblance of Coleridge's idea of Original Sin to the Dutch theologian Piet Schoonenberg's conception of the "sin of the world."

One of the most interesting rapports is with the French scientist and religious thinker Pierre Teilhard de Chardin. Both are profoundly Pauline in their theology; both see Christ as the final cause and matrix of the whole created world; both focus on the evolutionary movement of the world as a progressive development toward ultimate perfection, culminating in union with the God-man—for Teilhard the "Omega-point," for Coleridge the "divine humanity."

Coleridge seems particularly modern, too, in his conception of the relationship of Church and State. His idea of the Church and the State, each independent in its proper sphere of activity, is much like what modern theologians have only arrived at after almost two hundred years of the American experiment in pluralism. On this question, John Courtney Murray and Vatican Council II are distant from Coleridge only in time.

There is even a glimmering of the spirit of ecumenism in Coleridge. Although Coleridge was through most of his life a child of his nonecumenical age, he was always chary of the spirit of sectarianism, and when occasion demanded, he spoke out for tolerance and Christian charity. He opposed "popery" but could love papists. Against this background one should perhaps not be surprised—but perhaps inevitably is—to find Coleridge, at the end of his life, longing to find a bond of unity even with Rome. In one of the last of his notebooks (Notebook 54, f. [17]), he wrote in 1833: "Were I young, had I the bodily strength & animal spirits of early manhood with my present powers & convictions, I should not so far despair of a union between the *Protestant* and the now *papal* but still *Catholic* Church, as to prevent me from making it an object."

Perhaps this is the note on which we might fittingly close. Coleridge's whole life was a quest for unity, within a context of love. And perhaps, too, this is the reason why he may have an appeal for the Christian in the modern world. His capacity for love, of the world and of the men who work out their salvation in the world, was boundless. His realization of the oneness of the world was deep and moving. And his resolution of this love and this oneness into their relationship to God through Christ, the Word of God, was able to bring—even to a soul as long troubled as his—the welcome blessing of peace.

WORKS CITED   INDEX

❀ WORKS CITED

Abbott, Walter M., S.J., ed. *The Documents of Vatican II.* New York: Guild Press–America Press–Association Press, 1966.

Alonso Schökel, Luis. *The Inspired Word: Scripture in the Light of Language and Literature.* Transl. Francis Martin. New York: Herder and Herder, 1965.

Antoine, P. "Foi (dans l'Ecriture)," *Supplément au Dictionnaire de la Bible,* t. II (Paris: Letouzey et Ané, 1938), cols. 276–310.

Appleyard, J. A., S.J. *Coleridge's Philosophy of Literature: The Development of a Concept of Poetry, 1791–1819.* Cambridge, Mass.: Harvard University Press, 1965.

Arnold, Thomas. *Sermons.* 3rd ed. 3 vols. London, 1844.

Aubert, Roger. *Le Problème de l'Acte de Foi.* 3rd ed. Louvain: E. Warny, 1958.

Augustine, Saint. *Christian Instruction.* Transl. John J. Gavigan, O.S.A., in *The Fathers of the Church* collection (New York: Fathers of the Church, Inc., 1947). Vol. II. (Writings of St. Augustine, Vol. IV.)

Aulén, Gustaf. *Christus Victor: An Historical Study of the Three Main Types of the Atonement.* Transl. A. G. Hebert. London: S.P.C.K., 1931.

Bate, Walter Jackson. *Coleridge.* New York: Macmillan, 1968. (Masters of World Literature Series.)

Bea, Augustin, S.J. *De Sacrae Scripturae Inspiratione.* Rome: Pontifical Biblical Institute, 1935.

Beer, J. B. *Coleridge the Visionary.* New York: Collier Books, 1962.

Benoit, Pierre, O.P. "L'Inspiration," in *Initiation Biblique,* ed. A. Robert and A. Tricot. 3rd ed. Tournai: Desclée, 1954. Pp. 6–45.

——— "La plénitude de sens des Livres Saints," *Revue Biblique,* LXVII (1960), 161–196.

——— See Synave, Paul.

Black, Matthew, and H. H. Rowley, eds. *Peake's Commentary on the Bible.* London: Thomas Nelson, 1962.

Blunden, Edmund, and Earl Leslie Griggs, eds. *Coleridge: Studies by Several Hands.* London: Constable, 1934.

Boulger, James D. *Coleridge as Religious Thinker.* New Haven: Yale University Press, 1961.

Bromiley, G. W. *Baptism and the Anglican Reformers.* London: Lutterworth Press, 1953.

Brown, Raymond, S.S. *The Sensus Plenior of Sacred Scripture.* Baltimore: St. Mary's University, 1955.

Burghardt, Walter, S.J. "On Early Christian Exegesis," *Theological Studies,* XI (1950), 78–116.

Calleo, David P. *Coleridge and the Idea of the Modern State.* New Haven: Yale University Press, 1966.

Campbell, James Dykes. *Samuel Taylor Coleridge: A Narrative of the Events of His Life.* London, 1894.

Chambers, E. K. *Samuel Taylor Coleridge: A Biographical Study.* Oxford: Clarendon Press, 1938.

Charlier, Celestin. *The Christian Approach to the Bible.* Transl. H. J. Richards and B. Peters. London: Sands, 1958.

Clarke, W. Norris, S.J. "The Platonic Heritage of Thomism," *Review of Metaphysics,* VIII (1954), 105–124.

Coleridge, Samuel Taylor. *Aids to Reflection in the formation of a manly character on the several grounds of prudence, morality and religion, illustrated by select passages from our elder divines, especially from Archbishop Leighton.* Ed. Henry Nelson Coleridge, in *The Complete Works,* ed. Shedd, I.

—— *Biographia Literaria.* Ed. J. Shawcross. 2 vols. Oxford: Oxford University Press, 1907.

—— *Coleridge on Logic and Learning.* Ed. Alice D. Snyder. New Haven: Yale University Press, 1929.

—— *Coleridge on the Seventeenth Century.* Ed. Roberta F. Brinkley. Durham, North Carolina: Duke University Press, 1955.

—— *Collected Letters of Samuel Taylor Coleridge.* Ed. Earl Leslie Griggs. 4 vols. Oxford: Clarendon Press, 1956–1959.

—— *The Complete Poetical Works of Samuel Taylor Coleridge.* Ed. Ernest Hartley Coleridge. 2 vols. Oxford: Clarendon Press, 1912.

—— *The Complete Works of Samuel Taylor Coleridge, with an Introductory Essay upon His Philosophical and Theological Opinions.* Ed. W. G. T. Shedd. 7 vols. New York, 1856.

—— *Confessions of an Inquiring Spirit.* Ed. Henry Nelson Coleridge, in *The Complete Works,* ed. Shedd, V.

—— *On the Constitution of the Church and State According to the Idea of Each.* Ed. Henry Nelson Coleridge, in *The Complete Works,* ed. Shedd, VI.

—— *The Friend: A Series of Essays To Aid in the Formation of Fixed Principles in Politics, Morals, and Religion, with Literary Amusements Interspersed.* Ed. Henry Nelson Coleridge, in *The Complete Works,* ed. Shedd, II.

—— *A Lay Sermon, Addressed to the Higher and Middle Classes, on the Existing Distresses and Discontents. 1817* ["Second Lay Sermon"]. Ed. Henry Nelson Coleridge, in *The Complete Works,* ed. Shedd, VI.

—— *Letters of Samuel Taylor Coleridge.* Ed. Ernest Hartley Coleridge. 2 vols. London, 1895.

——— *The Literary Remains of Samuel Taylor Coleridge*. Ed. Henry Nelson Coleridge, in *The Complete Works*, ed. Shedd, V.

——— *The Notebooks of Samuel Taylor Coleridge*. Ed. Kathleen Coburn. 2 vols. New York: Pantheon Books, 1957–1961. (Bollingen Series L.)

——— *Notes on English Divines*. Ed. Derwent Coleridge. 2 vols. London, 1853.

——— *Notes, Theological, Political, and Miscellaneous*. Ed. Derwent Coleridge. London, 1853.

——— *The Philosophical Lectures of Samuel Taylor Coleridge: Hitherto Unpublished*. Ed. Kathleen Coburn. New York: Philosophical Library, 1949.

——— *Shakespearean Criticism*. Ed. Thomas Middleton Raysor. 2 vols. London: J. M. Dent, 1960. (Everyman's Library.)

——— *Specimens of the Table Talk of the Late Samuel Taylor Coleridge*, in *The Complete Works*, ed. Shedd, VI.

——— *The Stateman's Manual; or, the Bible the Best Guide to Political Skill and Foresight: A Lay Sermon, Addressed to the Higher Classes of Society* ["First Lay Sermon"]. Ed. Henry Nelson Coleridge, in *The Complete Works*, ed. Shedd, I.

——— *Theory of Life* [*Hints towards the Formation of a more Comprehensive Theory of Life*], in *Aids to Reflection*, Appendix C, in *The Complete Works*, ed. Shedd, I.

——— *Unpublished Letters of Samuel Taylor Coleridge, including Certain Letters Republished from Original Sources*. Ed. Earl Leslie Griggs. 2 vols. London: Constable, 1932.

Copleston, Frederick. *A History of Philosophy*. 7 vols. New York: Image Books, 1962–1965.

Cross, F. L., ed. *The Oxford Dictionary of the Christian Church*. London: Oxford University Press, 1958.

Denzinger, Henricus, and Adolfus Schönmetzer. *Enchiridion Symbolorum Definitionum et Declarationum de Rebus Fidei et Morum*. 33rd ed. Freiburg im Breisgau: Herder, 1965.

Dodd, C. H. *The Authority of the Bible*. London: Nisbet, 1928.

Dulles, Avery, S.J. *Apologetics and the Biblical Christ*. Westminster, Maryland: Newman Press, 1963.

Durand, Alexandre, S.J. "La Liberté du Christ dans son Rapport à l'Impeccabilité," *Nouvelle Revue Théologique*, LXX (1948), 811–822.

Durand, Alfred. "Inspiration of the Bible," *The Catholic Encyclopedia* (New York: The Encyclopedia Press, 1913), VIII, 45–50.

Forestell, J. T. "Bible, II (Inspiration)," *New Catholic Encyclopedia* (New York: McGraw-Hill, 1967), II, 381–386.

Gibson, E. C. S. *The Thirty-Nine Articles of the Church of England*. 2 vols. London, 1896.

Gotshalk, D. W. "The Central Doctrine of the Kantian Ethics," in *The*

Heritage of Kant, ed. George Tapley Whitney and David F. Bowers. New York: Russell and Russell, 1962. Pp. 181–196.

Griggs, Earl Leslie. See Blunden, Edmund.

Grillmeier, Aloys, S.J. *Christ in Christian Tradition: From the Apostolic Age to Chalcedon (451).* Transl. J. S. Bowden. London: A. R. Mowbray, 1965.

Henry, C. F. H., ed. *Revelation and the Bible: Contemporary Evangelical Thought.* Grand Rapids: Eerdmans, 1958.

Hodgson, Leonard. *The Doctrine of the Trinity.* Digswell Place, England, 1943.

Hooker, Richard. *Works.* Ed. J. Keble. 3 vols. Oxford, 1836.

Hunt, John. *Religious Thought in England from the Reformation to the End of the Last Century.* 3 vols. London, 1870–1873.

James, D. G. *The Romantic Comedy: An Essay on English Romanticism.* London: Oxford University Press, 1963.

Jonsen, A. R. "Faith: Patristic Tradition and Teaching of the Church," *New Catholic Encyclopedia* (New York: McGraw-Hill, 1967), V, 796–798.

Kant, Immanuel. *Critique of Practical Reason.* Transl. Lewis White Beck. New York: Bobbs-Merrill, 1956.

——— *Religion within the Limits of Reason Alone.* Transl. T. M. Greene and H. H. Hudson. Glasgow, 1934.

Kelly, J. N. D. *Early Christian Creeds.* New York: Longmans, Green, 1950.

——— *Early Christian Doctrines.* New York: Harper, 1958.

Küng, Hans. *Justification: The Doctrine of Karl Barth and a Catholic Reflection.* Transl. T. Collins, E. Tolk, D. Granskou. New York: Thomas Nelson and Sons, 1964.

Lacey, Paul A. "Samuel Taylor Coleridge's Political and Religious Development: 1795–1810," unpub. diss., Harvard University, 1966.

Lee, William. *The Inspiration of Scripture.* New York, 1857.

Léon-Dufour, X., ed. *Vocabulaire de Théologie Biblique.* Paris: Editions du Cerf, 1962.

Levie, Jean. *La Bible, Parole Humaine et Message de Dieu.* Paris: Desclée de Brouwer, 1958.

Lonergan, Bernard J. F. *Divinarum Personarum Conceptio Analogica.* 2nd ed. Rome: Gregorian University, 1959.

Lovejoy, Arthur O. *The Great Chain of Being.* Cambridge, Mass.: Harvard University Press, 1936.

Lynch, William F., S.J. *Christ and Apollo: The Dimensions of the Literary Imagination.* New York: Sheed and Ward, 1960.

Mascall, E. L. "The Doctrine of Analogy," *Cross Currents,* I (1951), 38–57.

Maurice, F. D. *Theological Essays.* London, 1871.

McDonald, H. D. *Ideas of Revelation: An Historical Study, A.D. 1700 to A.D. 1860.* London: Macmillan, 1959.

Migne, J. P., ed. *Patrologia Latina.* 217 vols. Paris, 1844–1855.

Miller, Craig W. "Coleridge's Concept of Nature," *Journal of the History of Ideas,* XXV (1964), 77–96.

Monden, Louis, S.J. *Signs and Wonders: A Study of the Miraculous Element in Religion.* New York: Desclée, 1966.

Mondin, Battista. *The Principle of Analogy in Protestant and Catholic Theology.* The Hague: Martinus Nijhoff, 1963.

Moran, Gabriel. *Scripture and Tradition: A Survey of the Controversy.* New York: Herder and Herder, 1963.

Muirhead, John H. *Coleridge as Philosopher.* London: Allen and Unwin, 1930.

Newman, John Henry. *An Essay in Aid of a Grammar of Assent.* New York: Image Books, 1955.

Owens, L. G. "Athanasian Creed," *New Catholic Encyclopedia* (New York: McGraw-Hill, 1967), I, 995–996.

Penido, T. L. *Le Role de l'analogie en théologie dogmatique.* Paris: J. Vrin, 1931.

Rahner, Karl. *Inspiration in the Bible.* Transl. Charles H. Henkey. New York: Herder and Herder, 1961.

—— and Herbert Vorgrimler. *Theological Dictionary.* Ed. Cornelius Ernst, transl. Richard Strachan. New York: Herder and Herder, 1965.

Rondet, Henri. *Gratia Christi: Essai d'Histoire du Dogme et de Théologie Dogmatique.* Paris: Beauchesne, 1948.

Rouet de Journel, M. J., ed. *Enchiridion Patristicum.* 21st ed. Barcelona: Herder, 1959.

Rowley, H. H. See Black, Matthew.

Sanday, William. *Inspiration.* London, 1893.

Sanders, Charles Richard. *Coleridge and the Broad Church Movement.* Durham, North Carolina: Duke University Press, 1942.

Sandford, Mrs. Henry. *Thomas Poole and His Friends.* 2 vols. London, 1888.

Schönmetzer, Adolfus. See Denzinger, Henricus.

Schoonenberg, Piet, S.J. *Man and Sin: A Theological View.* Transl. J. Donceel. Notre Dame, Indiana: Notre Dame University Press, 1965.

Storr, Vernon. *The Development of Theology in the Nineteenth Century.* London: Longmans, Green, 1913.

Sundberg, Albert C., Jr. *The Old Testament of the Early Church.* Cambridge, Mass.: Harvard University Press, 1964. (Harvard Theological Studies, XX.)

Synave, Paul, O.P., and Pierre Benoit, O.P. *Prophecy and Inspiration.* Transl. A. Dulles and T. Sheridan. New York: Desclée, 1961.

Tavard, George H. *Holy Writ or Holy Church: The Crisis of the Protestant Reformation.* New York: Harper, 1959.

Taylor, Jeremy. *The Whole Works of the Right Rev. Jeremy Taylor, D.D.* Ed. R. Heber. 15 vols. London, 1822.

Teilhard de Chardin, Pierre. *The Phenomenon of Man.* Transl. Bernard Wall. New York: Harper Torchbooks, 1961.

Thomas Aquinas, Saint. *Summa Theologica.* Ottawa: Commissio Piana, 1953.

Traill, H. D. *Coleridge.* New York: Harper, 1884. (English Men of Letters Series.)

Tulloch, John. *Movements of Religious Thought in Britain during the Nineteenth Century: St. Giles Lectures.* London, 1885.

Vorgrimler, Herbert. See Rahner, Karl.

Watson, Mrs. Lucy. *Coleridge at Highgate.* London: Longmans, Green, 1925.

Weigel, Gustave. *Summarium Doctrinale de Actu Fidei.* Woodstock, Maryland: Woodstock College Press, 1958.

Wellek, René. *Immanuel Kant in England: 1793–1838.* Princeton: Princeton University Press, 1931.

INDEX

Act, Scholastic idea of potency and, applied to problem of moral evil, 112–113n
Adam: fall of, 115–118; solidarity of all mankind in, 117–118n
Allegory, use in Scripture, 64n
Alonso Schökel, Luis, 67n
Alterity: God the Son as, 89–90, 93–94; role in Creation, 105–108, 113–114; as Ipseity's image of self, 106. *See also* Logos; Trinity
Anabaptists, on Sacraments, 169
Analogy of being: Scholastic concept of, 19–20. *See also* Consubstantiality
Angels, 106n
Anselm, St., on doctrine of Redemption, 142n
Antoine, P., 31n
Apocalypse (Book of Revelation), authorship and authenticity of, 76–77
Apologetics: Unitarian, 5–8; C related to history of, 37–38; nature of, 48; modernity of C's approach to, 196
Apologists, Greek, on faith, 31
Apostle's Creed: C's doubts about its apostolicity, 81, 101n; on Virgin Birth; C's adherence to, 135
Appleyard, J. A., 2, 4–5, 17, 23n
Aquinas, St. Thomas, 17, 20n; on faith, 32; on scriptural inspiration, 54n; on the Trinity, 92; on Original Sin, 124–125
Arianism, 101n
Arminianism, *see* Arminians
Arminians: C's objections against, 35; C's Arminian position on human freedom, 125; on Redemption, 146; on faith vs works, 155–156
Arnold, Thomas, on Scripture, 54n
Associationism, 4, 6, 7
Athanasian Creed: on the Trinity, C's reservations about, 101–102; authorship of 101n; compared to Nicene, 130
Athanasius, St., 101n
Atheism, 105
Atonement, *see* Redemption
Aubert, Roger, 32n
Augustine, St.: on faith, 31–32; on reason and faith, 48–95; on importance of literal sense of Scripture, 72; on the Trinity, 92; on Original Sin, 124; on problem of free will and grace, 151–152; on man's desire for God, 189

Aulén, Gustaf, 141

Bacon, Francis, 17, 21, 35
Baptism, *see* Sacraments
Barnabas, Epistle of, rejection from Canon of Scripture, 79
Bate, W. J., x, 13
Bea, Augustin, 65n
Beer, J. B., 12
Belief, *see* Faith
Benoit, Pierre, 55n, 73n; on scriptural inspiration and inerrancy, 65–67
Bible, *see* Scripture
Bishops, *see* Episcopacy
Blondel, Maurice, 196
Boulger, James, vii, 134n; on C's view of the Logos, 105–106; on C's view of relationships between God and man, 108; on C's idea of moral evil, 112n, 113n; on C's views of humanity of Christ, 130n; on faith vs works, 155–156
Boyer, James, 1
Bromiley, G. F., 57n, 169n, 170
Brown, Raymond, 73n
Bruce, F. F., 77n
Buber, Martin, 196
Burghardt, Walter, 71n
Burnet, Gilbert, 169n
Butler, Joseph, 5, 38

Calleo, David P., 162n
Calvin, John: on effects of Original Sin, 125; on efficacy of Sacraments, 170
Calvinists: on Predestination, 122, 152; on faith vs works, 155–156
Campbell, J. D., 162n
Cano, Melchior, 58n
Causality, meaning of in God, 88–90
Chalcedon, Council of, 100n
Chambers, E. K., 1n, 4n
Charlier, Celestin, 72n
Chillingworth, William, 82
Christ, *see* Alterity; Jesus Christ; Logos
Chubb, Thomas, 96
Church: C's acceptance of authority of over Canon of Scripture, 77–79; need of for interpretation of Scripture, 81–84; idea of, 160–168; distinction between National and Christian, 160; distinction between *ecclesia* and *enclesia*, 161; C's failure to apply idea of symbol to, 181. *See also*